"I'll Never Fight Fire with My Bare Hands Again"

Development of Western Resources

The Development of Western Resources is an interdisciplinary series focusing on the use and misuse of resources in the American West. Written for a broad readership of humanists, social scientists, and resource specialists, the books in this series emphasize both historical and contemporary perspectives as they explore the interplay between resource exploitation and economic, social, and political experiences.

John G. Clark
University of Kansas
General Editor

"I'll Never Fight Fire with My Bare Hands Again"

Recollections of the First Forest Rangers of the Inland Northwest

Edited by Hal K. Rothman

University Press of Kansas

Published by the University Press of Kansas (Lawrence,
Kansas 66049), which was organized by the Kansas Board of
Regents and is operated and funded by Emporia State
University, Fort Hays State University, Kansas State
University, Pittsburg State University, the University of
Kansas, and Wichita State University.

Library of Congress Cataloging-in-Publication Data

"I'll never fight fire with my bare hands again" : recollections of
the first forest rangers of the Inland Northwest / edited by Hal K.
Rothman.
    p.   cm. — (Development of western resources)
    Includes bibliographical references and index.
    ISBN 0-7006-0676-9 (cloth)   ISBN 0-7006-0677-7 (paper)
    1. Foresters—Inland Empire—Biography. 2. United States. Forest
Service—Officials and employees—Biography. 3. United States.
Forest Service—History. 4. Forest rangers—Inland Empire—
        Biography. I. Rothman, Hal, 1958–. II. Series.
                    SD127.I4 1994
                    634.9′092—dc20
[B]   94-18951

British Library Cataloguing in Publication Data is available.

Printed in the United States of America
10 9 8 7 6 5 4 3 2 1

for
Lauralee and Talia

Contents

Illustrations

Maps

Acknowledgments

L ike most works, this one required the assistance of many people and the patience and forbearance of others. Char Miller took time from his own work first to encourage me to undertake this project and later to critique it. John Clark offered insightful commentary, and Gerald Williams of the Forest Service suggested new avenues of inquiry. Terry West of the Forest Service guided me to numerous sources of information that would otherwise have escaped me, while Jud Moore and Mike Bragg of the Missoula office of the Forest Service helped me with the process of selecting appropriate photographs to accompany the text. The staff of the Forest History Society library fielded numerous bizarre queries, and a number of colleagues, in particular Bill Unrau and John Dreifort at Wichita State and Willard Rollings at the University of Nevada, Las Vegas, feigned ongoing interest in a project that surely taxed their patience. To all of them, I am grateful.

The real credit for this book and nearly everything else I've done goes to my wife, Lauralee, and our daughter, Talia. The two of them managed to keep me from being swallowed by my work, and their support and bemused interest kept me going when my own attention began to flag. As always, life would be much less rich without them.

One

Introduction

Toward a Social History of
the Forest Service

The history of the United States Forest Service has been told often and well. Created out of the throes of Progressive reform, the agency carved a mission for itself based on the axiom "the greatest good for the greatest number in the long run," a typical Progressive-era thrust at some combination of equity, efficiency, and a restructuring of society to reinvest the middle class with power and leadership. Under the dynamic guidance of Gifford Pinchot, a member of the nineteenth-century aristocracy, the first American trained in scientific forestry, and the second of his class and generation—after Theodore Roosevelt—to embrace the doctrine of noblesse oblige, the Forest Service became the leading conservation agency of the Progressive era. It embodied the spirit of the time as no other federal bureaucracy did.[1]

Much of the presentation of the agency's history has been monodimensional. Emphasis—from the turn of the century to the present—has been placed on the evolution of forest policy and management practices, the patterns of timber-cutting and response to threatening conditions such as major fires, changes in policy direction, and the status of the agency among its peers in the federal bureaucracy. Washington, D.C., is at the center of

1. Harold K. Steen, *The United States Forest Service: A History* (Seattle: University of Washington Press, 1976); Samuel P. Hays, *Conservation and the Gospel of Efficiency: The Progressive Conservation Movement 1890–1920* (Cambridge: Harvard University Press, 1959); Clayton R. Koppes, "Efficiency/Equity/Esthetics: Towards a Reinterpretation of American Conservation," *Environmental Review* 11:2 (Summer 1987): 127–46.

many of the stories told about the agency, with spheres of influence emanating out from agency headquarters to the regional office, district offices, and individual forests.[2]

Such a picture is distorted, particularly as a representation of the early years of the national forests and their management agency. Although the clamor in Washington was great and the directives from its offices clear and forthright, forestry at the grass roots was a different process that entailed finding a middle ground between the demands of locals and the policies of the agency. From its inception, the Forest Service was decentralized. Decisions about the nature of practice in the field were made at the regional and local levels. Leaders of the agency crafted policy in Washington, but applying their decisions meant allowing a degree of flexibility and even idiosyncrasy of which Washington officials might not approve. Balancing the demands of the agency and those of the place required a dexterity that has been largely unheralded in the histories of forest policy and decision making at the highest levels.

Forestry in the field was different than that planned by the leaders of the agency in the comfort of Washington, D.C. In the national forests, the policies of the agency were tempered by the realities of place, the limitations of the people who implemented policy, and the resources at their disposal. The networks of support upon which urban Americans relied were nonexistent in the national forests of the turn of the century. Forestry at the grass roots was far from an ideal situation.

2. David Clary, *Timber and the Forest Service* (Lawrence: University Press of Kansas, 1986), is the most comprehensive example; James P. Gilligan, "The Development of Policy and Administration of Forest Service Primitive and Wilderness Areas in the Western United States" (Ph.D. dissertation, University of Michigan, 1953), and Paul W. Hirt, "A Conspiracy of Optimism: Sustained Yield, Multiple Use, and Intensive Management of the National Forests, 1945–1991" (Ph.D. dissertation, University of Arizona, 1991), provide chronological and thematic boundaries of the kinds of topics undertaken by scholars; and Serge Taylor, *Making Bureaucracies Think: The Environmental Impact Statement Strategy of Administrative Reform* (Stanford, CA: Stanford University Press, 1984), presents another dimension. Social science scholars have also used history to explain various dimensions of Forest Service policy: Paul J. Culhane, *Public Lands Politics: Interest Group Influence on the Forest Service and the Bureau of Land Management* (Washington, D.C.: Resources for the Future, 1981), is one important example. In 1908, the Forest Service divided its holdings into six districts, now called regions. Each district was divided into individual national forests, managed by a district forester, now called regional forester.

The compendium of letters making up this book delves into the social history of federal forestry in the Inland Northwest. The letters were originally collected and published by a prescient regional forester, Evan W. Kelley of the Region 1 office in Missoula, Montana, in the 1940s, with subsequent volumes in the 1950s, 1960s, and 1970s. They recount the experiences of the people who worked in the national forests of northern Idaho, western Montana, and eastern Washington State between the 1890s and the 1920s. During Kelley's tenure as regional forester, he wrote the retired foresters in his area, asking them to put their experiences on paper for posterity.[3] In response, more than eight hundred pages of reminiscences concerning the period prior to 1940 came to the regional office, providing one of two such primary source collections in existence. Kelley mimeographed the letters and distributed them, mostly to people with ties to the Forest Service. The regional office library in Missoula also retained copies, where the documents became a staple of research into the history of the Forest Service. They offered a broad-based look at the life and experiences of early foresters in Region 1.[4]

Despite the seeming comprehensiveness of an eight-hundred-page collection of documents, the letters showed a certain skewing of the past that is a function of the nature of oral history. Time and nostalgia had altered perceptions, and experience had changed the way the authors viewed some of their activities and decisions. Even more telling, the foresters whose lives are here included selected themselves for the task; they wrote because they had fond memories or important points they wanted to make about their long careers in the agency. Some simply lived

3. Evan W. Kelley to "the People of Region 1," October 15, 1944, "Early Days in the Forest Service" (Missoula, MT: United States Forest Service, 1944), vol. 1.

4. "Early Days in the Forest Service," vol. 1, was subsequently printed each time enough letters came in. One "volume" exists for each decade of the 1940s, 1950s, 1960s, and 1970s. The other collection was compiled by Edwin A. Tucker and published by Tucker and George Fitzpatrick as *Men Who Matched the Mountains: The Forest Service in the Southwest* (Albuquerque: U.S. Forest Service, 1972). This excerpted volume captured the spirit of the interviews Tucker collected but sorely lacked detail and continuity. More than thirty years after the original interviews, David Gillio, an archaeologist in the Southwest Regional office, compiled all the interviews and had them printed in three volumes as *The Early Days: A Sourcebook of Southwestern Region History* (Albuquerque: USDA Forest Service, 1990–1992).

long enough to have their say, eulogizing colleagues who did not last as long.

The foresters who wrote these letters were not transients who passed through the agency, working intermittently or temporarily, but instead were those who gave their working lives to the secular religion embodied in early twentieth-century forestry. Most made it clear that they loved their careers and their agency, embracing its values and seeing no more honorable or important choices for themselves. They had been the backbone of the Forest Service in the Inland Northwest, the very people who interpreted and carried out the policies of the agency.

These early foresters lived a different kind of life than their superiors expected, faced a range of forestry issues with aplomb and confidence, and often became pivotal members of the loose-knit rural communities that depended on the national forests for an important part of their livelihood. As representatives of the federal government at the turn of the century, the foresters embodied the regulatory impulses of the twentieth century. Many were also natives of the areas in which they served, local people selected for some prowess and respected by their neighbors. This position, straddling the forests and the regulatory world, sought to bring order and efficiency to natural and human affairs and was a defining characteristic of early foresters in the field.[5]

The construction of a social history of an agency requires a different set of signposts than its traditional histories. The rhythms of a social history are different, far more tuned to vagaries of place than to policy directives, and its issues are as much personal and individual as institutional. A social history is not as smooth and direct as its institutional counterpart; there are many more side stories, tangents, and seeming idiosyncrasies. Yet out of such disorganization emerge clear patterns in the experiences of foresters in the Inland Northwest.

Between the establishment of the first forest reserves in the early 1890s and the 1920s, when agency practices became institutionalized, the Forest Service in Region 1 passed through three

5. Steen, *The United States Forest Service,* 77–82; Hal K. Rothman, "A Regular Ding-Dong Fight: Agency Culture and Evolution in the NPS-USFS Dispute, 1916–1937," *Western Historical Quarterly* 20:2 (May 1989): 141–61; Gifford Pinchot, *Breaking New Ground* (New York: Harcourt, Brace, 1947), 264–68.

distinct stages. From 1890 to 1905, the forest reserves—later renamed national forests—were managed by the General Land Office (GLO) of the Department of the Interior. The years 1905 to 1910 were the era of Gifford Pinchot and the expansion of his ideas; in the third stage, 1910 to 1920, there was a switch to professionally trained foresters and a spread of infrastructure and technical management. Before 1905, the GLO, long considered the most corrupt of bureaus in the most tainted of departments in the federal government, was poorly suited to the task of forest management. Its operatives ran the land offices where people could patent their claims, surveyed federal lands, reviewed claims, and performed numerous other similar functions. Overworked, poorly trained, and largely uninterested in scientific forestry, the staff of the GLO simply protected reserved forested lands from settlement claims.[6]

Nor were the bureau's appointees to administer the forests necessarily the best people for the task at hand. Most acquired their positions as the result of political patronage; many had never been west before they took their appointment; a significant number were unscrupulous, incompetent, or corrupt; and few had any experience in managing anything of substance. They had to supply their own horses and accommodations as well. Often given responsibility for more than a million acres, few had the experience or wherewithal to do more than simply look out at their domain from the comfort of a cabin.[7]

In the 1890s, scientific forestry was located in the Division of Forestry of the Department of Agriculture. Created in 1881, the Division of Forestry limped along under its first two leaders. In 1886, Bernhard E. Fernow, a German trained in forestry who first came to the United States during the national centennial and stayed to marry his American sweetheart, became chief. A tireless worker, the volatile Fernow built the Division of Forestry until he

6. E. Louise Peffer, *The Closing of the Public Domain: Disposal and Reservation Policies 1900–50* (Stanford, CA: Stanford University Press, 1950), 42–45; Hays, *Conservation and the Gospel of Efficiency*, 37–38, 156–57; Pinchot, *Breaking New Ground*, 161–72.

7. Steen, *The United States Forest Service*, 81–84; Pinchot, *Breaking New Ground*, 263–68; Tucker and Fitzpatrick, *Men Who Matched the Mountains*, 3–11.

became embroiled in departmental politics and left federal service to continue his quest in education and public policy. His replacement was Gifford Pinchot, the boy wonder of American forestry.[8]

With a personality to match his exuberant confidence, Pinchot wholeheartedly embraced the task he faced. The scion of a prominent and extremely wealthy eastern family, the young Pinchot was propelled toward public service by the guilt his father felt for the family's prosperity at the expense of the American landscape. Pinchot shared the belief in public service with Theodore Roosevelt, Mark Hanna's "damned cowboy" who became president after the assassination of William McKinley in 1901; Pinchot's sense of guilt seems entirely his own. Pinchot's currency grew with the ascendance of Roosevelt, culminating in 1905 in the transfer of the forest reserves to Pinchot's newly renamed United States Forest Service in the Department of Agriculture.[9]

Pinchot firmly embraced the ideas of Progressive conservation as the basis for his policy. He saw a world in which timber was wasted and feared that Americans would soon experience shortages of this critical staple. The goal of the professional forester, he believed, was to apply scientific management so as to preserve timber for the future while simultaneously assuring a constant supply for use. This dichotomy between management and use, which initially led to policy for the Forest Service, ironically became dogma as Pinchot's ideas changed. When the agency was later confronted with the public's desire for a broadened Forest Service mandate in areas such as recreation, re-

8. Steen, *The United States Forest Service,* 22–46; Andrew Denny Rodgers III, *Bernhard Eduard Fernow: A Story of North American Forestry* (Durham, NC: Forest History Society, 1991), 190–253; Char Miller, "Wooden Politics: Bernhard Fernow and the Quest for a National Forest Policy, 1876–1898," in Harold K. Steen, ed., *The Origins of the National Forests* (Durham, NC: Forest History Society, 1992), 287–300.

9. Char Miller, "The Greening of Gifford Pinchot," *Environmental History Review* 16:3 (Fall 1992): 1–20; Pinchot, *Breaking New Ground,* 1–122. Mark Hanna, the political boss of Ohio and a staunch supporter of President McKinley, feared Roosevelt and opposed his nomination for the vice-presidency. Hanna remarked upon Roosevelt's nomination that now the "damned cowboy was only a heartbeat from the White House." McKinley's assassination made Hanna's fears reality.

sponse was slow, in no small part as a result of the historic origins of the Forest Service.[10]

The creation of the United States Forest Service in 1905 inaugurated the second phase of early forestry. Committed to the ideals and aspirations of the Progressive era, Pinchot built the first genuine Progressive federal agency. His objectives included the prevention of timber famine, the wise use of natural resources, and the scientific and equitable management of the federal domain. Pinchot also sought to reshape local practices and to create a cadre of professionals who could teach the public as well as meet its demands for timber resources.[11]

At the grass roots, this meant rapid change. The forest reserves—soon to be renamed national forests to reflect Pinchot's sense that they were to be used instead of locked up—were paper entities with unclear boundaries, little organization, few programs, and fewer staff. By means of boundary and resource surveys, a national structure and clearly articulated chain of command, a range of management programs, and a greatly expanded staff, Pinchot sought to build an efficient agency that could lead by example. This required removing the incompetent, the avaricious, and the lazy; creating and implementing a set of rules and regulations; teaching new techniques; and winning the confidence of the public.[12]

None of this was easy to accomplish. In fact, in Region 1, comprising the forests of northern Idaho, western Montana, and eastern Washington State, it took the better part of twenty-five years to achieve such goals. Success was measured in increments, as foresters could only gradually bring order to the management of federal lands. The first areas brought under some form of management were either the most easily accessible, those closest to

10. Miller, "The Greening of Gifford Pinchot," 1–20; Rothman, "A Regular Ding-Dong Fight," 141–61; Hal K. Rothman, "Shaping the Nature of a Controversy: The Park Service, the Forest Service, and Cedar Breaks Proposal," *Utah Historical Quarterly* 55:3 (Summer 1987): 213–35; Clary, *Timber and the Forest Service,* 67–68; Steen, *The United States Forest Service,* 113–22, 152–62, 209–13.

11. Miller, "The Greening of Gifford Pinchot," 1–20; Hays, *Conservation and the Gospel of Efficiency,* 28–36.

12. Stephen Ponder, "Gifford Pinchot: Press Agent for Forestry," *Journal of Forest History* 31:1 (January 1987): 26–35.

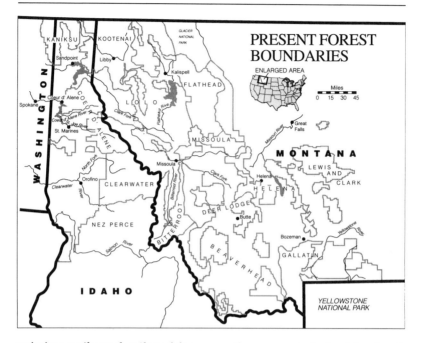

existing trails and railroad lines, or those most desired by local and regional timber companies. More remote lands, at the highest elevations or far from the lines of commerce, awaited the creation of infrastructure, the arrival of vehicles, and other accoutrements of modernity.

The spread of modern technology initiated the third phase of Forest Service history in the Inland Northwest. By about 1915, most new foresters hired in the region had a degree from one of the many forestry schools that had come to dot the West. Others were schooled at Duke University, Yale University, or another of the eastern schools that promoted forestry as a career for talented young advocates of "good government" and everything that concept entailed. Many had served in temporary or seasonal positions during their education, and a significant number were trained by professors who had put in their time in the woods. These young professionals, often called technical foresters by their predecessors, came to replace the unschooled but well-versed-in-the-woods types of the initial years of the Forest Service. With roads, trucks, equipment, a system of management, and an increasingly clear idea of the nature of forest resources in Region 1, the newcomers created a new, professional ethos that expanded not only the importance of their agency but their standing as individuals.

The difference that budding professionalism created became clear in the experiences of foresters in the field. In 1905, when the agency was founded, local men such as Elers Koch gave written exams and field tests to would-be foresters. The written section tested mere literacy; the field exam sought to find those with the proficiency and fortitude to survive the grueling and lonely life of an official assigned to administer one million acres of sparsely inhabited forest. Just fifteen years later new foresters had to have college degrees in their field, and they entered an agency with a cosmology, a set of procedures, a methodology, and a history of its own. When the authors speak of entry into the agency, the difference in their experience is a measure both of the passage of time and the institutionalization of the processes of the Forest Service.

Another way to mark the differences between these generations of personnel is by the nature of their personal lives. The initial foresters, those before 1905, were generally bachelors. The first of the post-1905 generation were more often married, but their wives rarely accompanied them to remote postings. By 1915 or so, it was increasingly common for rangers to take their wives to remote postings as telephone lines, communications networks, and a better system of trails and roads made life in the woods less than hellish. In the 1920s, young forestry school graduates received appointment to the agency, married their sweethearts, and headed off to their first posting in the same manner as any other college graduates of the time. Forestry had become a profession, its regimen as standard as that of other professions.

Throughout these three time periods (1890–1905, 1905–1910, 1910–1920), the experiences of foresters in the woods were distinctly different both from the ideals under which they were expected to operate and from the realities of life in a modern technological society. Until the 1920s, much of their work was performed under preindustrial conditions, without the broad array of transportation, communication, and material support that was so essential to the settlement of peripheries across the nation. Under these conditions, foresters were alone, applying a foreign value system to a land that lacked the commodities that had become basic components of existence in more settled parts of the nation.

Being alone in the woods in a more than million-acre domain gave foresters a kind of discretion uncommon for low-level federal employees. Foresters represented order, their so-called pine tree badge and the Use Book in which Gifford Pinchot standardized operating procedures becoming the equivalent of a sheriff's badge and a Bible. Foresters, in their capacity as official representatives, were often the sole purveyors of authority in remote areas in the Inland Northwest. They made decisions regarding the use of federally administered natural resources that were reviewed by their superiors, but on a day-to-day basis they interacted with the people of their area in a range of ways that reflected on the agency but could rarely be governed by the kinds of policies it made.

This location between cultures made for difficult choices. Often neighbors, friends, and acquaintances sought to play on their ties in order to bend and sometimes even break the rules of the agency. Standing up to such challenges required the kind of prowess that officials sought from those who wanted to be part of the agency. Foresters also had to be firm with a varied cast of characters—gunmen, claim-jumpers, trespassers, and squatters— many of whom had the ability to cause trouble for a ranger. The true test of a forester in the woods was the ability to make a decision, however much at variance with Washington policy, and make it stick.

The autonomy involved in the responsibility for one-million-acre forests gave foresters the opportunity to be petty tyrants, but such instances were apparently quite unusual. At the time, those who were selected for the agency or who chose federal forestry as a career possessed what might be termed "honorable character." The people culled from the small towns, logging camps, and farms of the Inland Northwest generally stood apart from their peers. They were known for their code of ethics, their prowess at work, reliability and temperance, or some similar virtues that were identifiable both to their neighbors and to the recruiters of Gifford Pinchot's Forest Service. Later forestry school graduates were imbued with zealous enthusiasm for utilitarian conservation and its ideals and entered an agency with a well-developed code. Although early foresters were not an incorruptible group, most felt so strongly about what they did that genuine miscreants were infrequent among them.

This devotion to duty was among the most prominent features of what could be called the cosmology of the early Forest Service in the field. Even when the official regulations did not answer local questions, foresters managed by a combination of common sense, confidence in authority, and local custom. The agency strove to implement ideals while foresters in the field sought to maintain the grudging respect they and their agency earned in small towns and logging camps. Combining both the principles of their agency and the value system of the places they lived, the foresters melded the best of the "pioneer" life with the highest principles of the Progressive movement.

Foresters did recognize that their role was unique for their time. As forest rangers, they served as a kind of primary authority, as a civilizing force in social matters as well as in resources management. Wholeheartedly embracing the ethic of Progressivism—for not to do so would surely have limited their effectiveness within the agency as well as their longevity in it—foresters served consciously and unconsciously as forces for "civilization." They represented federal authority and took that role seriously, encouraging both economic and social patterns of behavior that fit the dominant currents of their time.

These foresters were believers in progress through scientific management, the creed of efficiency so central to the entire concept of Progressivism. Selected from the mass of people in the woods precisely because they had exceptional value systems and skills, they felt little compunction about spreading the ideas of the new century. Reinforced by the extended network of foresters and led by the charismatic Pinchot, the men in the field rarely if ever questioned their duty as they saw it: to bring about change in the backcountry that would better not only the economic lot of people but their moral and ethical standing as well. Values such as these explain the common perception that the early Forest Service was a secular religion.

In the woods, foresters were subject to the changing whims of legislative and administrative policy made far away from them. Although the Forest Service valued its decentralized character and the autonomy its operatives had at the local and regional levels was astonishing, priorities could be and were changed without any input from the field. As one example, an often overlooked piece of legislation called the Forest Homestead Act or the Act of June 11, 1906—which made arable lands in national forests available to homesteaders—transformed the operations of the region and generated more work for early foresters than any other piece of legislation.[13] "June 11 work" necessitated the hiring of numerous people, took up most of the time not devoted to timber sales or fire fighting or management between 1906 and 1912, and compelled significant enforcement activity by the Forest Service. In the Inland Northwest, surveying, adjudicating, and administering June 11 claims took more time, resources, and money than any other task.

Fire suppression, prevention, and management constituted the other major demand on agency resources. The fires of 1910, in which more than eighty people died and more than 1.7 million acres were destroyed, were the most dramatic and dangerous, but significant and policy-altering conflagrations occurred in other years as well. The fires of 1910 were pivotal, and in subsequent years such as 1914, 1917, and 1919, foresters tried out the new technologies, practices, techniques, and procedures they developed in the aftermath of 1910. This process played an important part in developing agency culture, identity, and character.[14]

By the beginning of the 1920s, foresters in Region 1 had helped fashion an ordered world out of a vast domain of many trees and relatively few people. They had applied the doctrines of Progressive-era forestry and utilitarian conservation to a previously orderless world, developing a cosmology and a system of

---

13. This act provides an excellent example of the way in which forest history has been focused on upper echelon policy. Ramifications of the act appear in nearly every account of foresters in the field in this time period but generally rate little more than a footnote in the established histories of the Forest Service.

14. Stephen J. Pyne, *Fire in America: A Cultural History of Rural and Wildland Fire* (Princeton: Princeton University Press, 1982), 234–52.

implementation out of the values of their agency and their experiences, and created an agency culture that suited not only their self-image as foresters but the needs of their constituents.

In the letters in this book, foresters skillfully re-create this history in vivid detail. As a group, they were extremely literate, and a number possessed genuine literary skill. Most focused on their formative experiences within the agency, for it was those experiences that made the greatest impact upon them. The stories they told add new voices to the history of the United States Forest Service, American forestry in general, and the histories of Idaho, Montana, and eastern Washington. These individuals gave a clear picture of the nature of daily life in their agency, the pitfalls they faced, the means they used to solve professional and personal problems, and the nuances of finding a way to combine the demands of superiors with the customs and mores of remote places. In this, they laid the groundwork for a genuine interpretive social history of the early Forest Service.

Two

"The Whole Country Is Yours"

Federal Forest Land before 1905

T he set of principles that led to the need for the United States Forest Service began with the impulse to conserve and wisely use the natural resources of the American continent. The end of the idea of abundance, so dramatic a part of the westward movement of the American republic, left a large gap in national consciousness. The reality instead that the two coasts bounded the nation indicated to many in the 1890s that the practices of the past had become anachronistic. To those seeking positions of cultural, political, and economic leadership in American society, a future without the promise of more adjacent land into which to expand required a set of premises different from the ones embodied in the rapid and often arbitrary development of the American nation to that point.

The new premise, which came to be called conservation, had its beginnings in a long-established countertrend in American thinking. In his 1825 novel, *The Pioneers*, James Fenimore Cooper portrayed behavior he saw as typical of this new breed of human, the American. Unlike the productive farmer of Crève-coeur's neatly ordered eighteenth-century America, Cooper's nineteenth-century hunters were base individuals wholly unaware of the sentient nature of the world they inhabited. They shot aimlessly into a sky darkened by pigeons, felling hundreds, but not even bothering to collect them for food. Natty Bumppo, the Leatherstocking, and Chingachagook, the Last of the Mohicans, were joined by Judge Temple, the aristocratic character in the novel, in their revulsion at this scene. With a romanticized Enlightenment cosmology, Cooper linked the natural and the hierarchical in an ironic foreshadowing of the principles of the conservation movement.

There were far more real examples of misuse when Americans of the 1890s surveyed the world their industriousness had made. The great buffalo hunts of the middle of the century demonstrated an awesome capacity for waste. In the 1860s and 1870s, such hunters as the famous Buffalo Bill Cody and the lesser-known but often more effective Buffalo Bill Mathewson and J. R. Mead participated in the wholesale destruction of the American bison on the Great Plains. This adventure in hegemony, justified by the military rationale that the buffalo was the commissary of the Indian, left piles of stinking, rotting carcasses along the gleaming new railroad lines bringing settlers to the West.

Less imperialistic enterprises reflected the same value system. In the 1860s, the construction of the transcontinental railroad drew thousands of workers to the Rocky Mountains to turn trees into railroad ties, carving swaths out of the forests of the Rocky Mountains. By the end of the 1870s, timber was a prized commodity. The forests of New York, Pennsylvania, Ohio, and Indiana all were seriously depleted; the states of the upper Middle West faced the same fate. The 1880 Census reflected this new reality. In the census publication, the eminent botanist Charles Sargent wrote of the impending crisis in American timber; too much had been cut down too quickly and indiscriminately, he averred. Gifford Pinchot himself raised the prospect of a "timber famine" after one of his trips to Europe. While Americans still burnt trees to get them out of the way, Europeans desperately sought to manage the reduced quantity of timber that remained after thousands of years of similar behavior.

Nor were these instances unique. The spread of industrial society, which brought with it ever-widening zones of transformation and influence, also transported an avaricious tendency to reinvent landscapes. But the size of the continent and the seemingly endless expanse of land and natural resources had lulled Americans into a casual callousness. The New World was a land of plenty. Surely it would never run out of resources.

The announced end of the westward frontier following the Census of 1890 and the emergence of individuals and federal agencies that shared an expressed purpose to scientifically manage the resources of the nation began a move to change the attitudes and behaviors of the past. The closing of the frontier meant that Americans would have to use their resources more wisely to assure that part of their patrimony remained for future generations. In response to the rampant growth of industrial economy and the excesses of business leaders in an era of laissez-faire government, the federal government seemed the social agent best able to protect the public and its resources from the wiles of special interests.

Beginning in the 1890s, a small current of reform began to gather momentum in American society. Much of it focused on reclaiming moral authority, an arena previously given over to the leaders of industry—the robber barons in the parlance of some— and on creating a new sense of order. Reformers in many areas sought change in child labor legislation, education, and the responsibilities of government among a host of other causes. An activist spirit, emphasizing equity and efficiency, gained standing and stature.

Forestry was an ideal field to which to apply such a value system. By the end of the nineteenth century, the forests of the eastern half of the nation had been cut over and left for slash. As much as eighty million acres of timber land had been cut without being replenished; there were few if any provisions for reforestation. Wood was cheap, and as a result, there was no economic reason to cut timber efficiently. Huge quantities of wood simply rotted, for as long as the culture of abundance persisted it made little sense to take anything but prime timber. The thick forests of the eighteenth century had disappeared in an echo of the lifeless pigeons of Cooper's novel. As scarcity became a New World concept, many cried out for the efficient, efficacious management of American forests.

The forest reserves, those parcels of federal land reserved to protect timber and watersheds that were later renamed national forests, were an afterthought. Amendment 24 to the General Appropriations Act of 1891 authorized the president to set aside forest reserves, whether of commercial value or not, from public land in any state or territory. Ostensibly this was to protect people from the effects of flooding caused by deforestation, but in reality it began the process of creating a vast system of federally owned forests. This piece of legislation formed the original basis of the federal forests that American foresters have since managed. Yet the power granted in this legislation was not comprehensive, because it did not include the right to fund the administration of reserved areas.

Without funds, managers, or even rudimentary regulations, these reserved areas simply stood. Benjamin Harrison and Grover Cleveland both took advantage of their prerogative prior to 1897, when Cleveland's proclamation of twenty-one million acres in thirteen separate forest reserves on Washington's Birthday sparked the outrage of westerners. After an extensive battle over the president's right to issue such proclamations, the Senate resolved the question by presenting criteria for the establishment of forest reserves and, later, by allowing funding for the administration of reserved areas. This act, an amendment to the Sundry Civil Appropriations Act of 1897 now referred to as the organic act of the national forests, made a system of administration for the reserved lands essential.

Forester Walter A. Donaldson recalled the announcement of the new reservations in 1897:

> News came via Western Union that President Grover Cleveland signed a proclamation "reserving all public lands containing timber which was more valuable for timber than for other purposes." These were to be known as Government Timber Reservations, under the administration of the General Land Office, Department of the Interior.

The proclamation of reserved forested areas and the creation of a system of administration were separate procedures. The General Land Office (GLO) had myriad obligations, many of which its agents performed poorly, and forestry had become a specialized field. General Land Office agents lacked the training and often the inclination to manage timber. Nor did the agency have the kind of resources to support this new and seemingly complicated responsibility.

Exacerbating the situation was the reputation of the GLO as the most corrupt agency in the most crooked department in the

government. Two commissioners of the GLO resigned in separate scandals between 1900 and 1906, confirming what many already believed about the agency. Many of its positions were used
as patronage by politicians, creating a class of employees who
knew little about their duties. Some early employees regarded
their position as a sinecure or an opportunity for graft. None of
this made the life of federal representatives in the field any easier.
Saddled with such liabilities, they faced an ongoing struggle to
justify their presence.

Many who lived in the West signed on to manage the forests.
The job offered status and a dependable if not always ample pay-
check, both valued commodities. They found that they had vast
expanses under their immediate jurisdiction and very few tools
and amenities to support the work. Nor did they have access to
communications systems or significant budgets to support their
work. They faced trying circumstances. R. L. Woesner, who
knew some of what he called "the old-time rangers" and worked
for the United States Forest Service (USFS) after 1910, described
the life of the early ranger:

> In those days the "Forest Reserves" as they were called, were
> administered by the Department of [the] Interior. I recall when the
> old Lewis and Clark "Forest Reserve" took in all the territory now
> embraced in the Kootenai, Flathead, Lewis and Clark, and I be-
> lieve part of the Cabinet National Forest and [what has since be-
> come] Glacier National Park. The area north of the Great Northern
> Railroad was called the North Division and that south of the Great
> Northern was known as the South Division.
>
> This vast area was administered by a very few men. A ranger in
> those days usually had from a half million to a million acres of ter-
> ritory to cover, for which he received a salary of about $60.00 per
> month for himself and the use of as many horses as was necessary
> for him to operate, which was usually not less than two. He also
> was required to furnish his own camp equipment, his own tools
> and build his own cabin if he had one.
>
> Expense accounts were unknown in those days, and a Ranger
> usually carried subsistence supplies and camp outfit with him
> wherever he went. Most of the old-time Rangers I knew were

bachelors; however, I do recall having met a "squaw man" [a man married to or living with a Native American woman] or two in the Forest Service. They were all good woodsmen and could, and did live under rather primitive conditions. They were usually very good judges of horse flesh, and could drive a sharp bargain in a horse trade.

Trails or roads were few and far between. What trails there were, were mostly just trapper blazes [marks left on trees by trappers to show their way] across country and the few roads existing then were barely passable by team and wagon. In case a ranger wanted a trail any place, it was up to him to cut it himself with his own tools.

Long cross-country trips were often made through forested areas where there were no trails or roads with saddle and pack animals. We would probably hesitate some before starting out on those trips today, but it was all in the day's work to them.

Each ranger usually did his own fire fighting, or as much of it as he could, alone. Occasionally he received help from a neighboring district or the assistance of some trapper or settler who received no pay for his services. There were no "stand-by" crews then or emergency smoke chasers, or any smoke chasers at all. It was all up to the Ranger.

There were no telephone lines or other means of communication except by messenger on foot or horseback. This was so slow that by the time help arrived it was always too late. So the actual accomplishments in fire fighting in those days must be credited to the Ranger himself.

It was the custom of each ranger to keep a diary as far back as I can remember. I think these diaries would shed much light upon human behavior, human struggles and achievements of those days, and I quote a part of one ranger's diary I once read which was as follows: "Have been fighting fire up here above Lake McDonald [presently in Glacier National Park] two days now, with nothing to work with but my hands. Skinned both of my knees climbing up here over the rocks. Both of my hands are burnt and skinned too. My God, how much longer can I stand it?"

The next day's entry—"Got the fire under control. My knees have scabbed over and feel pretty good today, but my hands are in a hell of a shape. Dammed if I'll ever fight fire with my bare hands again."

Local people did not always feel kindly toward these government representatives who, it seemed, came west to tell people how to live. G. I. Porter, who joined the USFS in May 1907 and remained with the agency for thirty-five years, began as an adversary of the foresters:

As a prospector and miner in the territory now covered by the Nezperce National Forest, I, together with others of my ilk, was resentful of the restrictions imposed upon us by the regulations of the new Bureau of Forestry [actually the Division of Foresty, the arm of the Department of the Interior responsible for administering forest reserves. The Bureau of Forestry was the name of the division in the Department of Agriculture that Gifford Pinchot administered]. We had been accustomed to locating any character of land under our interpretation of the mining laws, cutting timber at will, without reference to the good of the forest, or viewing without alarm the frequent fires destroying timber, watershed cover and range.

Our intolerance (as I did not see it then in the nineties) was not mitigated by the character of administration of the lands withdrawn. Some—not all, be it noted—of the higher officials were totally unacquainted with the land and the inhabitants thereof, and some of the local officials were more interested in padding their expense accounts than in the proper performance of their duties.

The records of those early days are full of instances of arbitrary actions on the part of such officials. Further, some of the minor employees detailed for local administrative duties were politically appointed, without reference to fitness or knowledge of the land or the people.

To instance one such event: In 1900 a company which had been operating for several years had been accustomed to cutting timber for buildings, flumes, etc., without restriction. All lumber used prior to 1900 had been obtained from timber cut before 1897 and therefore was not cut in trespass. [This timber had been cut before the establishment of the reserve but was collected after-

ward.] By 1900 the flumes were damaged, and it became necessary to cut 100,000 feet b.m. [board measure] of lumber. Application was made through the local supervisor for this lumber. The
mine manager accompanied the supervisor in a casual preliminary
inspection of the area from which other timber had been cut, and
the official submitted the application—with his recommendation.
I still wonder what his recommendation recommended, since the
application was denied in Washington, the reason given: the
stumpage value would not cover the cost of surveying and administering the sale. The mining company went out of business, thus
depriving the community of benefits accruing from employment
of a number of men.

Porter knew; he was the mine manager. Like many others, he
learned through experience that the advantages of conservation
policies outweighed their disadvantages:

This long-winded dissertation may be indicative of the attitude
of the "old-timer" toward the early trials of the forest officers,
which attitude, in time, and through the efforts of the Forest Service, was changed—first, to tolerance, and then to intelligent acceptance and cooperation.

Roy A. Phillips remembered an early forester who seemed to
typify the breed:

George Ring was truly one of the pioneer rangers. In all the
early day photographs George is characterized by a derby hat and
a big chaw of tobacco that bulged out a cheek. He first worked in
1897 under the old political appointment system. His supervisor
ran a saloon in Grangeville and it was his daily custom to go out
on the porch of the saloon, where he could see the mountain
back of Grangeville, and then go back in to the saloon and write in
his diary, "Viewed the forest today." [This story developed an
apocryphal character. It has been attributed to most of the more
colorful personalities of the early era.] All the rangers had ranches
or other occupations and spent very little time out on the forest.
George said that his first summer was spent in a camp where he

thought the forest should be, but when the boundary was surveyed he found that he ate on the forest and slept off of it, as the
boundary line established a year later ran right through the camp.
George worked at the job and familiarized himself with the forest.
He was the only man on the forest who survived an inspection by
a Washington office inspector. When I went to the Nezperce in
1928, I found old boundary notices posted by George Ring in
1908.

Foresters faced genuine problems with local constituencies.
Albert Cole of the Madison Forest Reserve—now part of the
Beaverhead National Forest—told of his experiences:

In order to contrast the difference that "political pull" worked
in connection with the officers of the Forest Service at this time
with the situation a few years back when most all of the Forest Supervisors and rangers were appointed through the influence of the
different political organizations, there went to Washington three
separate and distinct petitions to Senators and members of Congress for the removal of the Supervisor of this Forest Reserve on
the grounds that he was too severe in his administration of the
timber-cutting and grazing uses on the Madison Forest Reserve. I
was shown one of these petitions, headed by the local district
judge, a Republican, and signed by Republicans and Democrats
alike, but all of these petitions were of no avail and Mr. [J. B.] Seely
continued to stay on as Supervisor for a number of years. Mr.
Seely was also warned by an anonymous letter not to show himself in the upper Madison Valley on pain of death by hanging. Mr.
Seely promptly rode up there on horseback and called on several
of the ranchers who he knew were after his scalp, but no one offered to harm him or even threaten him to his face. [Seely died a
natural death many years later.]
    In contrast to the attitude of some of the ranchers, there were
others, mostly the owners of the larger holdings, both sheep and
cattle men, who agreed that some regulation of the ranges had to
be made, as there was serious friction between the owners of both
classes of stock in the use of the range, and some bloodshed and

terrorism had been resorted to by both sheep and cattle men in the fight for grazing grounds.

One incident had occurred in the summer of 1904 when one outfit that ran both classes of stock had one of their sheep outfits raided, the herder beaten and told to clear out, and their sheep scattered through the timber, the camp burned and everything destroyed by cowboys belonging to their own ranch. The herder made his way back to the home ranch, but not before the cowboys had returned and boasted of their exploit. About the first man the herder met when he got back to the home ranch was the foreman, and as the herder had never been to the home ranch before, having been hired and outfitted on a small unit of the company ranches, the foreman asked him very profanely what he was doing there. The herder told his story of the raid and said that he had been herding for this outfit. The foreman and his cowboys were wearing large bandanna handkerchiefs over their faces when they raided the sheep camp, so that the herder did not recognize the foreman. The foreman recognized the herder all right but did not let on to him who had raided him. The incident was kept quiet for a long time, but the facts finally leaked out and other sheep outfits used the story as propaganda against the bloodthirstiness of cowboys in general.

Despite problems of this nature, the administration of the national forests continued. Old antagonists such as Porter gradually came to understand the concept of conservation. During Porter's time, he saw forestry undergo astonishing transformation. He also met the legendary characters of Region 1, not the least of whom was Major Frank A. Fenn:

Major Fenn was Superintendent of Forest Resources in that part of Idaho in which this scene was located.

Forest Reserves and the Bureau of Forestry, and the officials thereof, were not popular in those days and those places. Many residents, particularly small stockowners, miners, and others whose activities had not been restricted in relation to the cutting of timber, grazing of livestock and location of land, considered the new regulations as infringements upon their liberties and the pursuit of profits, and bitterly resented any interference therewith.

The results of one controversy, however, were beneficial to ranchers interested, and did much to bring about a better understanding of the principles and policies of the new administration of the public lands.

A mining company, of which the Miner was resident manager, had located under the mining laws, several hundred acres of meadowland, as placer mining claims, and two dredges of rather primitive design (although up to date at that time) had been erected on the meadows. Both had failed to make a profit, and were left to the mercy of the elements. The first, brought by pack animals over the old Nezperce Trail in 1893, was a total loss. The other, constructed in 1899, had the benefit of wagon-road transportation, and was of later model, but not more successful in bringing up paydirt from bedrock than the first.

The company, however, with the hope that time would develop better methods of gold saving, made the effort to protect its long-range interests by applying for patent to several 160-acre tracts of the meadow.

For a number of years prior to and during the operations of the mining company, several farmers had been cropping the land. Hay was the principal crop, for which there was a good market. They operated on sufferance of the mining company, which claimed surface—as well as mining—rights to the land. Since withdrawal of the lands from settlement, about 1897, the farmers had not been able to establish any rights to the land as agricultural land, but in the hope that future legislation would correct the existing laws, entered protest against issuing patent to the mining company.

The decision of the General Land Office of the Department of the Interior hinged upon the relative value of the claims as mineral or agricultural in value. Local administrators of the Forest Reserve took the part of the farmers, and the fun began. The case was decided in favor of the company in the local office of the Register and Receiver in Lewiston, Idaho, but upon appeal to the Commissioner of the General Land Office this decision was reversed, pending final proof by contending parties of the primary value of the land.

Here is where the Major stepped into the picture, having been a side-line observer, but with his own ideas on the subject up to this time. The company, having protected its rights by performing the required "assessment work" on the claims, prepared to continue this work in the spring of 1904. Men and steam engine and pump were started digging to try to locate the pay channel in the meadow. The Major was preparing to do the same sort of work to prove or disprove the mineral values, and here was his chance to achieve results at a minimum cost to the Bureau of Forestry.

Bureau funds were low, and such investigation to a point of definite decision as to value was impossible with funds and manpower available. So, what to do?

The Major and the Miner already were good friends. They combined forces. The Major supplied manpower to equal that of the Miner, and had the benefit of the power and pump. It is impossible to dig to bedrock at a depth of ten or twelve feet or more without a pump to keep the water down. During that summer they worked together, and determined, to the satisfaction of both, that gold-bearing gravel profitable to work did not exist.

The company abandoned its claims, application for patent was denied, the farmers gloated and the Miner lost his job. Later, the meadow was settled under the Forest Homestead Act of June 11, 1906 [which allowed the homesteading of arable land within national forests], the Miner being one of the settlers, and later receiving title to his homestead claim.

A sidelight: The local ranger, a bitter enemy of the Miner, threatened state's prison to the Miner, holding that the Miner's sworn statement as to the mineral value of the land when applying for patent, and his sworn statement as to the agricultural value when applying for homestead constituted justification for prosecution for perjury. But the ranger lost his job, through political action, the Miner took it over several years later (through Civil Service examination), and the Major and the Miner remained good friends forever after.

And in after years the Major took great pleasure in relating the story—of the only instance in his long official career in which one whose activities were under investigation assisted the investigating officer in proving the case to his own disadvantage.

The Major: Major Frank A. Fenn—may he rest in peace.

The Miner: Your relator.

Fenn was a revered figure among the first generation of for-esters. His combination of ingenuity, personal commitment, and skill inspired admiration. Nor was the respect granted Fenn lim-ited just to him. His wife, called "Grandma" Fenn, also engen-dered respect, as Ralph Hand of the Nezperce National Forest ex-plained:

> Major Fenn's wife, whom everybody called "Grandma Fenn," was equally active in the social affairs of the community during those years. As a sixteen-year-old girl, she had come to Mount Idaho from Portland to visit an uncle, just in time to get caught in the Nez Perce Indian War. It was said that at the battle for Mount Idaho she molded bullets for the defenders—a detachment of the Idaho Militia in which Major Fenn was then a first lieutenant. They were married about a year later. Grandma Fenn outlived her hus-band by nearly thirty years and died at the home of a daughter at Walla Walla at the age of ninety-five.

Grandma Fenn was something of an exception. For foresters, she embodied a kind of ideal, a combination of experience, steadiness, and grace under pressure that most of the other women they met did not share. The chances of meeting some-one like her were slim, for her urban background and learned ex-perience granted her unique status.

It was only after the development of at least a minimal infra-structure in the woods that rangers brought their wives with them. Initially, the group of men who worked for the General Land Office in the national forests were bachelors or men living with or married to Native American women. In the late nine-teenth century, to have the kind of knowledge necessary to work in the forests implied being on the periphery, a condition that mitigated against what would have been a conventional marriage at the time.

Such a condition limited the pool of potential spouses to which rangers had access. Young women from cities were un-likely to be attracted to a life of privation and isolation in the woods, and few middle-class women had the skills to make survival in the woods pleasant. When rangers were fortunate enough to marry, they usually wed women from the small towns and homesteads of their national forest. The men and women shared a kind of compatibility based on experience that was essential to their survival as a couple.

Ties of marriage also accentuated existing local relations, for the individuals with whom foresters dealt were often parents of the women they courted. The early rangers administered the claims individuals and businesses made for federal land. A range of laws helped individuals acquire the measuring stick of independent wealth of preindustrial people—land. Primary among these laws were the Homestead Act of 1862; the Timber Culture Act of 1873, which allowed settlers to substitute the planting of trees for some of the requirements of the Homestead Act; and the Timber and Stone Act of 1878, which allowed the sale of nontillable public timber land for personal use. There were frequent attempts to deceive the foresters, and people like O. O. Lansdale, of the St. Joseph National Forest, were sent to resolve the problems:

In 1901, Mrs. Lansdale and I moved to the forks of the St. Maries River, to what is now Clarkia [Idaho]. I hauled in groceries, supplies and equipment for pack trains to handle the timber rush of lumber companies and local people after homesteads and stone timber claims. Our first customers were C. W. Weyerhaeuser and two sons, and Mr. Rutledge and agents of the Howard Lumber Company with their cruisers to look over the Marble Creek drainage and Elk Basin. Then the local people from Moscow and Lewiston began coming. Plenty of locators waiting for them. The three Fry brothers, three Therault brothers, three Mix brothers, and Foly and Robinson. Fees ranged from $100 to $300 per claim. It was very common for two and three to be located on the same 160-acre tract—where the timber was thick and the ground rough.

In April Judge Pickrell and a party of eight went into the Little North Fork of the Clearwater after [to evaluate and deny] stone timber claims [those filed under the Timber and Stone Act of 1873]. I was to meet them at the snow line with saddle horses at a specified time to bring them out to my station. They failed to show up, and after waiting for them a couple of days I snowshoed [put snowshoes on] my horses and went looking for them.

When they reached the summit of Lookout Mountain, they had become confused and had followed their own tracks around the mountain. They were without anything to eat for four days, and were in bad shape when I found them. I understood that one of their party later died from exposure.

They went into the Clearwater via the Freezeout Pass and Hotel de Misery. The last name is inscribed on a large hemlock tree, many years before, possibly by Captain [actually Lieutenant John] Mullan, who blazed a trail from St. Louis to Astoria [to connect the headwaters of the Missouri River with the Columbia River system], or by General [Oliver O.] Howard while chasing Chief Joseph after the Whitebird massacre, for the following summer I found an old muzzle-loading cannon and one wheel near the tree.

In May 1902, logging started at the forks. [A man named] Knifong built a saloon and called the place Lansdale. We moved the old post office from Clarkia on the White ranch here, and called the place Clarkia.

There was no law south of Wallace, the county seat, and the place was getting wild. I was appointed judge there, and later was elected. I did not have much trouble with the lumberjacks; while the old-time jacks were wild and tough, they were credited with two virtues in particular—respect for women and the law. Clarkia was only fifty miles from the county seat through the St. Joe and Marble Creek country; one hundred seventy-five miles by boat, train, and stage. My principal trouble was with the natives there. A group of "hill-billies," Kansans and Oklahomans, had squatted there years before. Only a part of them could read, and they had no respect for the law, but made their own. Instead of a gavel to call court to order I used a No. 8 shotgun.

The Stone Timber Act and the homesteading law were sure a joke in the Reserve. I have packed homesteaders to their claims that did not know they were theirs. The peeled cedar log cabin in Elk Basin was where many applicants took their witnesses to look over the corners before proving up.

In the spring and summer of 1903, I was packing supplies for

A. H. Rianerson from Clarkia on the township survey on the Chamberlain and Forty-nine Meadows.

In October, the chief left the cook at Forty-nine Meadows, the head camp, alone. On Saturday I unloaded 15 pack loads of supplies. Monday I went back to the main camp and there were no groceries. The cook had set all the groceries on fire to force the party out. I went to Clarkia for another load; two days going out. Coming back, it had snowed 40 inches. I was eight days getting to the Clearwater and met the outfit coming out, leaving everything behind. We were seven days getting out. We started with 17 horses and shot 11 of them when they gave out breaking trail.

The law enforcement responsibilities of the rangers could become onerous. Even at this early stage, the woods were full of speculators who sought to gain access to timber land, sometimes at the expense of legitimate homesteaders. Lansdale continued:

The killing at Marble Creek climaxed the last stand of some of the large lumber mill companies to get control of the cream of the white pine before the Forest Service cracked down on stone timber and homesteading violations.

One company in particular hired C. Chambers to take a bunch (I won't call them men) to jump some of the best homesteads, picking out a section of virgin timber. For protection, they would build a four-room house in the center of the section. One room would be on each of the four 160 acres.

One of the jumpers, after seeing one of their gang killed, made his get-away out to Santa Town, leaving his wife to make the 30 miles alone carrying a youngster in her arms. I took this man back with me and met the Sheriff from Wallace.

I found a man by the name of Bulie dead in the trail, then his horse and dog. About a quarter of a mile farther was a man named Hendricks, also dead. The sheriff, a deputy and I stayed all night at Anderson's claim. The next morning they went back to Wallace, not even seeing the victims.

It was up to me, acting as coroner, to hold an inquest and bury them. Being all alone, the inquest was easy—just a case of dispensation of Providence. The burial was not so easy. Digging two graves with a piece of cedar board; then, with a rope around their feet, dragging them to their graves with the rope around the saddle horse.

Other early foresters dealt with disorder in the same direct manner. One, Frank F. Liebig, received his training as a forester in Germany and came to the Flathead, Montana, area around the turn of the century. His first district assignment in 1901 included one million acres. It was the approximate area of what is now Glacier National Park. He was the first ranger appointed to the area, serving three years with the Department of the Interior and thirty more with the Forest Service. Liebig was typical of the early forest rangers, self-reliant, determined, and persevering:

> In the early spring of 1902 on one of my trips to the foot of Lake McDonald, a man was waiting for me who said his name was F. N. Haines and that he was "looking for a good man that would like to work as a Forest ranger for Uncle Sam." He said he had heard much of me, that I didn't drink or get on a spree, and the main thing was that I knew the country and was not afraid of anything. He then asked me if I would like to tackle the job. He said the pay was $60 a month, board myself, and furnish a horse or two. I told him I made twice that much with my oil claims. But he insisted that I should take the job, as there would be some promotion and higher pay if I stayed with the Service. So I finally consented and went with him to Kalispell, where I had to fill out several forms nearly two feet long and go before a notary public, also get my citizenship papers all fixed up, and then the whole works was sent to the Department of the Interior in Washington, D.C. This was about the end of March or first of April in 1902.
>
> After that I went up the North Fork and the east side of the Rockies, and forgot all about my ranger's job. When I finally came home to the foot of Lake McDonald, I found in the Belton post office letters from Washington that I was a Forest ranger for over a month, and had to go to Kalispell to take the oath of office and get more definite instructions.
>
> The Supervisor gave me a notebook or two and a nice shiny silver badge. It said on it, "Department of the Interior, Ranger." The

Supervisor also gave me a couple of big sheets or forms, on which I had to state what I did every day, and send the sheet in at the end of the month to Kalispell. This report was sometimes half a month late, and the officials in Washington could not understand why I wasn't on time. I guess they didn't know that I had half a million acres to patrol, with very few trails in the area.

Then the Supervisor gave me a double-bitted axe and a one-man crosscut saw and a box of ammunition for my 45-70 rifle, and told me to "go to it, and good luck." He said, "the whole country is yours, from Belton to Canada and across the Rockies to the prairie or Waterton Lake and the foot of St. Mary's Lake." It comprised nearly the present Glacier National Park.

The instructions were to look for fires, timber thieves, which were plentiful all along the Great Northern Railway, and to look for squatters and game violators. I sure had my hands full, and then some.

A ranger and a mounted police were on the same footing. People always liked us a long ways off. More than once I have been waylaid, but, like the preacher and the bear, the Lord was on my side. My reputation as a good shot or Uncle's badge buffaloed the trespasser, and I always came out on top.

I guess the only time I was a little worried was once when word was brought to me by some homesteader that a bunch of Cree Indians had come across the Canadian border on the North Fork with about 10 or 12 lodges and 40 dogs and were killing all the moose and smoking the meat. I sent word to Ranger [Frederick] Herrig, stationed at Fortine, to meet me at Round Prairie near Bowman Creek. I also took F. Geduhn, a homesteader from the head of Lake McDonald, and we all met at the place mentioned.

Herrig was one of Roosevelt's Roughriders, and a quite imposing figure. He generally rode a dark bay horse, decked up with a silver-studded bridle and martingale. He wore mostly high-top boots, a big .44 strapped on his belt and a 45-70 in a scabbard, and he wore the ranger's badge always in plain sight, and a big Russian wolfhound was his steady companion.

Well, to make the story short, we found nine tepees north of Kintla Creek near a big willow flat. And we found plenty of meat over some poles with a fire underneath. Geduhn held my horse while I walked up to the tepees, where three or four Cree Indians were cutting up some meat. Ranger Herrig rode just fifty feet behind me, his rifle all ready for action. I had my rifle in my hands too. When we got close to the camp we were met by about twenty or more dogs. Men came from everywhere, and all the squaws and kids ran into the tepees.

I hollered for the chief to come out. Finally a diseased-looking Indian stepped out and made himself known as the responsible party. I told him that he came across the line and not to kill any more moose. He said they had a fire across the line which drove all the moose into the United States and they were hard up for winter food. I told him again that they ran all the game out of the country with their dogs.

Some of the Indians didn't want to go. I told them they had to break camp next morning or we would kill all the dogs. The Indians could not exist without the dogs. These dogs were trained to surround a moose and hold him until the Indian comes up and kills him.

We went to their camp next day about the middle of the forenoon, and no signs of breaking their camp. This time Indians were hiding behind tents and trees, no squaws in sight, but plenty of dogs. The old Indian chief was there to meet me and said they couldn't move for a week yet until all their meat was cured.

First thing three or four shots crashed out, and a couple of dead dogs rolled on the ground. Ranger Herrig couldn't stand it any longer, and wanted to mop up all the dogs. I got ready for action also, thinking that the Indians sure would get even with us. So I hollered to Herrig and Geduhn to hold their fire for a minute to see what the Indians had to say. Everything was confusion in the camp, and I thought lead would be flying in our direction any second. Then the chief hollered and told me they would move immediately.

The lodges went down, and in three hours they were on the trail up the North Fork and across the Canadian border. We hung around for several days, but the Crees stayed away.

Such an approach might seem drastic late in the twentieth century, but at the time the outlook of men who administered land dictated direct action. Foresters actually had little control over the land for which they were responsible, and resorting with a "might makes right" approach was habit, necessity, and common practice. The badge gave them authority; the circumstances of their existence often made negotiations both evidence of weakness and invitation to assault. That the trespassers were Indian certainly assured swift punishment, for at the turn of the century Indian needs did not exist on the scale of federal values. The level of force and the insistent manner used in this incident were typical of the way in which foresters dealt with the problems they faced. Anything less than a firm stance could make violators, Indian or otherwise, feel confident in their defiance.

The incident also highlighted the importance of good relations with local people. "F. Geduhn," a local homesteader, accompanied the foresters on this excursion; presumably he had a vested interest in the dispersal of the Cree people, and he inspired the confidence of these two hard-bitten foresters. Most accounts of conflict reveal the presence of others in the rangers' entourage. With so few rangers, the ability to form the equivalent of a posse was essential. Local people had to take a role in protecting the lands in question.

The foresters most likely selected people they could depend on in potentially difficult situations. People such as Geduhn were informal deputies, necessary for the uniformed rangers to make an impression and even more so if violence ensued. Rangers appreciated the commitment of such people and presumably were predisposed to returning any favors granted them when the opportunity presented itself.

This informal selection process may have embodied a class system in which people who were trusted by the rangers got a better hearing than those about whom the foresters had reservations. In these remote places, ties between people were important; enhancing those ties was a priority for the foresters. Those who cooperated with the needs of the rangers could be certain that camaraderie would yield advantages down the road.

This put the ranger's judgment of individual character on the level of that of a judge. People who seemed to be obstacles were treated as such. Their word did not carry as much weight as might that of someone with whom the rangers had cordial relations. Field rangers made recommendations on a range of policy matters. At any point, a negative view of an individual could color not only local relations but those with the agency and its resources as a whole.

The foresters who worked together under such conditions developed close personal relationships. They shared seemingly endless misery and discomfort and had to be able to depend on each other in such difficult situations as one Liebig described:

> The very next year Ranger Herrig saved me from drowning. It was in October, and bitterly cold nights. Sheet ice was floating down the North Fork. Riding up the river, I saw a big smoke rising up in the Coal Creek area on the west side of the river. I rode to the head of the Big Prairie to get a couple of settlers to help me on the fire. Just before I got to the place the horse stepped in a badger hole and nearly broke his leg. He was useless for a week. When I arrived at the homesteader's place nobody was home. I put the horse in the corral to look the fire over on foot.
>
> Before I got to the river here comes Ranger Herrig to pay me a visit. He saw the smoke also. And we decided to tackle the fire at once. We got a mattock and a couple of axes and left word for the settlers to follow when they came home. When we came to the river crossing, which was about 100 yards wide and two and a half feet at the deepest place, I had to wade across the river, as his horse would not stand for a double load. So he crossed over with the horse, and the big Russian wolfhound, and myself following. I had off my shoes and pants and underwear, to be dry when I got over. Before I got two-thirds across I got the cramps in my legs in the ice-cold water. My legs refused to move, and I had to drag myself on my hands to the shore in about 20 inches of water. Herrig just got across, when he was looking and saw what happened. He rode the horse right back and caught me just in time and dragged me to the shore. I lost my memory for 20 minutes, and when I came to Herrig was rubbing my body and legs to get circulation in my body started. After an hour I was in shape to hit the trail again, and had quite a stretch of the fire surrounded when the settlers arrived. One settler had a horse which didn't mind a double load in crossing the river, and I sure made use of it. The fire was either a lightning hangover, or started by hunters. I think it was the latter.

Our first ranger meeting, if I remember it right, was held at the foot of Lake McDonald in 1904, with about five or six assistant rangers helping out, a Mr. [E. A.] Sherman and a Mr. [Earle] Clapp from Washington, D.C. [both of whom later held high-level posts in the Forest Service] visiting us, and mostly supervising the meeting, telling us there would be a great change in the Forest Service in the near future, which was true. The very next year the Forest Service was transferred from the Department of the Interior to the Department of Agriculture.

Under the old Department our Forest was called the Northern Division of the Lewis & Clark Forest Reserve [north of the Great Northern Railroad tracks]. The present Flathead and Lewis & Clark Forests were once one Forest and called the Southern Division of the Lewis & Clark Forest Reserve. Its first Supervisor was a man by the name of [Gus] Moser. He lived in Ovando, and he made the round trip through the Forest once in a year—at least I only saw him every other year in Belton. And the first Supervisor stationed in Kalispell was Page Bunker.

A man by the name of B. Daughs [who] started at Lake Mc-Donald as a guard, now retired also, helped me in the early days of 1904–06 on trail work. We were working at one time on the Continental Divide near the headwaters of the Belly River and Mineral Creek when we spotted a big smoke in the North Fork Valley between Quartz and Bowman Creek, so we cut across country, below Vulture Peak and down Logging Creek and Lake. The shortest distance not over 20 miles, but what a country. We made it, but that was all. Horses nearly all in, and ourselves too. Not much clothes left on us either. Half the time a trapper's trail and the other half a mountain goat's trail. And when we finally got to the fire a thunderstorm came up. Lord, how it rained, and how cold we were. We didn't say much, but we thought a lot—nothing pleasant either.

One of the most formidable tasks that early foresters faced was surveying land to determine what should be reserved by presidential proclamations. In Region 1, largely unsettled, this was a task of paramount significance. Elers Koch was a Montana native who attended Montana State College in Bozeman, went on to receive a master's degree in forestry in 1903 from Yale University, and became one of most important figures in the first generation of American forestry. He described the surveying process:

There may be some historical interest in the early boundary examinations which laid out many of the Region One National Forests. Even before the Department of Agriculture took over the Forest Reserves from the Department of [the] Interior, Gifford Pinchot realized that without further loss of time the remaining forest land in the West which was still public domain should be reserved. With Theodore Roosevelt as President, it was only necessary to get the necessary data as to general suitability of the land as Forest Reserves and the location of the boundaries on the map.

To this end a rush job was put over, principally in 1903 and 1904, to make the necessary field examinations. F. E. Olmstead was put in charge of the work. The personnel were all young men, mostly just out of forest school, and, considering their lack of experience, they did a mighty good job. The men engaged in that work in those years, as I remember them, were Smith Riley, Coert DuBois, Frank Reed, R. E. Benedict, W. H. B. Kent, John Hatton, R. B. Wilson, R. V. R. Reynolds, a man named Hereford, and myself. There were probably one or two others I have forgotten.

It was probably the best and most interesting job there ever was in the Forest Service. A man was given a State map of California, or Montana, or Idaho, with a green-colored block indicating the general area he was to cover. The first job was to go to the local Land Office and take off on township plats the status of the land. At the same time rough copies were made of the drainage and topography from the township plats of such of the area as was surveyed. Sometimes a USGS [U.S. Geological Survey] map was available, or some sort of a county map. Then the examiner proceeded to ride the country and see it for himself. The area was covered usually at the rate of about two days to a township, and we really saw and rode every township. A rough type map was made showing the general classification of the cover. If there was no map, the examiner made a map as he went along.

Each man worked alone on a separate unit. He was allowed complete latitude as to how he covered the job. He might engage a packer with pack horse and saddle horses, or he might ride the country on a saddle horse, stopping at ranches, sheep camps, mines, or whatever offered when night overtook him. It was surely enjoyable work, each man his own boss, and seeing new country every day. The mapping was expected to be only approximate and there was no great amount of burdensome detail to worry about.

Considering the rapidity with which the work was done, it is surprising how well the original work has stood up. Most of the boundaries so established have had little modification in subsequent years.

We spent the summer and fall in the field, and in late fall all repaired to Washington with our notes and maps and spent the winter getting the data on paper. As fast as a unit was completed a proclamation was drawn and sent to President Roosevelt for approval. It was a quick and efficient job, and before Congress got around to repeal the authority of the President to proclaim Forest Reserves [in 1907], nearly all the remaining forested public land in the West had been safely covered into the Reserves.

In 1904, I covered the Gallatin, the Tobacco Root Range, now in the Beaverhead, and the Castle Mountains, now in the Lewis & Clark. In the fall I looked at an area in the breaks of the Little Missouri in North Dakota. It contained only a few stringers of yellow pine, and I recommended against it, but it was proclaimed as the Dakota Forest Reserve, and a few years later was released [back to the public domain].

In the late fall of 1904, Lew Barrett and I examined and readjusted the entire boundary of the Big Horn Reserve in Wyoming.

All of the Reserves in North Idaho were created before the regular boundary job. In Montana, as I recall, Coert DuBois did the Lolo. John Hatton did the Helena, R. V. R. Reynolds did the old Missoula, now in the Lolo, north of Missoula. DuBois also did the old Hellgate, now part of the Lolo, Bitterroot and Deerlodge. A man named Hereford did most of the Beaverhead.

About the only considerable area in Montana which was not covered in time was the range northeast of Missoula between the Blackfoot and the Clark Fork. This was lined up for examination, but we did not reach it before Congress took away the President's authority.

In 1905, DuBois made a quick ride up the West Fork of the Bitterroot and eliminated a strip along the river which was alleged to be agricultural. It turned out to be mostly a mistake. In the same year I recommended some reduction in the area of the Madison and the Absaroka to eliminate some straight grazing land.

It would be interesting to know whether any of the old boundary type maps and reports still survive.

I do not recall much opposition which developed while the examinations were being made. I guess it was all done so fast that the local people didn't quite know what was happening till T. R. signed the proclamation.

When the Department of Agriculture took over the Forest Reserves in 1905, nearly all of the old boundary crew were made general inspectors, and 1905 and 1906 were spent in inspections which resulted in a high percentage of the Land Office Forest Supervisors being dismissed. It was quite a shake-up.

Most of the boundary men took places in the new District Office organization when it was put into effect in December, 1908.

By 1905, an air of expectation permeated the Bureau of Forestry. There were inklings that changes were imminent, but in the Inland Northwest—the area that would become first District 1 and later Region 1 of the Forest Service—few could have estimated the scope. When Gifford Pinchot maneuvered the transfer of the forest reserves to his new agency in the Department of Agriculture, the people involved with the forests of the future Region 1 could anticipate great change.

Three

"Pitchforked by Pinchot"

A New Agency Defines Its Boundaries

F ounded in 1905, the United States Forest Service embarked on a mission of service and enlightenment. One major thrust of Gifford Pinchot's new agency was to teach the methods of scientific utilitarian conservation. Another emphasis was to meet the needs of local constituencies in the West, many of which depended on federal timber and grazing land for their livelihood. This bifurcated mission put the agency in a difficult position. It had to teach without preaching while managing without alienating its potential constituency.

The agency had a powerful leader in Gifford Pinchot, the man responsible for its founding and the first American trained in scientific forestry. Scion of a wealthy family that made a large part of its fortune in the great timber cuts of the first half of the nineteenth century, Pinchot took a different track from most of the young American pseudoaristocrats of his generation. After being turned toward forestry by his father, he embarked on a career of public service, guided by a sense of noblesse oblige that he shared with Theodore Roosevelt. Pinchot went to Germany to study forestry and returned to the United States determined to implement the teachings of the emerging discipline.

With this idea, Pinchot had captured the tenor of his time. At the turn of the century, the nation, and particularly its leadership, was obsessed with the concept of efficient management regulated by trained experts. It was an age of accreditation, when training was considered equal to or, in some cases, more important than experience. Pinchot's agency initially blended people with experience and people with credentials, developing a healthy mix. Despite the strong central leadership Pinchot offered, the new agency from its inception sought to develop decentralized authority. The majority of decisions affecting local areas were made in the field, and a commitment to flexibility characterized and defined policy making. The first employees of the USFS had to be selected from the states in which the national forests were located. Elers Koch, who had already proved his mettle both in school and in the field, was one of the originals:

When Gifford Pinchot in 1905 took over the Forest Reserves from the Land Offices [General Land Office of the Department of the Interior], he took with them all the personnel, good, bad, and indifferent. The new Reserves, their proclamations fresh from the President's pen, had to be organized, and at the same time those already under organization inspected and checked up.

To that end, a lot of us young fellows in our twenties, with the vast experience of two years on the boundary job, were pitchforked by Pinchot into jobs as general inspectors and sent West to see what we could find out. Being a native son of Montana, my field of action was in Montana and Wyoming. During the years 1905 and 1906 I made general inspections of the Gallatin, Big Horn, Absaroka, Madison, Lewis & Clark South, Lewis & Clark North, Big Belt, Little Belt, Deerlodge and Highwood Mountains in Montana, and the Big Horn in Wyoming. [These areas included most of the timberland in western Montana, northern Idaho, and northwestern Wyoming.]

I have run across a few of my old inspection reports in the files, and perhaps with due modesty, I am really surprised how good they were. Perhaps our youth made us bold and self-confident, but also the knowledge that, aside from G. P. himself and Overton W. Price [Pinchot's chief assistant], we had about as much experience as anybody else, although under present standards our experience would not qualify us for a job as district ranger.

It was more or less taken for granted that the politically appointed Supervisors of the GLO [General Land Office] would be found incompetent unless they could prove otherwise. Most of them were, but some of them proved to be pretty good men.

One of my first jobs was the Gallatin, in my own home country.

At that time it was only a spot on the map—four or five townships. Mike Langohr, the Supervisor, was the sole Forest officer. Mike wasn't so bad at that, but there really wasn't much to do on this small area, and he shouldn't be blamed for also running a greenhouse and florist's shop on the side. However, after my inspection report Mike had to choose between the supervisorship and the greenhouse, and he chose to resign.

My first inspection of the old Lewis & Clark South in 1905 was an interesting job. This included the wilderness of the Blackfoot, Swan River, South Fork of the Flathead and the Sun River—and it was truly a wilderness at that time. Headquarters were at Ovando [in northern Montana].

The previous Supervisor had been Gus Moser, and many tales are told of his performances. It is alleged that he and his wife used to meet the rangers coming in for their monthly pay checks and mail, and that her wiles and other attractions, together with Gus' superior skill at poker, usually resulted in separating the rangers from most of their pay.

Moser was succeeded by Bliss, who was Supervisor at the time of my inspection. He was a nice old man, but quite incompetent, and his only excursions to the forest were drives in a buckboard over the only road on the Reserve to Holland Lake in the head of the Swan. Fortunately for him, he had an excellent and vigorous head ranger in Page Bunker. Bunker and I outfitted in Ovando with one pack horse and a saddle horse apiece. We rode up through the North Fork of the Blackfoot, across the range to the Dearborn, and north along the east side. Jack Clack [later a Forest Service employee] was then buying Government timber and operating a small mill west of Augusta. We went up the Teton and down the North Fork of Sun River. We tried to cross into White River, but a snowstorm drove us out and we went back over the Dearborn. It was interesting that we saw no big game on that month's trip, though we ate grouse nearly every day, knocking their heads off with our 30-30 rifles.

As a result of my inspection, Bliss was removed and Bunker made Supervisor and headquarters moved to Kalispell.

Others remembered similar circumstances. John F. Preston, who worked in the Lewis & Clark National Forest, the District

Office in Missoula, and at agency headquarters in Washington, D.C., recounted:

> While in Sumas, Washington, I received a wire to report to Supervisor Todd, Neihart, Montana, for timber sale work. I arrived in Neihart, Montana, the latter part of September 1907.
>
> The branch train from Great Falls arrived at Neihart, Montana, after dark, which in the fall of the year meant about six o'clock. Neihart proved to be a silver mining town with a population capacity of 3,000 to 5,000 people, but with an actual population at that time of perhaps 50. Montana had a great many silver towns in a similar or worse condition than Neihart—plenty of mines, abundance of ore, ample refining machinery, homes, schools, stores, all of the physical structure of civilization. One serious defect in the man-made economy had caused life to dim and all but go out; the price of silver (undoubtedly caused by overproduction) was insufficient to allow the mining industry to operate and all was silent and ghostly where once had been noise and intense activity. The something which gave the life impetus to this physical hulk of civilization was gone and only the corpse remained.
>
> There was a great deal of Neihart, physically speaking; it stretched along the canyon for about three miles and was never more than 1/4 mile wide at any point. With the collapse of the mining industry, the population had dwindled to about what could be supported by the business of raising cattle and sheep, the production and shipment of smelter poles and a little summer tourist trade.
>
> I sought the one little hotel and boarding house in the town and was content to look up the Forest Supervisor the following morning. The train stayed all night in Neihart and returned to Great Falls the next morning, leaving about 8 o'clock. I found the Supervisor's Office about a mile up the canyon from the little hotel, located in a private residence. I remember the train was pulling out as I walked up the street.
>
> Upon arriving at the office, I found that I was a little in advance of the office hours and had to wait for the arrival of the clerk. I introduced myself and found there was no one in the office except the clerk and she informed me that the Supervisor, Mr. Todd, was

on the train leaving town that morning bound for a two-week's elk hunting trip in the Sun River. I inquired if he had left any instructions for me. There were none although we found a telegram on his desk from Washington informing him that I was reporting to him on this date for timber sale work. I searched the files to try and find where the timber sales business was located, because the young lady who was acting as clerk could give me very little help.

Fortunately, about the middle of the afternoon, Ranger Guy Myers rode into town over the divide from the Judith River, [with his] saddle horse and pack horse. The pack horse was carrying a deer. Myers had a little timber business and he invited me to return with him. He helped me to get a saddle horse and before 10 o'clock that night I was over on the middle fork of the Judith River at a little cabin that measured about 12 × 18, camping with Guy Myers.

The next two or three days we cruised and marked timber for a little sawmill and made up a contract on the proper forms ready for the Supervisor's signature. The limit on sales without advertisement was $100, but this sale came well within that limit. The telephone line had just been completed from Neihart to the Judith River. About the third day a telephone call came from Neihart from George Cecil, telling me to return to Neihart. Cecil was one of the inspectors working under Mr. E. A. Sherman's direction out of Missoula, Montana. As I recall, Mr. Sherman, as Chief Inspector, had a force consisting of G. H. Cecil, F. A. Silcox, R. Y. Stuart, and Paul G. Redington and I think C. H. Adams was one of the inspectors. [Stuart was chief forester of the U.S. from 1928 to 1933; Silcox succeeded Stuart, remaining in office until his death late in 1939.] Cecil told me upon my arrival at Neihart that he had been sent there to fire Todd, and that he would like me to stay in town and help him gather the evidence. This I did, with the result that when Supervisor Todd returned from his hunting trip he had a telegram from Washington suspending him and appointing Cecil acting Supervisor. The suspension was properly followed up and Mr. Todd was either dismissed or forced to resign. This incident proved valuable to me, since it established my confidence in the civil service system and proved that drastic personnel action could be taken when necessary.

Earl V. Welton of the Deerlodge and Helena National Forests found more than incompetence:

> The Supervisor [of the Helena National Forest] and his brother had a ranch in Belt Park and they had about 60 head of cattle. The ranger at Belt Creek had this brother made application for their 60 head. When it reached the office the Supervisor said, "Here is where I save a little money," so he tore up the application but issued the permit.
>
> The storekeeper in Neihart had a few head of stock, and his application was approved. One day the Supervisor was in the store and the man said, "Here is the money for my permit." The Supervisor said, "Never mind the money; just give me credit for it on my account."

Under the administration of Pinchot and his vanguard, such action was tantamount to treason. Those caught in such an activity were dismissed from the agency as quickly as possible. Recognizing the folly of harboring unacceptable behavior in Pinchot's domain, Elers Koch and his peers weeded out the incompetent, the avaricious, and the foolish. Those who remained were part of an elite group, local people who embraced a dominant cultural current of the time, and they generally seemed to recognize the importance of what they did and of maintaining proper standards of conduct.

The foresters who accepted Pinchot's cosmology of forestry and all it embodied made themselves different from many of the people of the West. Their neighbors knew little of utilitarian conservation, nor did they care about its principles of wise use of resources embodied in the axiom "the greatest good for the greatest number" in the long run. Most simply sought to make a living from the seemingly vast natural resources of the West.

In the American mainstream, scientific forestry had growing appeal at the turn of the century, for its tenets of management were of a piece with those of the era. A generation trained at the emerging forestry schools of the East soon joined the initial practitioners in the woods, fashioning an agency full of scientific expertise and local knowledge. Gifford Pinchot put his mark on all of them. The best of the holdovers from the old Department of the Interior administration were brought to Washington, D.C., along with the new recruits to learn their craft at the feet of the ever-demanding chief. Koch was among them. Here he described Pinchot the taskmaster and life in his realm:

> While investigating a complaint case I ran onto an old fellow name Geiffer who lived up on the North Fork. He told me a story about Gifford Pinchot, who had explored this country in the 1890s. Anyone who knew G. P. will appreciate it. It seems that Geiffer met G. P.'s party on the trail and Mr. Pinchot was riding one of Geiffer's horses. Geiffer said to him, "What are you doing on my horse?" G. P. said, "Is this s.o.b. of a horse yours? Well, you can have him. The blankety-blank-blank bucked me so blank-blank high this morning I thought I never would come down."
>
> I spent the spring of 1906 on administrative work in Washington. At that time the western forests were divided into three administrative districts—the Northern Rockies, the Southern Rockies and the Pacific Coast. A sort of a Chief of Operation was made responsible for each. I had the Northern District, Smith Riley the Southern, and Coert DuBois the Pacific Coast. These positions were later rotated frequently as inspectors came in from the field.
>
> Gifford Pinchot was a hard taskmaster to us young fellows. We had a buzzer system for inter-office signals, but G. P. had a special buzzer of his own in our quarters—one buzz for me, two for Riley and three for DuBois—and this buzzer had a tone like a rattlesnake that fairly lifted one out of his chair and across the room when G. P. pressed it. When we wrote a letter for G. P. to sign we always awaited it in fear and trembling. If he signed it without change, it was an occasion of triumph. Often the letter came back with a big blue question mark scrawled across it. Then we had to figure out if it was basically wrong or merely a punctuation point out of place.
>
> G. P. was merciless with careless errors. I recall one reply I prepared to a Senator asking for the total area of the National Forests. The stenographer got an extra zero in my figure, which I failed to detect, and G. P. gave me a panning for carelessness which I will

never forget. It was a hard school, but good training for us, and the surprising thing is that we never lost our devotion and high respect for G. P.

I often think what a wonderful thing it was to have a Government bureau with nothing but young men in it. Most of the men, aside from G. P. [Overton] Price and [Albert] Potter [Pinchot's top assistants], were in their twenties, and there was no sign of Departmental inertia or red-tape inhibitions in our cosmos. I believe much of the efficiency for which the Forest Service has been notable among Government bureaus was due to this condition. With the lapse of forty years, our Service has grown old, and the men in it. I sincerely hope that the present retirement policy will help to rejuvenate the Service, and that in filling vacancies seniority will not be given too much weight.

Pinchot was committed to solving local issues at the local level, and once he determined that he had trained a cadre of people committed to his methods and goals, he moved to an even more decentralized form of management than that established in 1905. Elers Koch continued:

In the spring of 1907 all the general inspectors who had been making headquarters in Washington were moved permanently into the West. Six inspection districts were set up. District One, which coincided approximately with the present Region One, was given to E. A. Sherman. General inspectors under him were Paul Redington, George Cecil, F. A. Silcox and C. H. Adams.

I could have remained on as an inspector, but I had been knocking around the country for four years. I wanted to get married, and I had concluded that being a Forest Supervisor with definite responsibility for a particular tract of forest was the most attractive and soul-satisfying job in the Service. Pinchot encouraged me in the idea, since he had promised the West that the Reserves would be placed in charge of Western men.

Finding such people was a story of its own. One of the primary responsibilities of USFS inspectors such as Koch was to administer examinations to candidates for ranger positions. A job with the USFS was highly prized in many parts of the Inland West. It offered regular pay, some status, and for westerners, the ability to work out of doors, something many soon found to be a much overrated commodity. People in all kinds of occupations turned out for the examination. Yet forestry jobs required specific skills, and Koch and the other inspectors had to be sure that the people they selected could do the work:

In 1905, when the National Forests were transferred to the Department of Agriculture, one of the first essentials was to obtain a competent staff of men to man them. The personnel employed by the Land Office on the earlier created Reserves were all taken over, but as some of them were incompetent political appointees there was a good deal of immediate weeding out, which left vacancies to be filled. There were, to be sure, some mighty good men under the Land Office—fellows like Than Wilkerson of the Bitterroot, and Frank Haun and Page Bunker of the old Lewis & Clark. We gladly retained such men. There were also a lot of new Reserves, such as the Lolo, Cabinet, Hellgate, Helena, Beaverhead, and Deerlodge, which had to be organized and manned from the start.

Gifford Pinchot had promised the western people that so far as possible the Reserves would be put in charge of local men who knew the country and its traditions. As pioneer conditions prevailed, the aim was to select competent woodsmen for rangers—men who could shoot straight, handle horses, travel with a pack outfit in the hills, and generally take care of themselves outdoors.

The first job of the newly appointed general inspector for each region was to hold a series of ranger examinations. In 1905 I conducted three such examinations in Montana, at Missoula, Bozeman, and Neihart.

In contrast to the present-day purely written Civil Service examination, the original tests included two days' field events and one day for the written portion. The field test included rifle and pistol shooting at a target, riding a horse, putting on a pack, a simple exercise in compass surveying and pacing, the use of an axe, and cruising of a block of timber.

From twenty to thirty men turned out at each place of examination. They included all sorts, from packers and bar-keeps to first-

Elers Koch, the consummate ranger, on horseback in 1941. (Photo by K. D. Swan courtesy USDA Forest Service)

class woodsmen or cowpunchers. We usually proceeded first to the local target range for the rifle and pistol shooting, which aroused great interest and competition. Walt Derrick tells with great glee how his first pistol bullet struck a rock thirty feet in front of him and ricocheted to the target to become firmly embedded in the bulls-eye. He claims I allowed him the bulls-eye, since the bullet was there to establish it.

Most of the men got by fairly well with the horseback riding, since everybody rode in those days, but from the way a man approached a horse and swung into the saddle it was not hard to tell the good horseman.

The packing was the most fun. Obviously, some of the men had never put on a pack before, and they were required to cargo up a miscellaneous outfit of camp equipment and grub and pack it properly without the use of alforjas [saddlebag]. Many and curious were the hitches [knots] used. I remember one fellow at Missoula who, after precariously balancing the two packs on the saddle, took the lash rope and wound it full length around the horse and over the pack. I asked him what he called the hitch, and he said it was the "Oregon wind."

The second day everybody mounted saddle horses or buggies and we proceeded to the nearest timber for the axe and cruising work. I usually picked a tough Douglas-fir for each man's chopping demonstration. Some of them, of course, put the tree down in workman-like manner. Others went at it like some of our green CCC boys [the young men brought to the national forests by the Civilian Conservation Corps program during the 1930s]. I recall one barber who, after painfully beavering around his tree for ten minutes, stopped to wipe his streaming brow. One of the boys called to him, "Joe, it's about time for you to stop and hone your razor."

After the timber cruising, which finished the field test, we generally had a horse race back to town. I especially remember the race at Bozeman. I was riding a hard-mouthed, raw-boned black horse we called Nigger Baby which belonged to my brother. We came down out of Sour Dough Canyon hell for leather, and nobody succeeded in passing me in the ten miles to Bozeman.

Those examinations really were effective. The written test eliminated the illiterates, and the field tests insured that we got experienced hands. We got a lot of good men from these examinations. Several similar examinations were held over the next few years, generally conducted by the Supervisors. I think I held the last field examination in Missoula in the spring of 1910.

Those tested had a different point of view. Thomas Myers was one of the applicants that Elers Koch examined at Neihart, Montana. He survived the ordeal and went on to serve thirty years in the USFS:

I had put in my application to take this examination [in Neihart in August 1905], and as I wished to get some pointers on the job, I went up to the Belt Creek Ranger Station about three days before it was to start. Wellman Holbrook and a lad by the name of Ratliff were there, and I had them show me how to read the Forest Service compass and other things that had a bearing on the examination.

The first night I was there I went out to cut up some wood and found the handle in the axe broken. I spoke to the boys about it and they both asked, "Can you hang an axe?" I told them I could, so they dug up four with broken handles and I put in new handles and ground up two of them.

Well, the day of the examination we were all at the office at Neihart. As I remember, there were fifteen of us waiting for the officer to arrive who was to hold the examination. He finally showed up. One of the axes was leaning against the office building. He picked it up and said, "I suppose the axes will have to be rehung before they can be used." I spoke up and said, "Brother, if you can do a better job I'll take my hat off to you." He said, "It is a good job."

We were to have three days to take the examination, but the officers cut it to two. We had a half day of written work, a half day to see if we could pack a horse, and one day in the field, estimating and mapping an area of timber and reading the compass, then cutting down a lodgepole pine tree each and telling where it was to fall. My turn came and he pointed out a tree with three bends in it and asked me where it would fall. I pointed to one of the boys and said I would use him for a stake, but he stuck a stick in the ground and moved away. My guess was good; my tree almost hit it.

Not everyone was as solid an applicant as Myers. Koch examined Albert Cole in 1905. Cole remembered his initiation:

I received my discharge from the army on May 30, 1905, and although I was urged by my company commander to reenlist and go back to Alaska, I returned home and lost no time getting in touch with Forest Supervisor J. B. Seely, who had his headquarters at a small ranch about three and a half miles below Virginia City, Montana. After quite a long talk with Mr. Seely I secured an application for the forest ranger examination and mailed it to the Civil Service Commission. While awaiting the date for the examination,

I brushed up on packing a horse and other possible subjects which I hoped would help me in the examination.

The examination was held in the Virginia City schoolhouse and the field test was held at different places adjacent thereto by Elers Koch. The written test consisted of questions pertaining to the knowledge of cattle, horses, and sheep, knowledge of the different brands and location of ranches and the different ranges where the stock were run during the summer months, also how to cook, the baking of bread, and how to take care of oneself in the mountains and woods. The field test included timber estimating, riding and packing a horse, shooting with rifle and pistol, surveying, mapping, pacing a measured distance, cutting down a tree with an axe, compass reading, and more. Since I never had any mapping or surveying or compass work, it was all rather a lot of guess work with me.

There were only three of us that took this examination, a man named Knight, another named Cole, and myself. Mr. Knight was a lawyer who thought he would rather have outdoor work, Cole was a rancher, and I was a Jack-of-All-Trades and a master of none of them.

The exam showed that Cole was what he said he was: a master of none. He failed this exam, working as a seasonal employee until the opportunity to try again came around:

> As I had not passed the ranger examination, I was laid off in December of 1905 and worked at different jobs during the rest of the winter.
>
> Early in the spring of 1906 Mr. Seely notified me that another ranger's examination was to be held at Townsend, Montana, and urged me to take it as he thought I would be able to pass it this time. Accordingly I went to Townsend and took the examination, which was given by a man by the name of Moore, who was Supervisor of the old Elkhorn Forest Reserve. On my return, Mr. Seely again hired me as a Forest guard.

But Cole did not pass that time either. Despite his work for the agency, he seemed unable to meet its standards for permanent employment. Then Cole received an opportunity:

Early in October [1906] a man named Northey made application for a large tract of timber on the headwaters of the Boulder River on the district where I was working. Mr. Earl[e] H. Clapp came out from the Supervisor's office in Helena to survey this tract and I was assigned to give him what assistance I could. We worked together for about two weeks making a triangulation survey, and I never worked with any man before or since who taught me as much about surveying and timber estimating as he did during those two weeks we worked together. He was the finest and most patient teacher and instructor that I have ever had the good fortune to be associated with. May his shadow never grow less. When we finished the job Mr. Clapp told me that he was practically sure that I would be kept on all winter as the Service was short of help, and that I could tackle the examination again next spring with every hope of passing.

After Clapp returned to the Supervisor's office I received word to return to Madison County and get my horse, as it had been decided to keep me on all winter. I think Mr. Clapp had much to do with that decision, for which I have never ceased to be grateful.

In April 1907, the ranger examination was held in Helena, and I took it for the third time. This time I passed with a very satisfactory grade.

Albert Cole benefited from the type of mentorship for which Pinchot's USFS was famous. In seasonal work, Cole had proven that he could do the work and had the skills to survive as a ranger. What he lacked was training in specific aspects of forestry. In this he was not alone. Most of the men the USFS recruited in the West had similar deficiencies. They had little opportunity to go to forestry school, and so were selected on the basis of skill and local reputation. In situations such as Cole's, the lack of formal knowledge was overcome by an informal network that functioned as a way to recruit people the agency needed. The time Cole spent with Earle Clapp, who later headed the Branch of Research and served as acting chief of the agency from 1939 to 1943 and associate chief after that, was typical. Through Clapp, Cole acquired the last of the knowledge he needed to reach full status in the agency.

This testing situation, despite its strict standards, was a window of opportunity for people of the places where foresters served. The field exam did persist for many years, but it ceased to have the importance that it did in the early years of the agency. As forestry schools became more common, the agency had a pool of scientifically trained young professionals from which to chose. They too had to pass the field exam, but it was not the proof of their merit in the way that it was for the local men recruited to the initial generation of foresters. By 1930, those who entered the agency as a result of a field examination were anachronisms, replaced certainly at the managerial level and often at the forest level by the graduates of forestry schools. Experience in the woods remained important, but not as important as understanding what had become the science of forestry.

Albert Cole's position reflected that reality. His skills fit the needs of the Forest Service at the field level. In his day, foresters were not yet the scientific professionals that they later became. People management was as important as timber management while the agency was working to spread its message. Cole could be taught forestry; he could not be taught the characteristics that made people in the area respect him. These he had to supply on his own.

A decade later, the field exam was still an important way to separate serious applicants from those who lacked the skills necessary for life in the Forest Service. Elers Koch still ran the tests and the location was different, but the procedure remained similar. David Olson, a forestry school graduate who served at Savenac Nursery and in the Lolo National Forest, recalled his examination in 1914:

> Stopping off at Missoula en route to school, I learned that a Ranger's examination was to be given the following day so I decided to take it—"just for the heck of it." Elers Koch gave the examination. Fourteen took it, among them Jim Bosworth and Tom Crossley. I don't remember what subjects were covered in the written portion of the exam but I do recall some of the field tests. After identifying some range plants and scaling logs, we went out to Koch's home on Beckwith Avenue. From his barn north to the

river was a prairie. First we took turns to run traverse with compass, around a staked area, and pace the distance. Then each took
a turn at packing a horse. The final test was to saddle a horse and
ride it as hard as it would go across the prairie toward town. A
cockle burr was placed under the blanket to liven things up a bit.

After passing the examination, the new rangers then had to do
the job for which they had been hired. Often it was under difficult or trying conditions. Despite the presence of a transcontinental railroad, consolidated as the Great Northern Railway in
1889, there was little other infrastructure in the Inland Northwest. What existed did not work very well. Edward G. Stahl remembered one train trip:

> We moved westward to classify lands along the foothills south
> of Port Hill. The Great Northern Railroad had a branch line from
> Bonners Ferry to Creston, British Columbia. I read someplace of a
> slow train that was easy to overtake but hard to meet. It was likely
> a reference to the Kootenai Valley Branch line. The train ran tri-
> weekly, went north on Monday and tried all the rest of the week
> to get back. But on the day that Robert [McLaughlin] and I rode
> the train, the schedule was reversed. About ten miles north of
> Bonners Ferry we were stopped by a mud slide that covered the
> rails. The crew and some passengers proceeded to clear the rails.
> Robert and I decided that walking was easier than shoveling. We
> walked ahead to Copeland, then on to Port Hill, and still no train
> in sight.
> This story illustrates the train crew's idea of a time schedule. A
> traveling man said the train was stopped on the main line and
> while he walked the aisle and gnawed his fingernails, the train
> crew sauntered up the open hillside, each man carrying heavy
> twine to snare gophers. They got one cent bounty for each tail.

The work foresters were asked to do was also difficult. Elers Koch
experienced a winter inspection trip atypical only in its urgency:

> One of my most arduous jobs was in January 1906. For some
> unknown reason the Washington office wired me to make an in-

spection of the Highwood Mountains Reserve at once. A field trip in the Highwoods in January is no picnic. I drove out from Fort Benton thirty miles or so to Highwood in an open bob sleigh, with the thermometer thirty or more below zero and the wind right off the North Pole. A man named Thain was Supervisor, and we took saddle horses and rode the Reserve, stopping at ranches. It was a poor time to see the condition of the range, but at any rate I got acquainted with some of the ranchers and got their reaction to the administration, which was generally favorable. I don't think it got above thirty degrees below on the whole trip, and if the Washington office merely wanted to find how tough I was, I certainly demonstrated.

Also in 1906, I made another inspection of the Lewis & Clark South. I started from Kalispell with one of the rangers up the South Fork. By that time the rangers had pushed a trail of sorts up river as far as Spotted Bear, and from the head of the river down to Black Bear. Between these two points there was no trail, but we made it through on elk trails as best we could. Again, in a month's travel in the late fall we saw no big game. Bunker was doing good work opening up the country with trails so far as his limited funds permitted.

On the 1906 trip I again crossed the main range and rode up the east side, returning to Kalispell by a rugged trail along the Great Northern. I camped one night near Nyack, and during the night both my horses were run over and killed by a Great Northern train. I put in a claim, but through neglect in following it up the case expired by statute of limitation and I never collected a cent from the railway company.

The Lewis & Clark North in 1905 included all of what is now Glacier Park and the country northwest of Kalispell. F. N. Haines was Supervisor. Mr. Haines told me how he came to be appointed. He had been active in Republican politics in his home town in Indiana, and one day one of the Senators from that state called him in and said, "Mr. Haines, I have two positions at my disposal. One is a postmastership, the other a Forest Supervisor in Montana. You can have either one." Haines said he did not know a spruce tree from a pine, but he wanted to go West so he chose the supervisorship.

Actually, in spite of his background, he made a good Supervisor for the times. There was little or no timber business, and he did not need to be a forester. The main job was opening up a wilderness, and Haines turned out to be a mighty hunter, and did a lot of good work in building trails, bridges and ranger stations. He had some mighty good men as rangers. I specially recall "Old Death on the Trail" Reynolds, who afterwards became Acting Supervisor of the Big Belt Reserve, and Fred Herrig, one of Theodore Roosevelt's old ranch hands.

Joseph B. Halm recounted similar stories of his initiation into the agency:

> After graduating from the Forest School at Washington State College in June 1909, I accepted a position under Supervisor W. G. Weigle on the Coeur d'Alene to do boundary survey work. I was assigned to work under Ranger Edward Pulaski at Wallace, Idaho.

Pulaski became the most famous of the first generation of foresters for his leadership in fighting fires. Innovative and creative, he was a leader by temperament. He received credit for designing the combination of mattock and axe known to anyone who has ever fought fires as a Pulaski and showed a generation of young foresters how to do their job. Halm's narrative continued:

> Strong, active, full of enthusiasm, broke but happy, I reported for my first job in the Forest Service. I recall my entire field wardrobe consisted of a cheap cloth summer hat, a silk dress shirt, khaki pants, and a good pair of "Bass" shoes, [one] size too small. I must have presented a most bedraggled, pitiful, but amusing sight. Little wonder the miners stared at me as Pulaski and I entered Burke, Idaho, one rainy day in June. My hat had become a shapeless rag, my wet, transparent shirt stuck to my skin, I had no jacket and I limped badly from those never to be forgotten boots. I am sure Ranger Pulaski didn't think highly of his raw recruit in those first days, but I carried his pack, tried not to show my discomfort, and in a short time won him over.
> Our pack consisted of two blankets, bread, and a little bacon,

coffee, onions, and a few dishes; no milk, butter, or sugar. We each carried a small ax, maps and notebooks.

I recall early one morning, going along a ridge near Big Creek on the present St. Joe National Forest, my eyes were nearly swollen shut, the result of recent mosquito bites. I was in the lead trying to follow down the main ridge. Every little while Pulaski would suggest that the trail was to the right or to the left. I could see no trail, and green as I was, I couldn't figure in my mind how he knew where that ridge went. He kept saying, "There the blazes are, over there." It dawned on me after a while in my prairie-trained mind that those barked places on the trees were blazes and so gradually through his patient tutoring I learned something of the ways of the woods.

It was on this trip that I first met Rutledge Parker, State Forester of Montana [in 1944]. Having completed our assigned portion of the boundary survey, we were headed back toward Wallace over an old little-used 30 mile trail. Mr. Pulaski said, "We should be meeting up with Rutledge about here." I knew Mr. Parker was running the eastern forest boundary and that we were supposed to meet him, but how or where, I did not know. Hardly had Mr. Pulaski spoken when, as if by magic, out of the heavy timber and underbrush, popped a man with a compass and small pack. He was somewhat scratched and torn. Neither Mr. Parker or Mr. Pulaski appeared surprised; to me this meeting was a miracle. What impressed me most at that time was how Mr. Parker or anyone else could ever find his way about alone in that vast, trailless uninhabited wilderness, and after days, time himself to meet us at this particular uncharted spot. I doubted then if I could ever qualify as a ranger or be able to perform such a feat.

In July after the boundary survey was completed, I was assigned to fire-patrol duty between Mullan, Idaho, and Lookout Pass. Lookout is on the state line between Montana and Idaho. My camp was near Dorsey, a side track and water tank along the N. P. railroad switchbacking to the summit. When my train had puffed away around the mountain out of sight leaving me standing alone at the Dorsey water tank, I sat down on my pile of equipment, confused in mind, bewildered. Was this what I had studied so hard to achieve? Was this my goal—Forestry? Well, I had set out to do a job and I would see it through. I found my camp site and made camp near a spring along the old Mullan road.

This was to be a busy summer for me with my scaling, patrolling, small fires, trips to my lookout and packing supplies. My instructions were to patrol the twelve miles of railroad on foot after each of the two daily passenger trains (this, of course, was impossible), and as often as possible to go to my lookout, Stevens Peak, a five-mile climb up a sawtooth ridge to the peak, a bare unimproved lookout. I did manage to make this trip once a week. I had a stull [a round or squared timber used as a roof or side support in mining] sale near my camp, the Gustafson sale which required a portion of my time.

The first person with whom individual foresters worked often became mentors to the newcomers. Edward G. Stahl of the Flathead, Kootenai, and Kaniksu National Forests had vivid memories of his introduction to forest work:

I was among the group at Kalispell, Montana, that took the first Civil Service examination there for Forest Ranger, in 1905. My rating placed me at the top of the eligible list, and early the following spring I received appointment as Forest Ranger, assigned to work under the direction of Fred Herrig at Ant Flat.

Fred Herrig was a veteran of the Spanish-American War and served with Roosevelt's Rough Riders. He was the largest man in the regiment. He had punched cows for Teddy on the Little Missouri. When Roosevelt was organizing the Rough Riders, Fred was packing ore in British Columbia and Roosevelt wired him from San Antonio, Texas, to come down and join them.

Herrig was breveted second lieutenant [in the Spanish-American War] for special services for tracking some mules loaded with machine guns that got away during a skirmish. Several full-blood Indians had given up the job, and Fred tracked the mules into Spanish territory and recovered them and the guns. He was from Alsace Lorraine, very dark and wore a handlebar mustache, giving him a villainous look. Roosevelt was making a tour of the West one time when he saw Fred in the audience. Roosevelt motioned him to come up on the platform. Fred said before he got nicely started, two plainclothesmen had him by the collar.

With Byron Henning, we cut trail the spring of 1906 up the Stillwater Valley. It rained continuously. Fred told me that the year before, he sent in his monthly diary with a lot of daily records reading, "Rain, stayed in camp." His next check was quite a bit short and it never rained so hard again!

We camped at Fish Lake. I packed my horse in and walked while Fred and Byron Henning rode. We planned to go to Ant Flat for the weekend, but I was handicapped with a mean horse and no riding saddle. I rigged up a bridle with small rope, but got bucked off at the first attempt. Fred said, "Eddie, you might as well stay in camp. You're crazy as hell to try to ride that horse bareback." A school ma'am boarded at Fred's place and I had a date to take her to a dance at Gateway, so I felt honorbound to get to Ant Flat in time. I cinched a lash rope around the horse for a handhold and blindfolded him. When Fred pulled the blind, I whacked the horse over the ears with my hat and arrived at the station far ahead of the other two.

On June 15, I received orders from Supervisor Haines to transfer to Indian Creek in the North Fork District by way of Kalispell. The trip covered about 120 miles with saddle horse and pack horse. Mr. Haines traveled with me from Kalispell. The South Fork of the Flathead was in flood, and we swam the horses across from a rowboat.

I cut trail for a while along the north shore of Lake McDonald. Charlie Russell, the cowboy artist, had a summer home nearby. Four years later, in 1910, this District, a ram pasture [an area so rocky foresters considered it mountain goat country] of about 1,600 square miles—including the main range of the Rockies— from the Great Northern Railway to the Canadian line was designated as Glacier National Park.

I crossed the river to the west side at Henshaw Ford, now Pole Bridge, and traveled for about a week to learn the country. There was no road there at the time and it was a beautiful country, with meadows and parks near the river, and deer, moose, bear and other game plentiful, as well as trout in the streams. I camped at Hay Creek and was bothered by some Government pack mules left there by Chapman who had made a geological survey of the country. They wandered at large all summer and were wintered by Long Jeff [Tom Jefferson]. At night they fought my horses until the pack horse broke loose. The next day I tracked them ten miles north, only to learn they had crossed the river at the Henshaw Ford.

I had to pack my equipment on the saddle horse. At the ford I made a raft, chased the stallion in and threw rocks at him, then put off on the raft. He did not follow the ford and could not get up the opposite bank. I was forced downstream by the current and when I landed, the horse had started back. I jumped into water up to my waist to catch him, and had a hard time getting him up the bank. Later Theodore Christensen and I cut trail up the South Fork of Coal Creek to the summit of the Whitefish Range.

The pairings of USFS personnel often made for fast friendships. When two people took to each other, they developed close ties and often became inseparable. Stahl remembered one of his favorite companions:

In the spring of 1908, Robert McLaughlin was sent to the Moyie District on special duty to survey Ranger Stations and classify homestead lands. I traveled with him as sort of Boy Scout and Man Friday. We were kindred spirits in that we both had a perverted sense of humor. (I mean—what we considered funny might not seem funny to you.) Bill Nye best illustrates the idea when he tells of Peck's bad boy, laughing at a funeral—until his dad knocked the hell out of him and convinced him it wasn't funny. We didn't make it pay as Bill Nye did, but carried on for our own amusement. I never saw another man enjoy a joke or gag so much as did Robert McLaughlin. He was short and heavy-set, with clear blue eyes and a square, jutting jaw. When telling a yarn, he was very serious and seldom smiled, but the next day on the trail would laugh heartily. We led a hobo life traveling afoot, by speeder [a small, usually gasoline-powered vehicle that traveled on the railroad rails] or in a boxcar. Sometimes at night we camped out but more often stopped at settlers' cabins.

We were surveying a Ranger Station near Meadow Creek when he awoke me early one morning, saying, "We have a cougar treed." There was a big forked tree near camp with a small dead cedar lodged in the forks. We all wore calked boots and he had walked up the leaning dead cedar to the forks and poked my clothes far out on the upper end with a pole. They figured I would have to chop the big tree down to get my clothes but I got them without chopping. I climbed to the forks, retrieved the clothes with a long pole with a nail in the end as a hook.

Robert studied law at night (when he wasn't thinking of nonsense) and was later appointed Montana State Forester.

After a forester had worked with someone and proved he could do the job, he was often sent to work alone. One of the worst tribulations faced was loneliness. In his inimitable way, Stahl described the nature of their lives:

In the spring I was sent to Gateway to cut trail across the Purcell Range, to the Yaak River via Dodge Creek. I bought two matched black ponies and packed to the base of Yaak Mountain, crossing the Kootenai on Mills' Ferry, located in British Columbia.

It was a lonely job cutting trail until a man named Cody was sent up to help me. He was the best all-round woodsman, packer and horseman I ever met. He had two half-broke horses loaned to him to break for their use. He did not agree on the route I picked for the trail so I told him he could move over to the western slope and cut trail where and how he chose, which he did. We met on weekends to go for supplies.

It got so lonely my dog couldn't stand it. He went down to the Kootenai River and howled 'til the ferryman from Gateway came over and took him across to town. When a man's dog shows up at the settlement without his master, the settlers in the valley assume, and often correctly, that it is an indication of tragedy. Jack Barnaby lost his life in a snowslide, and when his dog came out, a posse went to look for him. A man named Matty lost his life on Kishanehn Creek and a bear devoured him. His dog came out to Big Prairie, the first indication of tragedy. The mystery of Matty's death was never fully solved. Late in the spring, when his dog showed up at Big Prairie, several of Matty's friends went up to his trapper cabin to investigate. They found the door latched, a large hole in the roof and, upon opening the door, found bones scattered over the floor—all that remained of Matty. They found considerable blood stains on the bunk, also an automatic .45 pistol set near the cabin for a bear. By the signs they found, they decided he had shot himself accidentally and died on the bunk. When the weather got warm, the bear, attracted by the smell, had torn a hole in the roof to get in and devour him.

When my dog showed up at the river, Mother Mills pestered her man until he got Harvey Young to join him and come up to my camp. Perhaps they were disappointed to find me swinging a mattock on the trail but I was thankful to know that someone took an interest in my welfare.

I almost forgot to tell you about my dog. He was a mongrel, part terrier with long hair, and I called him "Tommy Whiskers." I taught him several tricks. He would sit up, balance a pine cone on his nose and at the count of three, flip his nose sideways and catch it. He didn't like to swim the rivers and soon learned to get up behind me on the horse. He was more than just a pet. He could tree a mountain lion or nip a bear on the stern end until it would sit up and roar. He stayed away from skunk and porky. I taught him to smoke a pipe by first putting sugar on the stem. A dog as well as a man can learn one trick too many, and when I moved into town, he got some costly ideas. I didn't mind taking him to the barber shop once a month to get his moustache waxed and his beard trimmed Van Dyke, but when he wanted high-priced cigars, I had to draw the line and broke him of the smoking habit by giving him Peerless tobacco. [Peerless tobacco was a powerful concoction some say was part barn sweepings.]

Loneliness was one hazard of the foresters' lives, but the sense of being part of something larger than themselves reminded individuals of the importance of their many tasks. As representatives of the government in a time when few rural people had contact with federal officials, foresters played a pivotal role in rural life in Region 1. This particular function had little to do with forestry per se, but did much to shape the status of the federal government in remote peripheries. The forest ranger—combining law officer with "Uncle's badge," skilled woodsman, and simply another person in the woods—was a welcome sight in the remote parts of the forests of the Inland Northwest.

Four

"He's the Ranger in Charge"

Foresters and the Creation of Order

One of the most complicated tasks for forest rangers was the enforcement of the rules and regulations of their agency and of the U.S. government. In many cases, foresters were the only official representatives in a vast area, and besides their ordinary responsibilities, they functioned as de facto law enforcement officials and general problem-solvers. These roles, which some rangers readily accepted and others took on more tentatively, reflected the ambiguous nature of being of a place while simultaneously being loyal to the goals and objectives of a larger society.

Yet that status, of keeper of order and arbiter of rules and regulations, was one of the most definitive that representatives of the new agency could claim. It labeled foresters and forestry as being of the new, representing the future and its ordered cosmology and challenging the status quo. As foresters accepted this role and sought to embody the system of order that was making inroads across the West, they became different from their neighbors.

During the first years of the new agency, its implementation of the Forest Homestead Act of June 11, 1906, which allowed homestead claims to be entered for arable sections of national forest land, best reflected the new value system. Gifford Pinchot's philosophy dictated helping local users and respecting their needs, and this law, which he engineered and supported, engendered the trust and respect of many previously suspicious westerners. It showed local people that the reserved areas belonged to them as well as to the government.

The passage of this legislation created great difficulty for forest rangers and caused important changes in local administration. The law added a new and different kind of responsibility to the existing duties of the overtaxed field officers of the Forest Service. Few in number and with myriad existing responsibilities, forest rangers faced the additional burden of evaluating homestead claims. That task was a complicated obligation that entailed closer contact with a broader public than did typical timber and grazing administration.

The new responsibilities also accentuated the importance of having a quality workforce within the Forest Service. The caliber of its staff was critical to the success of the agency's plans. Foresters had to understand the woods as well as be able to deal with people. Often, in a variety of disputes, rangers functioned as arbiters. In the field, they had tremendous discretionary power, for they *were* authority. They carried the force of the federal government behind them at a time when that power had increasing meaning. Sometimes foresters were accused of being arbitrary and capricious, but usually they could explain their actions. As local people, they were respected for their ties to the place, and in cases when the Forest Service selection process worked well, for some prowess. They were representatives of the new order of the twentieth century with clear and distinct ties to the ways of the places they administered. One such situation, dating from the 1920s but reflecting the importance of local stature, was described by W. K. "Bill" Samsel of the Clearwater National Forest:

> By about June 1 most of the lookouts and smokechaser stations had been manned and the trail maintenance and construction crews were being placed. All together we had about 50 men in the Lochsa area and around 25 in the Lolo area. These regular district maintenance and construction men were also our first line defense forces when a fire escaped the smokechasers. If these men could not handle the fire, then it was necessary to recruit crews of what we called pickup fire fighters. Usually they were recruited in Missoula, but sometimes it was necessary to draw from the Spokane labor market. To put it mildly they were a very poor caliber of men, agitators, "I.W.W.s" and derelicts.

The Industrial Workers of the World (IWW) was the most radical of western labor unions, and its members represented the most alienated parts of the labor force. The IWW was inclusive in character, representing men and women, blacks and whites, migratory timber workers, miners, and harvest laborers in large numbers. Spokane was one of the centers of IWW activity; IWW workers (often called Wobblies) protested unfair labor practices there by chaining themselves to lampposts and reading the Declaration of Independence. Arrested by the hundreds with more arriving on the next train, the IWW workers crowded the local jails and eventually forced reform.

Most foresters, allied with government interests, regarded the IWW as a nuisance and its workers as weak and of inferior caliber. Foresters saw themselves first as skilled workers and second as part of an organization that had positive, progressive goals. "Wobblies," they believed, sought only to tear down the very institutions necessary for advancement of life in the Inland Northwest. Bill Samsel shared this view:

> We would truck them from Missoula to Mud Creek and hike them to the fire. Ed [McKay] would personally take charge of the fire and the crews, using his district men for foremen, straw bosses, etc. It was on such an occasion as this that Ed with his district men had been battling a stubborn fire for a couple of days. The pickup crew arrived just before supper and sat down for a little breather. Mr. Agitator decided that now was the time to get with his program. Accordingly he mounted a stump and began to orate with an Adolf Hitler gusto. Just as he was getting full steam ahead and seemed to have his captive audience coming his way, Ed walked in from the fire line. He stood for a moment just sizing up the situation. Then very quietly and nonchalantly he stepped over to the speaker, tapped him on the shoulder and said: "Hey, fella, pipe down, you might start something that would be hard to stop." Completely disarmed by Ed's cool, matter of fact expression, the man turned to see Ed slowly walking away. What type of man the speaker expected to see I do not know. What he did see was a man who stood better than six foot, weighed 225 lbs. and carried no surplus fat. With two weeks growth of whiskers, his

blue shirt open at the throat, he was smeared with pitch and blackened with soot and ashes. His filson pants stagged off [cuffs cut off] above the tops of his logger boots likewise were soiled from the grime of the fire. His pine tree badge rode inconspicuously on his left belt, not noticeable by the orating agitator. All this dirt and grime seemed to enhance the image of this superman of the woods. Behind it was a tower of strength, a man of sincerity, firmness and determination, who led his men to victory on some of the toughest forest fires. Most of all Ed MacKay was a man who good men were proud to follow. When our erstwhile orator regained his composure, looking into the faces of his audience, whose expressions had changed from seriousness to amusement, he asked: "Who is that guy?" Someone answered, "He's the Ranger in charge."

Although this exchange may later have taken on a mythic character, it reflected the ideals foresters set for themselves. As conscious purveyors of order, the people of the Forest Service had a crucial role in difficult and often unpredictable circumstances. They inhabited a part of the world with lawless tendencies. Many of the situations they faced could quickly turn violent, and they had to be aware of potential danger, as Roy Phillips told in this tale about legendary ranger Frank Haun:

To be resourceful, self-reliant and overcome obstacles no matter how overpowering they might seem was another trait essential in an early day ranger. For example, a couple of hombres with a bad reputation decided to file a squatter's claim on a bar having agricultural possibilities and Frank took me along to help move them off. They were busy building a cabin and scarcely paused to talk to us, but told us in no uncertain terms to get the hell off their land before they put us off. Frank sat down on their coats, which at the time I thought was strange, and after we had talked and argued with these fellows for a couple of hours their activity on the cabin finally ceased. Finally one said "You win," and to his partner, "These S.O.B.'s won't leave us alone. Let's go" and picked up their coats, under which were two .45 Colts. Frank had suspected this so sat down on their coats to make sure. [No shootout ensued.]

The exploits of Frank Haun would fill a volume. He was one of the colorful early day rangers. I was fortunate indeed to serve as his assistant for about 2 years and consequently got some very good training that was of great value many times in later life.

The patience, fortitude, and will power to overcome human and physical obstacles, a la Frank Haun, was indeed necessary in the repertoire of an early day ranger. In those days the [rural] public was very antagonistic toward the Forest Service, since it was generally believed by those with whom we came in contact with the creation of the national reserves, [that] resources heretofore free to the public had been locked up from entry and exploitation. I learned that to mingle with these people and to avoid heated arguments would almost always get the desired result, and that once you gained their respect and confidence you could get them to do anything within reason. Therefore, over the nearly 30 years I was a supervisor, I tried to instill within the rangers under my direction the lessons taught me by Ranger Frank Haun. As a result, very few complaint cases ever got past us and those so settled, with few exceptions, never became known to a higher authority.

Foresters also were compelled to mediate personal disputes. Their authority over natural resource use seemed to extend to the private realm in unexpected ways. They symbolized order and authority to people far from the structures of society. As a result, many came to serve as informal justices of the peace.

Charged with creating a system of order out of a series of paper proclamations, the foresters became forces of change. The decisions they made affected the lives of the people of their region, and they answered to those people as well as to their agency. They also had to address changes in policy and new legislation that emanated from Washington.

The passage of the Forest Homestead Act of June 11, 1906, which opened arable land in national forests to homesteading, created a new context for the work of USFS rangers. In an instant, the new law made the foresters responsible not only for inventorying the resources of their forests and marking its timber for sale and its grasses for grazing but also for evaluating homesteads. No increase in appropriation accompanied this daunting new task, nor were additional foresters hired. As a result, limited agency resources were stretched even further. Clarence Swim was one of many pressed into service as a result of this act:

At Missoula my first assignment was a homestead to be surveyed on the East Fork of the Bitterroot—Johnson's ranch. It seemed that Mr. Johnson had a bad reputation. He was an old-timer, and had caused more or less trouble. I did not know this. District Forester E. A. Sherman said, with a twinkle in his eye, "Swim, we will bid you goodbye; you may not return." En route up the Bitterroot, I was asked on several occasions where I was headed for. I would reply, "Johnson's ranch on the East Fork." In each case some guarded remark was made. I stopped at the ranger station near Sula to get Ranger Glogoly to help me in the work. We rode to the Johnson ranch. Mr. Johnson was home and invited us in. The place had been occupied for many years. His house was never locked. There were many articles of value lying around; among them, as I recall, were several quite large gold nuggets. We surveyed 160 acres, with lines established highly to his satisfaction. Everything was lovely.

I was assigned to the Helena Forest and spent the remainder of the working season examining [Act of] June 11th applications there. The work on the Helena was difficult since there were many border-line applications covering poor scabby land, and many tracts including questionable mining claims. Dwight Bushnell was Forest Supervisor, and Wellman Holbrook his assistant.

The increase in workload meant that the Forest Service had to find more personnel. Some failed to live up to expectations, but many worked out well despite a number of shortcuts taken in the process of getting into the agency. O. C. Bradeen of the Helena National Forest recalled his entry:

I was literally "kicked" into the Forest Service—no college degree, no logging experience—just kicked by a mule. In 1912 I met at Polson, Montana, by accident a school friend of my father's who was the Assistant State Forester of Montana. They had logged off to some extent such river drainages in Maine as the headwaters of the Penobscot, the Mattawamkeg, and other rivers in the vicinity.

My Dad went to Boston to get rich and the Assistant State Forester followed the logging through Wisconsin and Minnesota, and wound up in the woods around Kalispell. He wanted a compassman to help him on a cruising job of some state timber and asked me to take it. Finally, when the job was finished we went to Helena to see what was next and he surprised me with the question, "How would you like to go to Africa for three years?" I didn't care about going to Africa so he took me up to the Supervisor of the Helena and said, "Jasper, give this boy a job." I went to work with [Walter J.] Derrick's June 11 crew the following day. In moving our camp we used a team of mules and a buckboard and one of the mules caught his hoof between two rocks and bent his shoe out so that each time he stepped he would gouge the shoe into his opposite leg. We had no tools to use so it was decided that if we wished to go on, the shoe had to come off. After the usual round-table discussion, I proposed that I get hold of the shoe and pull it off by main strength, etc., which resulted in a kicking exposition but I wound up on the ground with the shoe in my hand and the mule's foot out of the shoe.

Finally the June 11 work was completed for the time being and the crew dispersed except I was given a job as acting Ranger which eventually led into a permanent job, if 32 years of service can be classed as permanent. I have always maintained that I was actually kicked into the Forest Service.

My first headquarters was an old guard cabin which hadn't been used since the preceding fall, and in the meantime a family of skunks had made a home under the floor. We got along fine together for a few days, but finally the skunks couldn't stand it any longer and moved out. I felt real lonesome for some time until a pack rat showed up and filled in the niche in my existence formerly held by the skunk family.

My first assignment to a fire was on the St. Joe during the I.W.W. troubles. We were having an awful record of men quitting because they were "sick." Consequently, by reason of this fact the fire fighters would demand travel time in and out amounting to 16 hours travel time and a round-trip ticket. Something had to be done to stop this faking.

The Adams portable telephones were first used about this time and, as you recall, if you put your two fingers on the posts and pressed the buzzer you would get quite a shock. So it was finally decided to use this means to determine whether a man was faking "sick" or not. We would explain to the "sick" I.W.W. that we had an instrument which would determine whether or not he was faking sick, and if we thought we could win in a scrap, we would open the "sick" man's shirt and put the two posts on his bare skin and press the button. The dumb ones would accept the "result" and the wise ones saw the joke and after a cup of coffee and a piece of pie at the cook tent would go back to work.

Some sought to take unfair advantage of the new homesteading law, and the foresters learned to be suspicious of certain kinds of claims. Fraudulent homesteaders made frequent attempts to deceive rangers, as Joseph B. Halm of the Coeur d'Alene National Forest in Idaho recalled:

In those days, 1909–1912, we had a swarm of timber homesteads to check on and most of those so-called claims we knew to be fraudulent, but it was our job to get the evidence. In the Little North Fork, Marble Creek and Big Creek, we were extremely unpopular as rangers and had to use discretion and diplomacy. We never knew when a bullet might meet us in a thicket or on the trail. Most of these claims had a small cabin with shake and some with dirt roof.

One cabin, on each of our periodical visits, had a comb and looking glass outside the door; the ferns outside had been mowed down and to the casual passerby the cabin looked inhabited. The two small windows had a cloth over them so no one could look in; a heavy chain and lock secured the door but to us it was easy. We pulled the chain around, unhooked the hidden part and walked in. The interior was lighted by the cracks through the shakes overhead which were only single-laid side by side and the rain and snow came straight through. The floor was natural earth and the stubs of brush left in clearing the spot were still sticking up in the middle of the cabin, as were chips made in the construction several years before. A small shake table supported by two cleats driven between the wall logs, a pile of dry boughs for a bed and a rusty tin stove comprised the complete furnishings. We would take a piece of pine wood, write our names and the date on it, put it in the rusty stove and check to be sure it was always there on our return. After taking careful note of dates, we would close the door, hook the chain, pull it around in place again and go our way.

Old-timers will remember those places well, no clearings, only the trees necessary for a 10' × 12' cabin had been cut. The cabins stood almost hidden by great ferns under beautiful giant virgin white pines which were the prize sought by the timber home-steader who, except for a possible fishing trip once a year or more likely every other year, never visited these claims. Later when he tried to secure patent and was confronted by honest evidence, he often perjured himself in his endeavor to get the claim, which, if he were successful, he sold for several thousand dollars to lumber companies.

The Culp claim [the one previously described] was outstanding in that it was the key to perhaps a hundred others in the Little North Fork of the Coeur d'Alene. The year before applying for patent, Mr. Culp moved into his cabin with his family. Few others had ever made any show of residence. There were a few who actu-ally lived on their claims and made a showing of clearing and farming; these few claims were never protested and we never bothered them.

Mr. Culp cut a few trees and cleared a small patch of ground be-tween the stumps about the size of a small city lot. I photographed his garden at times. Even radishes and lettuce would not mature. We watched his claim closely and when he applied for patent, Messrs. Rutledge, McGowen, Swartz, Girard, Skeels, Haines, Farmer and myself went in, made camp and made a careful de-tailed final study of the claim. It was carefully mapped, timber counted, and the clearing measured. I did the mapping and the photographic work.

During the hearing on the case in Coeur d'Alene, they asked each witness just where he went each day and it so happened that in tracing our routes in our evidence each and every one had gone around a small strip of bottom land near the cabin because it had no paths into or through it and was so dense no one had ventured into it. We had, of course, looked into it from both sides of the gulch. There wasn't anything there except willow, alder, dogwood and a few dead snags. When all the testimony was in and each had shown he had not crossed this acre or two, Mr. Culp was called and asked by his attorney about this particular spot and he stated that was his meadow where he kept his cow and horses. What a blow! It was 4:00 P.M. and Mr. McGowan [our attorney] called for a recess, which was granted until eleven the next morning.

Charlie Farmer and I volunteered to go in there that night. We took a car to Hayden Lake. The only power boat was across the lake and would not be back until about 9:00 P.M. We finally got the boat and at 9:30 met the ranger at the upper end of the lake. He had horses and flashlights ready. We dashed off up the inky dark trail, up the mountain and over the divide. We held to the tail of our horses and ran behind, switching them at a trot, then down the other side, always on the run following the windings of the trail through the dense timber. We forded the North Fork several times and at break of day arrived at the claim. We fought through the alleged meadow back and forth, climbing over the brush which tore our clothes to shreds. Needless to say there wasn't a spot in the whole area where a cow could have laid down. After half an hour, we were again on the trail. We called our attorney, Mr. McGowan, by Forest Service telephone and told him what he had expected to hear. He asked if we could make it back by eleven. We could. Then by daylight we dashed back over the trail to the lake, a round trip of 70 miles and arrived in Coeur d'Alene, 105 miles round trip, at exactly eleven amid shouts of our friends. When we got our breath, we testified, begrimed and tired but happy. I recall a statement I made, "I defy any one to go there and find the meadow referred to." [The claim was denied.]

That seemed to settle it, but this was not to be the end. The Registrar of the local Land Office said he would go in and have a look. The Registrar's statement was very simple. "I went to Mr. Culp's claim and found the meadow as described by Mr. Culp." [This again made the claim patentable.] Perjury? Yes. The Secretary of Agriculture then came west and accompanied by Mr.

Rutledge, the Registrar and others made a personal investigation, and needless to say he found that the government witnesses had told the truth and he reversed the decision. This, of course, meant that all the claims protested [because of the registrar's decision] were declared invalid.

As in the case of the registrar, the Forest Service and local authorities sometimes ran afoul of each other. This often resulted from the process of developing a system of management where none had existed before. Many of the national forests were established hastily, with little regard for inholdings—areas already claimed within newly proclaimed national forest boundaries—and often state, local, and USFS officials had to work out compromises. One such case resulted in the Battle of Belton, as foresters waggishly referred to one situation. Jack Clack of the Flathead National Forest, a participant in the "battle," explained:

When the Lewis & Clark Forest Reserve was created, the township south of Belton, or West Glacier, was unsurveyed; therefore, when it was later surveyed, section 36 which bordered Belton on the south did not become a school section [the section reserved for support of local public schools in the Northwest Ordinance]. This, however, did not stop the State of Montana in the spring of 1909 from selling 40 acres of said section 36 to the Great Northern Railway Company for the purpose of building chalets thereon. [This land had increasing value; the move to create Glacier National Park—with its own railway depot—was well under way.] When Supervisor [Page S.] Bunker of the Flathead National Forest, of which the area was a part, heard of the sale, he at once wrote the District Office in Missoula, told them of the deal and asked for an allotment to fence the area as evidence of the government's claim to ownership. This was granted, and I took a crew to Belton and fenced the tract. About this time a suit was started in the federal court to determine the ownership. We stationed a fire guard at the spring on the tract during the summer of 1909. Everything ran smoothly until fall.

During August I was at Coram locating a trail which a crew was building from Coram to Hungry Horse. Bunker left Kalispell by train to go to Essex. During the wait between trains at Columbia Falls he bought a copy of *The Spokesman Review* [the Spokane newspaper], and in it saw an article which said that the Governor of Montana was sending a company of militia to Belton to take possession of section 36 and hold it in the name of the State of Montana. Jack Kruse, ranger at Coram, happened to be in the depot at this time, so Bunker wrote a note to me and gave it to Kruse to deliver. The note read: "Col. Falls—9/27/9. Clack: Take Kruse to Belton tonight and the trail crew on No. 4 tomorrow. Rustle all the pick handles, firearms and ammunition available and use every man to see that no unauthorized person enters the enclosure at Belton. Use force if necessary but do not shoot unless you have to. Move all night if necessary. Am going to Essex after Bradley and McNary. Make this stick. —Bunker."

I knew that the only train which would bring passengers from Helena would be the Burlington, which reached Belton about 11:00 P.M., so Kruse and I had supper before we left. When we reached the fire guard's tent at Belton we found him lying on the cot dead drunk, so far gone that we could not waken him. Kruse and I therefore had to meet the train alone. Shortly before train time we parked ourselves back of a pile of logs just inside the gate which gave entry to the tract and from which we had a good view of the depot and platform about 100 yards distant. When the train stopped the first two men who got off were in soldier uniforms. "Well," I thought, "here they come," but no more men in uniform followed. In fact, the only other passengers to get off were Bradley and McNary. When the train pulled out the two soldiers went across the track to the Dow Hotel. When Bradley came over I asked him if there were any more soldiers on the train and he said no. I then went over to the hotel to find out who the two were. I learned they were a Lieutenant of the regular Army and his dog robber [attendant], who were going through the newly created Glacier Park. As there would be no more trains until the next day, we went to the tent and turned in. We met the first train the next day, but the only passenger to get off was Bunker, and he told me that he had wired the Governor from Essex, asking if he intended to try and take possession of the tract by force or await action of the court. The Governor wired back that he would wait action by the court. The court decided in favor of the Government. Thus ended the Battle of Belton.

The rapid change in responsibility and the integration of forestry school graduates into an agency made up of westerners sometimes produced situations that were at their heart clashes of culture between professionally trained foresters and those with experience in the woods. Thomas G. Myers of the Lewis & Clark National Forest remembered two such incidents:

> Ranger Bonham and I had an argument with a grazing inspector from the Regional Office in 1911 or 1912 about the use of rock salt for cattle while on the Forest. The inspector did not approve of the use of rock salt. When we asked his objections he said it took too much of the cows' time. Bonham said, "Hell, what is time to an old cow?" We kept on requesting the use of rock salt.
>
> I was on a grazing inspection with one of my Supervisors at another time (I only had fifteen of them during my twenty-five years at the Judith District). It was quite early spring. We had covered most of the lower C & H range and rode out on the divide going over some S & G range. [C & H denoted cattle and horse range; S & G, sheep and goat.] I was ahead with the pack horse when the Supervisor called to me, saying "Myers, you have bedded sheep too long here." I pulled up and said, "What did you say?" He told me again. I said, "My God, man, sheep have never bedded here." He said, "What is the matter? The grass is all killed out." I said, "The snowdrift has just melted, that's all." A few years later we were riding over the range and he said, "Myers, there was a hell of a lot I did not know when I came here." I laughed and said "Yes."

Stock herds in the Inland Northwest were relatively small compared to the size of the range available at that time. In 1906, the Forest Service allowed 93,514 cows on federal range in Montana for the summer season and 6,862 for the entire year. In Idaho, 20,053 cattle ran government range in the summer, with permission given for 531 all year. Washington State had similar numbers: 25,520 in the summer and 1,209 all year. Of the fourteen western states and territories, Montana ranked fourth while Idaho and Montana were near the bottom of states with large areas of federal land. Sheep were also common on western range, with the 878,550 sheep grazing in Idaho ranking third behind Oregon and Utah. Montana and Washington, both with roughly 250,000 sheep that summer, ranked at the bottom of western states and territories where sheep ran on federal land.

The numbers attested to the complexity of the job of foresters. Sheep herds were generally large, but cattle permits in the area averaged less than 100 head; in Montana, the average permit was for 68 head; in Idaho and Washington state, the average was 50. The small size of herds in the vast acreage of national forests made assuring compliance a time-consuming task.

There were also members of the Forest Service who had difficulty adjusting to the kind of order the agency increasingly required. Myers recalled one such unfortunate individual, who found himself faced with responsibilities beyond his capabilities:

In the fall of 1909, I think it was, as that was about the time we were getting new Supervisors quite often on the old Jefferson, I did not have much work on hand and was in Hobson one evening when the train to Great Falls arrived, so I went to Great Falls. As I had not had any letters from the office in some time, I thought I would give them a call. Got in quite late and no lights in the office, so I took in the town that night. Next morning I went up to the office, and found a new force in charge—a Mr. H. Graff as Acting Supervisor, and a new clerk (I do not remember her name). I told them who I was and where I was stationed. Graff spoke up and said, "Gosh, I am glad you came in," and handed me two telegrams from the District Office, both requesting that his office submit the annual grazing report. Graff asked me what he should do about it. I said that should not be very hard, and he said, "Hell, man, I have been out on a timber cruising crew in Idaho the whole time I have been in the Service." He had got a wire from the District Office to go to Great Falls and take charge of that office. Well, he had all right, as he had all the files out of the cases

and piled on the window sills, and whenever he wanted to look
something up he would start at one end and go through the folders until he found it. Some job. The clerk was having an easy time.
Well, to make a long story short, I told him to get out a letter to the
rangers requesting them to submit a grazing report. He wrote the
letter out in longhand and gave it to the clerk to type. I got a
chance to ask her if she could not take dictation, and she said,
"Sure, but he can't dictate, so there you are." I often wondered
why that poor boy was put on the spot like that, for I never heard
of him after he left Great Falls. We got out the grazing report, but it
was a little late. I know there were three of the boys on the Forest
force who could have handled the job much better. But in those
days the forest was a mess, and probably the D. O. [District Office]
thought an outsider in charge would be best for the job.

Despite intermittent internal conflict, the Forest Service presented a formidable front to the people of the Inland Northwest.
The ranger corps also served in other capacities. Part police
force, part public welfare agents, the foresters furthered the cause
of order at every opportunity. Joseph B. Halm recounted typical
duties:

One day Mr. Weigle sent me to assist a Mr. Brown in looking up
a miner working in the Big Elk, a prospect several miles from my
camp. We went in to the canyon where the mine was supposed to
be located. The mountains here were honeycombed with tunnels
and abandoned prospects. We arrived at what we took to be the
Big Elk and with lighted candles entered. The place did not appear
to have been worked recently but it was the most likely looking
place we had found so we went in several hundred feet until we
came to a cave-in, this couldn't be the place, but having gone this
far, decided to explore farther. We scrambled over the cave-in and
wading through slime and muck, kept on until suddenly I felt a
timber strike my shoulder. I had fallen against the side of the tunnel. This startled me. I could hear my heart pounding in my ears.
Brown, my companion, was staggering and fell to his knees, he
shouted, "After damp, we've got to get out of here, look at those
candles." Only a tiny glow remained. We staggered back down the

tunnel and out. Another few seconds and we both would have perished in that gas-filled tunnel. It might have been days before we would have been discovered. We found our man later, but not in that tunnel.

Another responsibility involved assuring that the people who used national forest lands did so legally. Many in rural communities resented the intrusion of the government into their lives, and foresters were the living embodiment of the agency that caused the resentment. Albert Cole recounted some of the difficulties inherent in managing the forests:

By the time this job was finished it was nearly August 1 and my partner had already been ordered to another ranger district, so I wound up the work and on my way back to headquarters I stopped and got my mail. I was surprised to receive a telegram, which had been mailed to me, to come to the Supervisor's headquarters at once. I left the Ruby Ranger Station early the next morning, and with my bed roll on the back of my saddle rode to the Supervisor's headquarters, a distance of about 40 miles. Mr. Seely informed me that I had been transferred to the Helena Forest Reserve to assist in checking on trespass timber cutting [Forest Service slang for timber cut illegally from national forest land] on the Dry Cottonwood District of that Forest. As soon as I could put my horse in a suitable pasture I went to Butte by train and hired a livery outfit to take me out to the Dry Cottonwood District. I reported to Earl[e] H. Clapp there and got acquainted with him and Walter J. Derrick, L. D. Williamson and Mallory N. Stickney, who were already working on the trespass timber cases in that part of the country. Derrick was in charge of the Dry Cottonwood District, Williamson of the adjoining district. Clapp was from Washington, D.C., and Stickney was a recent graduate of Ann Arbor, just assigned to the Helena Forest.

The work that these men had been doing and which I was to help them with consisted of scaling stulls, counting lagging [small round or split poles, rough lumber, or brush placed above the caps and along the sides of mining props], measuring cordwood and mine props and converter poles, and investigating the ownership of the cut products and making out trespass reports and propositions of settlement for the timber cut. The disposal of slash was a "bone of contention," inasmuch as most of the cutters were very much opposed to piling brush as most of them had cut the material on a contract basis and had not counted on the extra work involved in that activity. W. J. Derrick, being the ranger in charge of the district, had many hot arguments with the Austrians and Italians who had cut this timber for the mines in Butte, and once or twice he was threatened rather seriously but generally prevailed on them to conform to Forest Service regulations.

An amusing incident occurred when we crossed over the hill from the Dry Cottonwood Creek side to the head of Flume Gulch. Derrick had given us to understand that an Austrian family by the name of Casagranda, who lived at the head of Flume Gulch, had stated that there would be bullets flying when we invaded their place to scale stulls, etc. I think Derrick told this mainly for Clapp's and Stickney's benefit, as they were from the East and he wanted to impress them with the hazards of the Forest ranger's life in this wild and wooly western country. We did not dodge any bullets, but the whole Casagranda family and some of their relatives sat or stood around us as we worked. Stickney was crawling around a pile of lagging, getting a count on it, when he crawled right into a yellow jacket's nest and was badly stung before he could get away from them. He always insisted that the Casagrandas deliberately planted the wasp's nest there to sting us for revenge.

We worked in the Flume and Browns Gulch country until late in September and succeeded in cleaning up most of the trespass material. We had no trouble with any of the residents of those areas, but a few of them talked very big about what they would do to us both physically and through legal means but that was the last of it.

When we finished the work on Derrick's district I was assigned to work with Ranger Williamson on the Bernice District, which adjoined the Dry Cottonwood District. I took up my headquarters at a ranch in Elk Park, which was an area about 10 miles long by three miles wide lying between the railroad stations of Elk Park and Woodville, practically on top of the Continental Divide and well watered by Bison Creek and tributaries and bounded on the east and west sides by high, rugged hills and mountains. The park was thickly settled by Swedes, Italians, Finns and a few French Canadians. The main activities were ranching and cutting timber for the mines in Butte.

Forest Supervisor Bushnell was kind enough to let me have the use of one of his good saddle horses and riding equipment, and thus equipped I rode herd on the timber cutters and measured timber and made out trespass reports and argued with the many different denizens of that locality as to brush disposal and payments. The hardest man to deal with was a French Canadian named Dave Dubie who hired choppers to cut timber for him on a contract basis. Dubie also ran a saloon at Elk Park and a small store. He generally managed to keep the choppers in perpetual debt to him so that he did not have to lay out much money for their work. Both Ranger Williamson and I had many hot arguments with this man, and he was always trying to bribe us with cigars and the offer of drinks to shut our eyes to a portion of his activities. One trick he used was to send his bartender out, while we were arguing with him, and fill our carrying cases with cigars and bottled goods, hoping we would accept them and make things easy for him, but Williamson, who was easy-going most times, would take the stuff back into the saloon and tell Dubie in no uncertain terms what he thought of such underhand proceedings.

The combination of mines and railroads created a lucrative market for timber companies. The amount of timber cut in the region grew dramatically from the 40 million board feet harvested in Montana and Idaho territories in 1879. By 1899, after the construction of the Great Northern and the Northern Pacific and all the branch rail lines, the cut jumped to 320 million feet. In 1910, production reached 1 billion feet, remaining above that level and peaking at 1.5 billion in 1925 before a decline during the depression of the 1930s. Competing for advantages small and large made practices like those of Dave Dubie common.

The permits for timber required much Forest Service management and often an even greater amount of explanation, as Albert Cole recounted:

Toward the end of October, 1905, I was transferred from the upper Ruby Valley to Sheridan, Montana, to assist the ranchers in obtaining permits for posts, poles, house logs and small amounts of saw timber for use on their ranches. These permits were all free use, but they had to be issued by the Washington office and it was months before they were returned after the applications were made. [The Forest Service had not yet accomplished its goal of administrative decentralization.] However, generally the timber was marked and cut and on the ranches before the permit came back. This was necessary, as the rancher had to get out this stuff before the snow got too deep for such work. I was kept plenty busy covering the country from Sheridan to Whitehall, all on horseback, a distance of about forty miles with numerous ranches all along the way.

While sitting in the hotel office in Sheridan one evening talking to the men who habitually loafed there, a gentleman came in and, seeing me, asked if we could go up to my room, as he had something to ask me in regard to the Forest Reserves. I was well acquainted with this man and knew him to be an influential rancher, stockman and businessman, although he did not run any stock on the Forest ranges. We talked until nearly midnight, and I explained to him the aims and objectives of the Forest Service. He seemed very much impressed and asked numerous questions about the grazing practices and timber uses on the Forest Reserves, and I furnished him a copy of the Use Book and explained that the Forest Service was not adopting a policy of arbitrary restriction but that we were to try to help the ranchers and timber users to a better use of the Forest resources. He expressed himself as being fully satisfied that we were on the right track and said that he would talk to other stockmen, ranchers and businessmen and let them know what he believed was to be gained by this new movement in the conservation of the timber and forage resources of the country. It was men like him that overcame the prejudice of the more intelligent stockmen, ranchers and businessmen toward the Forest Service objectives.

There were also difficult and dangerous people in the woods, and often foresters had to serve in official capacities in tragic situations. Edward Stahl remembered one such instance on the Kootenai:

> A Frenchman named Solo Joe was placering [placer mining] near the summit of the Purcell Range. He warned me that if I ever ran across a trapper named Olson in the Yaak River District to mistake him for a mountain lion and shoot him. If I had followed Joe's advice it would have saved a lot of misery. But I never saw Olson. He was crazy. "Dingle on the bean," Joe said. Olson had once set a bear trap in the trail for Joe. A year later Ranger Raymond wrote the Supervisor at Libby to have an officer pick up Olson as he was dangerous. The Supervisor, a new man from the east, kidded Raymond for being afraid of Olson but took no action. Two of Raymond's laborers on trail work, upon going to their homestead for the weekend, met Olson coming out the door. He said he had called to borrow some soda, but he had put strychnine in the sourdough can. One man died that night but the other one survived. Their names were Todd and Hensley. Raymond took Olson in and he was placed in an asylum, where he later died.

Developing an institutional structure also required accoutrements such as buildings. The rangers themselves often lived on their homesteads, using a private structure there as the ranger's office. When they traveled, they stayed in shacks or line camps. By 1909, the agency had begun to develop facilities of its own, as these excerpts from the *Range Gazette,* Camp Crook, South Dakota, and Ranger Shevling's writings attest:

> May 8, 1908: The office of the Long Pines National Forest was completely destroyed by fire.
> May 14, 1908: Forest fires burned over a stretch of ground 10 miles long and 2½ miles wide, covering over 10,000 acres. It was out of control from Friday night until Sunday morning. All the women and men in the vicinity who were able turned out to help. Nearly all the timber burned. This fire was the young growth of trees that had come up since the fire of 1886.

In the fall of 1908, the forest office was in the W. B. Padden residence which burned; the office was moved to the hospital and later the same year to Shuning's store which burned at a time when a large forest fire was burning in the Long Pines. All the supervisor's records and equipment were destroyed; the forest offices were then established in the old post office building.

W. H. Benton, construction engineer from the Washington office, came to Camp Crook and drew up plans for a Government-owned supervisor's office, and by a special appropriation of $1,100, this building was constructed during the fall and early winter of 1909. In the erection of this building, Camp Crook has the proud distinction of having the first building erected in the United States solely for Forest Service office purposes. The building is 24 × 28 ft.; all rooms are commodious and well lighted and were planned for the future as well as the present needs.

Joseph B. Halm remembered another kind of complication:

> After the fire season of 1909, I was sent to the St. Joe Ranger Station near Grand Forks, where we cleared ground and built a large house for drying and extracting white pine seed. The lumber for the cone house was salvaged from abandoned camp buildings along the nearly constructed C. M. & P. S. Ry. Much of our materials in those days was salvage.
>
> Our crew consisted of five men, Ed Holcomb, Sam Milsap, Gus Yeager, John Long and myself. We batched in the lean-to of the cone house. Cones were plentiful that fall. The 110-year-old clear stand of white pine yielded a splendid crop. We robbed the squirrel caches and got as high as fifty bushels of cones from a single cache. I can to this day see those disgusted squirrels with their pitch-smeared whiskered faces scolding at us as we plundered their caches. How they must have sworn in their squirrel language as those big hulks robbed them of their hard-earned winter storehouses.

The chattering squirrels did not reflect the depletion of wildlife in the area, although their distress at the actions of humans surely typified reaction of wildlife to an increased human presence. By 1900, American wildlife had been depleted by the combination of a large eastern market, a relatively open West where game was plentiful, and a lack of any serious restrictions on hunting practice. Many species, including whitetailed deer, moose, black bears, bighorn sheep, and bison, were extinct or in danger of extinction as wild game and fowl came to comprise an important part of the diet of even urban Americans. Squirrels were exempted only because they were not fashionable as market food items.

This process was less comprehensive in the forests of the Inland Northwest. Harder to reach and difficult to traverse, particularly during the seven months of the year that could legitimately be called winter, the mountainous areas of western Montana, northern Idaho, and eastern Washington provided a barrier against the kind of exploitive hunting that occurred on the Great Plains. There was serious impact in pockets in the region; along the railroad tracks and in concentric rings emanating outward from mining towns and the timber camps that served them, game was clearly depleted. Even in Yellowstone National Park, at the south end of this area, poaching became such a problem that federal legislation to protect animals there was first enacted in 1894. This situation was a harbinger of the consequences of an unregulated future, and in the worldview of the time, legislation was the means to rectify it.

In many ways, law was at the center of the worldview of the USFS. New laws were the means to restrict wanton behavior as well as to define the terms of future debate over issues of efficiency and management. Foresters had an attachment to law that the realities of their peripheral status could not always uphold. In law was order, in order the combination of sustainability, efficiency, and fairness that drove foresters in particular and Progressives in general.

As a result, local communities and their idiosyncratic laws and mores were one of the greatest threats to the kind of order foresters represented. At the turn of the century, many westerners perceived themselves as wholly independent, far from the rules and regulations of the nation. Some of the people in small towns or on homesteads were those left behind after "boomtime" jobs in railroad construction or mining disappeared; others were independent people who sought solace from the mainstream. Still

others were families who saw in the ownership of land the promise of independence if not always prosperity.

The currents of the time had left them behind in remote places
in the woods. Without being aware of it, they were consigned to
the national scrapheap by economic and social forces far away.
Wall Street, the opening of new markets and the discovery of
new natural resources elsewhere on the globe, local and regional
economic depression, and other factors all combined to socially,
culturally, and economically strand people on land from which
they could only eke out the barest of livings. They were trapped
by lack of infrastructure, personal skills, and understanding of
market forces into an anachronistic life on difficult and often in-
hospitable land.

These people developed a culture and identity of their own.
They embraced the Forest Service for what it could offer them,
and they resented its ability to legislate their lives. These independent westerners lived in a world of first-come, first-served,
where they could do as they pleased as long as they did not im-
pinge on any other person. This dogmatic iconoclasm made relations with individuals and communities into one of the most difficult responsibilities for rangers.

The relationships between the people of the woods and the
Forest Service were tinged with ambiguity and ambivalence.
Each needed the cooperation of the other, but they were mutu-
ally wary. The foresters sought local respect as they taught new
practices, the locals support for their way of doing things as well
as access to whatever amenities of the outside world—mail,
news, roads and trails, tools, and anything else that made their lot
easier—foresters could provide. The relationships were tenuous,
based as much on the character of individuals as on respect for
the badge representing federal authority. In one-to-one relations,
foresters could improvise; faced with widespread assault on the
laws and policies they were sworn to uphold, they responded
vigorously. When necessary, they took the position of enforcing
the law rather than administering land in the manner to which
they were more accustomed. As federal employees, they could
be easily deputized as marshals when needed. Most were more
than prepared for the task, as Joseph B. Halm of the Coeur d'A-
lene National Forest attested:

The bore of the Taft tunnel on the new Milwaukee railroad through the Bitterroot mountains was nearing completion. Grand Forks [now the site of Falcon] was a wild mushroom construction town on the Idaho side. The main section of the town had no streets. It was built in the form of a hollow rectangle around a sort of court. Both sides and ends of this court were almost solid with rough lumber and log buildings. During the mornings the court was deserted except for a few sobering stragglers sitting on empty beer kegs piled in front of the twelve or fifteen saloons. Some of these saloons also served as eating places and one or two had store annexes. Behind the saloons, scattered all around through the woods were nondescript assortments of tents and shacks which served as dwellings for all the town's population.

Toward evening the town would begin to show signs of life and as night came on, gas and oil lamps began to glow, player pianos began their tinny din, an orchestra here and there began to tune up. Women daubed with rouge came from the cribs upstairs and sat at lunch counters or mingled with the ever increasing throng of gamblers and rough laborers from the camps. As the hours wore on the little town became a roaring, seething, riotous brawl of drinking, dancing, gambling and fighting humanity.

During the fall, while located at the cone camp about two miles from town, we received instructions to close all the saloons at Grand Forks and arrest the operators. Ranger Kotkie, at Supervisor Weigle's request, gave each saloon owner due notice. They paid no heed, simply laughed at him and said to do his worst. Kotkie arrived with warrants, then arrested the owners and assisted by several of us, marched them over the mountains to Taft, Montana, thence by train to Wallace, Idaho. They were duly tried in court and fined.

Upon our return to Grand Forks, we found most of the saloons still running full blast, operated by hired assistants. Warrants were again secured and these new men were taken out for trial. This went on for several weeks and we became extremely unpopular. When one saloon was closed, another sprang up next door under new management and we had it all to do over again. Finally, however, only two saloons remained—one operated by a burly tough and his equally tough assistant. One day Ranger Kotkie, Mr. Holcomb and I went into this place to arrest the owner who had threatened to shoot us on sight. Mr. Kotkie stepped up to the bar and showed his warrant and said, "Mr. Blank, I am sorry, I will have to arrest you." The man replied, "The hell you say, you can't take me." Kotkie, who spoke slightly broken German, answered, "Vell, I can try, can't I?" Then he told Mr. Blank to be ready at nine o'clock next morning and we walked out.

Supervisor Weigle was notified. He rode all night on horseback from Wallace arriving at our camp early in the morning. He organized us into a posse of six, including Kotkie, Holcomb and myself. We were all armed but kept our guns concealed. At nine o'clock we walked quietly up to the saloon; no one was in sight. We went to the rear, one stayed in front and four of us went in. Only two or three men were in the room. Holcomb stood just inside the door. I took my post against the wall opposite the bar while Weigle and Kotkie stepped up to the bar and Mr. Weigle said, "Are you ready to go, Mr. Blank?" The man reached under the bar, things looked bad for a moment; when he withdrew his hand he had a towel, wiped his hands and said, "I'll go just as soon as I can change my clothes." I am sure we all breathed more freely then. Mr. Weigle had also secured a warrant for the arrest of the bartender. He asked them if they would go peaceably and they said they would.

Weigle, Kotkie and the two prisoners walked over the mountains to the Northern Pacific Railway at Taft. At Taft Weigle and Kotkie took their prisoners into the train and just after the train started, the bartender dove out of a car window and was never heard of again. The subsequent search brought out the fact that this man was a desperate character with a long prison record—an escaped convict with at least one known murder to his credit.

With this final arrest the saloons disappeared and with their demise the boom town of Grand Forks faded to a few lunch counters and stores. The town burned during the great fire of 1910 and is now only history.

Foresters learned that they had to accommodate the needs of people in remote places. On occasion, this reality contravened both their training and their best instincts, as in this apocryphal tale:

In 1908 the U.S. Forest Service was just getting organized. There were few men in the field to manage the millions of acres set aside as National Forests in the rugged West of those days. The problems encountered were, to say the least, different, and sometimes as difficult for the bosses near the Great White Father in Washington to solve, as for the young upstarts who encountered them.

A young forester newly assigned to a vast wilderness through which a transcontinental railroad was being constructed learned that some women had moved in close to a large construction camp and were occupying National Forest land. He asked them to vacate. They told him to "go to hell." Then he wired his chief: "Undesirable prostitutes occupying Federal land. Please advise." He received this reply: "Get desirable ones."

Five

"A Badge and a Use Book"

Foresters in the Field

With the outlines of a system established, individual rangers still faced an immense task. More than representatives of an ordered bureaucratic society, they were people selected to administer forest lands by a specific set of rules and regulations. Their domain was vast, and the modern network of forest roads and state and county highways that now graces the Inland Northwest did not exist. In many areas, neither did trails. What foresters most often faced was a world to which little formal structure had been applied. Their job was to implement rules and regulations not only in a symbolic but in an actual sense as well.

Their responsibilities and problems were many and varied. Rangers built ranger stations, faced unusual and sometimes abominable living conditions, and traveled to perform inspections, map boundaries, survey land, and meet their peers at ranger meetings. They organized timber sales and issued grazing permits, served as an informal network of communication for people in the woods, and often were the bearers of both good and bad news.

These rangers and their activities were critical to the development of the Forest Service. To the public, their individual actions represented the agency, and the way they conducted themselves in unusual and distant locations with little help determined how successful the new agency would be. Not only were they representatives of the Forest Service, they often stood for the entire concept of government in a section of the country that still generally lacked an institutional structure and the mechanisms that had come to dominate the nation. As a result, they routinely faced daunting responsibilities alone, as Roy Phillips explained:

> A fire guard in those days often had to patrol areas the size of present-day ranger districts, and the task of getting around over his district represented days of severe physical effort. No lookouts existed and the patrolman viewed his area from high vantage points as he traveled around on his beat. If he sighted fire he went to it and if true to his trust, stayed with it until it was out, with the hope uppermost in his mind that nothing would happen elsewhere until he again got back into circulation. Sometimes with hands and feet blistered and even his body galled by sweat he kept on day by day with little to eat and almost no sleep.

In the early years of Forest Service administration, rangers were much like independent contractors. Not only were they not compensated with funds to cover depreciation of their personal property, they were expected to provide much of their own equipment. Although the salaries they received were reasonable, they certainly were not ample. Despite the commitment of forest rangers to the ideals of utilitarian conservation, they were often economically marginal individuals. Albert Cole recalled:

> I want to mention that the Forest guards and also the rangers and Supervisors had to furnish their own horses and equipment, our own subsistence and lodging, feed our horses and pay all of our own expenses, whether we were at our headquarters or in the field. Forest guards at that time started at $60 per month. The only equipment that was furnished was a marking axe (and, oh, what an axe!), a notebook and a book of regulations called a Use Book. This marking axe was about the clumsiest tool I think I have ever had to use in all my life. It was shaped something like a pole axe or single-bitted axe, and the side opposite the blade had the letters "U.S." and was the marking part of the tool. It was out of balance and was so hard that it could hardly be sharpened and on account of its hardness the blade broke and chipped off at the slightest provocation. The marking hatchet in use now is a far cry from the clumsy tool of the early days.

Getting to a new ranger station could pose real problems. Clyde Fickes of the Lewis & Clark National Forest recalled his first posting:

> I applied for work on the old Lewis & Clark National Forest in the spring of 1907. Appointed a Forest Guard on July 1 at $60 per month and supplying myself and two horses, I was assigned to a survey party on Swan River with D. C. Harrison of Washington, D.C., as Chief of party, and Forest Rangers Jack Clack and Ernest Bond, as well as a cook. On July 23 and 24 I took the Forest Ranger examination at Kalispell and was directed to go to the Hanan Gulch Ranger Station on the North Fork of Sun River. It has always been my impression that I was not a very promising candidate for ranger to A. C. McCain, Acting Supervisor while Supervisor Page S. Bunker was on detail to Washington, D.C., so he figured, "I'll give this kid an assignment that he won't want to accept, or else he will never get to Sun River and we will be well rid of him."
>
> They gave me a badge, a USE BOOK and a GREEN BOOK and told me, "When you get to Hanan you can take charge of the Sun River District." That's how I became a forest ranger in 1907.
>
> Well, I fooled McCain by making my way to Hanan Gulch on the North Fork of Sun River. Leaving Kalispell on July 26th, with saddle and pack horse we traveled eastward along the Great Northern Railroad which was about the only feasible way in those days to get from Kalispell to Sun River. Swam the South Fork, which was high, and camped the first night at the old Fitzpatrick homestead about where the present highway bridge is located.
>
> Most of the trail followed the old tote road used in building the railroad, and there were places where the trail lay between the iron rails which made travel by horse a little hazardous at times. Arrived at the Lubec Ranger Station on the 30th, and leaving there on August 1st rode south along the foothills, arriving at Hanan on the 5th. According to my diary I had traveled some 190 miles in ten days to reach my post of duty. Several years ago I

drove approximately the same route in a little over four hours.

At Hanan I found Ranger Henry Waldref in charge and the two cabins comprising the living quarters occupied by the A. C. McCain family of five. There were several acres of timothy meadow at the station and Waldref was putting up the hay, a job which I helped him finish during the next three days. Henry gave me a general outline of the conditions on the district as he understood them and some idea of what the job load was, although that expression was unheard of by either of us at that time. (His home was at Lincoln where he had a prospect [a mining claim] that he worked winters since his appointment was only for the summer months.) He had a black saddle horse and a span of bay mares, one with foal at side, that were the fattest pieces of horse flesh I believe I ever saw. And if one of them raised so much as one wet hair on the trail, he would stop until it had dried.

By the next year I had acquired five head of horses with necessary riding and pack equipment, some furniture and kitchen tools. The Hanan Ranger Station consisted of an old log cabin 16 by 20, and dirt roof, a 14 by 16 hewed log with box corners, a cabin, barn, corral, hay meadow and pasture all taken over from a former homesteader or squatter named Jim Hanan who allegedly operated a station on the old Oregon-Montana horse rustling trail. Hanan Gulch was ideal for such a purpose because a short stretch of fence sealed the gulch up to make a tight horse pasture from which there was no escape. For a ranger station no more isolated or lonesome spot could be found anywhere. Visitors were practically unheard of for months at a time. About all I had to do was rustle enough wood to keep warm, throw out a little hay for the horses on a stormy day and ride 25 miles to Augusta every two weeks to get mail and supplies.

In some cases all the rangers had was a job that put them in charge of an area of forest. There were no buildings, trails, or equipment that they did not supply. Thomas G. Myers of the

A remote ranger cabin. (Photo courtesy USDA Forest Service)

Lewis & Clark National Forest found himself in such a situation. He described what he found on his arrival at the forest and the process he experienced of initiating some form of administration:

> I finally heard from the Civil Service that I had passed the Ranger examination. The next thing was to get an appointment. I wrote the Supervisor at Neihart about a job on the Little Belt Reserve, now part of the Lewis & Clark. Along about the following March, I received my appointment, to take effect May 1, 1906, at $900 per annum. I could not report for work until June 1, which was O.K. with the Supervisor, so that was when I started work for the Forest Service.
>
> There were four new men besides myself, and we started in at the Belt Creek Station building fences and fixing up the old house and barn there. From Belt Creek we went to Dry Wolf, and built a log house and fixed up an old barn, and built quite a lot of fence for pasture and meadow.
>
> The first of August I went over to the Judith, as I was to have charge of that district. There was an old log cabin that was built in 1876, I found out later, that was to be my home, and there was an old log barn and a shed, but not any pasture under fence, so I started in cutting posts.
>
> The other boys arrived and we gathered up a lot of barbed wire

scattered through the timber, left by the sawmill outfit that had been located here for years. I wrote the Supervisor about money to buy wire to finish the fence. He replied he had no funds for that, so I bought it myself.

I had my own axe and a few other tools, as there was only one hand saw, one one-man crosscut saw, and an old pole axe.

I was in the office at Neihart when a Mr. Darling, engineer from the Washington office, was making up a list of tools and equipment that would be needed for building the telephone line on the Forest. When they came to the reels for paying out the wire the engineer said we ought to have one single and one double reel. I laughed and asked him what we needed the double reel for. He said, "You might want to string wire out both ways." I said, "Can't we do it with one single reel?" We got both. I asked the engineer if he was working for the Forest Service or the outfit that had the stuff to sell. He did not have much use for me, I was told later.

Paul G. Redington took charge of the Forest in November 1907, and after he got things lined up he put W. S. Perrine in charge, and Perrine put me in charge of completing the telephone line to Judith Station. I got through with it the last of November after cutting the crew from 28 to 12 men.

In 1908 I received my authorization for $450 for building the dwelling at the Judith Station, blueprints and all made by an engineer by the name of Work. The building was 24 x 24 with hip roof. The lumber was bought in Great Falls, shipped to Benchland, and I had to have it hauled from there by team 26 miles to the station. It was about 13 miles to where the logs were cut, at a cost of $1.25 per log, which was not bad.

What got me down was when I started studying the blueprint and found it called for the hip rafters to be 24 feet long. I called the office and told them I thought the hip rafters should be cut 20 feet long, but I got the "No, don't do it" answer, but to follow the blueprint; so I used the full 24 feet for pattern, but when I put two of them up I saw the roof with that pitch would split a raindrop. So I cut off 2 feet and tried that, but they were still too steep, so I cut off 2 feet more and it was still quite steep, but I let it go at that.

I did not have a level so I wrote in to the office for authority to buy one, but got word back no money to purchase level, so I bought one myself.

Building a remote cabin. (Photo courtesy USDA Forest Service)

When I got the walls up and roof on, all I had was one big room downstairs and plenty of room upstairs but no floor. I had a good neighbor at the American Sapphire Mine who said I could use their team and sled to haul logs to their mill, so I went over and cut about 3 M [thousand] feet of logs and sawed them into boards and 2 × 4 and put in partitions and a rough floor upstairs. I still had lumber left, so I put a porch across the front and one half-way on the rear of the house; but no shingles for the roof. The Supervisor came into the station, and in looking things over asked me where I got the lumber. I just said the porches looked awful without shingles, and by gosh I got them. When the fiscal year ended the office had to turn back about $3,300 of unspent funds. Was I mad? NO. I finally got the dwelling in fair condition.

On my first advertised timber sale, I was to have help from the office in working up data, but no help arrived. So I studied my Use Book on "Timber Sales," and went at it alone, surveying the area, making my estimate of stand and notes for forest description. Finally got my field work done and came back to the station and started in writing up estimate sheets, forest description in longhand (no typewriters in those days). Well, I worked on the damn thing and after getting it finished, map and all, I thought it looked good. So I sent it in to the office. In about ten days or more I got the thing back from the office with a six-page letter, telling me how much I did not know after being in the Service for six months and about all the mistakes I had made. Well, I got mad and the next morning I saddled up the pony and that night I was in Neihart, but did not see the Supervisor until next morning, when I went into the office, put his letter and everything on his desk, and asked him what the hell he wanted. We went over the papers together and he approved them, and the sale went through.

My first year, 1907, with grazing applications and permits, I only had six cattle and horse permittees, so I rode from ranch to ranch getting their applications. I rode in to Mr. Ethen's ranch; got there in time for supper. When I told him my business he said, "I'll be damned if I will apply for 500 head." I asked him who said anything about the number he should apply for, and he dug up a letter from the Supervisor stating his application would not be accepted for less than 500 head on and off. During the fall and winter I had been counting the number of head of his stock I found on the Forest, and I never found 350 head on at any time. His stock were not near the Forest through the summer, but he said he was willing to apply for 350 head on and off yearlong. I handed him the application and told him to make it out the number he wanted, and he applied for 350 head on and off yearlong. I O.K.'d his application and sent it in to the office. A few days later I received a letter telling me I should not have O.K.'d this application and to get another for the 500 head. Well, I made another trip to Neihart, taking with me my counts of the number of head I had found on the Forest. The application was approved for the 350 head.

I think it was in the fall of 1909 that two rangers were picked from each Forest to attend the ranger school at Missoula. So I was put in charge of the Belt Creek District while Ranger L. T. Morgan was at school. There were all kinds of timber sales from one end of the district to the other—sawtimber, smelter poles, mine props and ties and cordwood. At that time the district extended from the Divide south of Neihart to Ming Coulee southwest of Sand Coulee.

The office sent this Forest assistant out here to map and estimate a large block of lodgepole pine for props and tie timber on O'Brien Creek, and requested me to assist him in getting started. So I went up and helped him run or survey out two lines almost one mile in length and about a quarter mile apart for a working base. Then I had to go to scale up sawlogs at Logging Creek and

Ming Coulee. When I got back there was a letter from the office
telling me to assist the boy with his estimating. I spent three days
with him and found out he had not done a thing since I left him.
There was about three feet of snow up there. I had to go into the
Barker country to measure up cordwood and up into Belt Park
and scale up sawtimber and mark trees for cutting. Plenty of snow
here too. When I got back to Belt Creek Station and got my mail
sent down from Neihart I found a wire from the office saying,
"Please help Forest assistant with his work." Well, I almost hit the
ceiling. I went up to Neihart and told the boy if he would just take
over my work and do it I would try and do his for him, but I
helped him for a few days more. I had to stand my own expense,
while he had his paid. He was in Neihart through December, January and part of February. The Service never got anything from his
work as Ranger Morgan completed it after he came back from Missoula. We had plenty of snow that winter. I traveled on skis all the
time.

Foresters often had to explain the regulations of their agency
to friends and neighbors who had known them all of their lives.
This authority over the way westerners used their land engen-
dered resentment. Others did not understand the principles of
government service and scientific forestry, and rangers often had
to set them straight. Earl V. Welton of the Helena National Forest
described one such instance:

   I received an appointment as forest guard on the old Helena
   National Forest effective October 1, 1907, and started work that
   day at the Dry Cottonwood Ranger Station under Ranger W. J.
   Derrick.
   I was familiar with all the country, for I had ridden the range
   here when I was a boy. I was also quite familiar with survey lines,
   as I had been employed for four seasons on a GLO survey.
   I had been reared in the Deer Lodge Valley and was well acquainted with nearly everyone. Naturally, I had to explain the Forest Service regulations, especially those relating to timber and
   grazing. An old sheep man who I had known all my life said to me
   one day, "Earl, if it wasn't for these Forest Reserves I'd show you

some sheep raising." Up to that time, this man, to my own personal knowledge, had for several years maintained a sheep camp, some time during the grazing season, in nearly every gulch from the "Hump," 12 miles north of Butte City, to Peterson Creek, a stream that flows into the Deerlodge River at Deer Lodge. He had been restricted by permit for only one or two seasons at the most at that time, and still ran the same number of sheep.

Another man said to me, "You sure have a good job now, and I'm glad you have it." I said yes, it was a pretty fair job, something new, and better than ranch work. "Oh, but think of the graft there'll be in it," he said. I asked him how he figured that. "Well," he said, "that's easy. Take for instance a cattle and horse permit. I want to graze 100 head. All you have to do is to charge me for 50 and split the difference with me for the balance." In those days a charge of 27 cents a head was made for horses and cattle for a six-month period beginning April 15. I said to him, "If you pay for the full 100 head it would cost you $27; for 50, $13.50. Then split the $13.50, and you make $6.25 and I make $6.25. And what can I tell the grazing inspector this fall when he sees all the stock on the Forest, grass all eaten off, and about one-half the amount of the grazing fee collected? No, I'll stay in the straight and narrow path."

Albert E. Cole of the Deerlodge and Helena National Forests remembered similar problems with local constituents:

> After taking the examination Mr. Seely hired all three of us as Forest guards and sent us to the upper Ruby Valley to work for the Forest Service, to finish building a small one-room cabin to serve as a ranger station, and to get out posts and poles for a pasture fence and do other work in connection with developing the ranger station site. We were to ride over that part of the Forest Reserve, as they were called at that time, to contact ranchers, stockmen and other Forest users to acquaint them with the rules and regulations of the Forest Reserves and to help them get accustomed to the procedure for getting permits for grazing and timber.
>
> Almost all of the ranchers of that part of the country were very hostile to the Forest Service objectives and were very bitter in

their denunciation of the rules, but were not necessarily hostile or dangerous to us as individuals nor to us as Forest employees, as they knew we had to do our job and they realized we had no personal feeling toward them in the performance of our duties. They all thought that the Forest Reserve idea was a crack-pot scheme of some politicians in Washington and that it would be done away with as soon as a Democratic administration took over the government of the country, and even President Theodore Roosevelt, who had been quite popular in that country before, was severely criticized and lost considerable prestige and support because he had supported the movement.

As I had been born and raised in this county and was well acquainted with most of these ranchers, and my father, being a carpenter, had erected buildings on a number of the ranches and I had been with him on several jobs, it seemed to surprise many of the Democrats, as they knew my father was a staunch Democrat, to see me employed by a Republican administration, as all of them thought that all Government jobs were obtained through political pull. One old man said, "I am very much surprised to see you hiring out to the Black Republicans and lowering yourself by working for such a bum outfit; but you'll lose your job sure when we put in a Democratic President, and this Forest Reserve business will be done away with and we free American citizens can cut our timber and run our stock as we always have."

In December 1909, a rather momentous event occurred in that our first Forester, Mr. Gifford Pinchot, resigned. This was the result of the Pinchot-Ballinger controversy. Antagonists of the Forest Service were sure it meant the end of the Forest Service life. One such man said to me: "The rest of you fellows will soon follow your leader into oblivion." He meant, of course, we would all soon be discharged and that the Forest Service was through. I replied, "My dear sir, the Forest Service will be functioning long after you and I are under ground." Well, I am still alive, but I believe he has passed on, and the Forest Service is much stronger and doing much better work than ever before. The old antagonisms are about all dead now and some of our old enemies have nothing but praise for the way in which it brought order out of chaos, especially in the grazing end.

The early foresters also worked under abysmal conditions without amenities such as permanent shelter and reliable communication systems. It was hard to maintain remote operations such as the few fire lookouts, as W. K. "Bill" Samsel explained:

Most of the Forest Service's early day lookouts were above timber line, in the cap rock, where timber did not obstruct their view. In the beginning, of course, these points were unimproved. There was no protection from the elements, for man or equipment. It was common practice then for the lookout man to camp in the nearest sheltered place below the lookout point, from where he could quickly hike up and take observations. During periods of high fire danger and lightning storm activity he might make several such observation trips in a day's time. In such cases the man would hike from one point to another taking observations on each point and return. Such stations were referred to as patrol routes and the person manning such a station was known as a patrolman.

Living quarters on these early day detection points were most primitive. The Forest Service furnished a tent, a few cooking utensils, and a bed, consisting of 3 OD army type wool blankets and a tarp, a double bitted axe and fire tools. It was up to the man to use his own ingenuity and skill as a woodsman in making his quarters as comfortable as possible.

The first three summers I worked for the Forest Service I was stationed on one of these unimproved points. I was fortunate, however, that there were two of us stationed at the same point. In such cases one man was designated the lookout and the other the smokechaser. I played the latter role. One advantage of two being together was that we could throw our bedding together and make a much better bed. We built a good substantial bunk up off the ground and covered it deep in fir boughs for springs and mattress. We stretched our tent in a good sturdy manner so it would afford us, our bed, food, and personal belongings the maximum protection from the elements. Believe me, the elements can be rough at an elevation of 8,000 feet, what with wind, lightning, rain and even hail and snow.

Since the Forest Service did not furnish a stove, we built a rock fireplace where we did the fry cooking and boiling, then an oven in the rocks for baking bread. This done, our quarters were complete, still quite primitive, but we managed to get along and be quite comfortable most of the time. It has been said before and I am sure it is true, that it took a special breed of men to live under such primitive conditions. They had to love the mountains and be possessed of the old pioneer spirit. Starting wages for a first-year lookout man were $70 per month, including room and board. And, at first, room was "all outdoors."

The first structures to be built on the early day lookouts were small, crude log cabins for man shelter [a common term at the time]. The observatory might be just a ladder up a tree to where a small platform with a railing called a "Crow's Nest" was built. On this Crow's Nest the lookout man had his map board and alidade and could do his fire spotting. On points where there were no trees suitable for observatories a crude tower was sometimes fashioned out of poles. These structures were built by the lookout man and smokechaser with no plans or blueprints. Many of them did serve the purpose for quite sometime. The first somewhat modern lookout structure to be used in this region was a 14' × 14' frame structure with windows on all four sides. This type of structure was placed directly on top of the lookout point and served both as living quarters and observatory. It was a vast improvement over any previous facilities. Several versions of this structure were built during the period ending World War I and the early 1930s. Many were constructed from logs and native material with a cupola added on top. This cupola was used for an observatory and made the structure much more functional.

At this point I should say something about the food which was furnished by the Forest Service. Because all food had to be packed in by mule train, which took from 4 to 6 days from the road end, and because there were no facilities for keeping fresh foods, they had to be of a non-perishable nature. A typical grub list would run about as follows: Flour, baking powder, salt, sugar, coffee, beans, rice, dried apricots, prunes and raisins. Sometimes there were dehydrated potatoes. For meat there was ham and bacon, and sometimes a little canned corned beef. Other canned foods consisted of corn, tomatoes, milk and syrup. Some years later when the Forest Service began to furnish canned fruit and applebutter we thought this was really high living. It is only fair to say that we supplemented our diet with huckleberries and fish when we were able to get where they were. Also when grouse season opened that helped, too.

The water supply was often a problem. Most lookout points were located a considerable distance above a source of water, so keeping an adequate supply on hand for drinking and for camp use was quite a chore. In the beginning about the same system was used by all. The Forest Service furnished a 5–gallon water bag with shoulder straps attached. This was called a man-pack water bag; old-timers referred to it as a "coon." At any rate, the lookout backpacked his water to his tower up from the nearest mill, creek or lake. This might be a distance of 2 or 3 miles. In these cases, water had to be conserved. No bathing was done; dishwashing was cut to a minimum. Such utensils as frying and baking pans were never washed—as soon as a slick glaze was burned on them they were simply wiped out with a cloth. Other dishes were scraped and wiped as clean as possible before they were put in the dish water. In this way the water remained clean enough so that it could be used two or three times.

In later years better methods of supplying lookouts with water were developed. One of the better systems should be credited to Jack Clack, who was assistant supervisor on the old Missoula National Forest at the time he developed this system. He fabricated a 200 gallon tank from galvanized sheet metal. This tank, cylindrical in shape, was sunk in the ground on the leeward side of the lookout. The top plate was perforated with nail holes and was then covered with a 4 to 6 inch layer of gravel. When the drifted snow melted in the spring this snow would filter down through the gravel and fill the tank.

In the beginning, communication was just as primitive as other facilities on these remote points. The Forest Service first attempted to use the heliograph. For many obvious reasons there was little success with this instrument. Next we tried to tie in telephone communication with a fine insulated wire which we hung on tree limbs. This was called emergency wire telephone. It was a little more dependable than the heliograph. However, it was vulnerable to breakage by windstorms, falling trees and by wild animals, such as elk and deer, tangling in it. The first fairly dependable communication did not come until the advent of the standard Forest Service tree line. In this, No. 9 galvanized wire was used. It was hung on trees with a split tree insulator which, when a tree fell across the line, could render through and go to ground rather than break the line.

Rangers depended on each other for much more than supplies and news. In District 1, they were forming the backbone of a permanent organization with obligations to local, state, and national constituencies. Remote rangers often felt removed from the agency and occasionally fell out of touch with changes in procedure. Ranger meetings became a central form of communication at the national forest level throughout the agency, and particularly in District 1, where many rangers spent much of the year out of contact with their peers. These annual convocations gave rangers the opportunity to keep abreast of change in their agency, learn about problem areas and innovative solutions, and experience the camaraderie of a fellowship of people doing a job in which they strongly believed. Sometimes getting to a ranger meeting was a chore in itself. Clyde Fickes recalled one of these experiences:

> One of my most interesting experiences was my first ranger meeting, held at the mouth of White River on the South Fork of the Flathead River from October 14 to 18 inclusive, in 1907.
>
> On September 30th, notice was received from Supervisor Page S. Bunker at Kalispell that the meeting would be held. The supervisor had just returned from a six-months' detail to the Washington office and I guess he wanted to find out if his rangers could get around in the mountains satisfactorily. E. A. Woods, who was the ranger on the old Dearborn District, was in town at the same time I was and we agreed that, in company with Waldref and Guards Nixon and Converse, we would assemble at the mouth of the West Fork of the South Fork of the North Fork of Sun River and all trail over the Continental Divide together. Nixon had been over the route with a hunting party and was to be the guide. I call it a "route" advisedly, because there was no such thing as a located trail except along the main river. The appointed day of meeting

was October 8th, but due to an unforeseen circumstance I could not get there. A. C. McCain had been appointed supervisor of the Custer and I had agreed to see that his outfit was shipped to him. Lincoln Hoy, the ranger from the old Teton District, rode into Hanan on October 3rd with Mac's saddle and pack horses which had been at Lubec. Hoy prevailed upon me, when he learned of the ranger meeting, to wait for him while he went home and got his outfit for the trail.

We left Hanan the morning of the 9th and camped at the beaver dams on the West Fork. The others had not waited for us so it was a case of finding our own trail over the divide. My diary for the 10th reads, "moved up West Fork Trail, camped on top of the divide under the cliffs. Jumped about 5 miles of logs. Bum trail." I was riding the best mountain horse I think it was ever my pleasure to fork. A gray mare, 3/4 Arabian, 8 years old, that I bought from McCain, who had acquired her from Gus Mosier [Moser, once a forest supervisor] of Ovando, via a poker game, so I heard. Sure-footed as a goat, never excited, could jump any log she could put her nose on and, best of all, was never known to leave her rider afoot. The next day we pulled down to the mouth of White River to be the first arrivals at the meeting site. Woods and the others had stopped on the head of the river to try to get some meat, which they didn't.

Like all its successors, the ranger meeting on White River was mostly talk. We also did a ranger station survey under the direction of Harrison and on the third day all moved down the river to Black Bear where a new cabin was being built for the ranger headquarters.

Snow was beginning to cover the high country so those from the east side—some nine of us—pulled out for home. No one wanted to buck the logs on the West Fork so we went up to the Danaher Ranch and crossed through Scapegoat Pass and some 16 or 18 inches of snow.

The White River meeting was where I first met Tom Spaulding, who was later to be Dean of the Montana Forest School. Tom accompanied me to Hanan, as he had been sent from the District Inspector's office in Missoula to examine some June 11 claims and survey several administrative sites on Sun River and Dupuyer Creek. Tom was my first contact with anyone who even pretended that he knew something about forestry. He introduced me to Swappach and Pinchot's Primer of Forestry, books which I later acquired and read, or shall I say, devoured [*Forestry* by Adam Swappach was translated from German and first published in English in 1904].

Not all ranger meetings were positive and productive. Tom Myers was glad when this one was over:

About the last of August [1906] the Supervisor and his ranger assistant, that was supposed to be at the Belt Creek Station, came into the Judith Station on their way to the Musselshell for a ranger meeting at the Spring Creek Station. So it was pack up and go with them. We left the next morning, going up the South Fork of the Judith. It started in raining by the time we got to the Trask ranch. I wanted them to stop there for the night where we could cook our supper out of the rain, but no, we had to go on and make camp in the rain. No tents, and we had to cook our hot cakes over a campfire in the rain. We had them fried, boiled, and spoiled; but they were good. The Supervisor told us we must not sponge off of the permittees. I said, "Hell, all we would do is use the house to get in out of the rain." There was no one living there.

Well, the next morning we pulled out for the head of Haymaker Creek, but before we got there the fog got so thick you could not see the fellow twenty feet ahead of you. I brought up the rear and every time they found the trail I put up a fire-warning notice (the old cloth type).

We did not make it into Haymaker that day as the Supervisor got lost. He was the only one who had ever been through that way. We finally made it to the old Spring Creek Station after four days' traveling. I found later that the trip could be made in one short day's travel. Grub was getting low so two of us had to go to Martinsdale for supplies. Five days. Went fishing the sixth day; had good luck. There was a rancher the Supervisor wanted to see, so we all rode up the Musselshell fifteen miles. Seventh day gone.

The eighth day we pulled out for Hoover Springs; camped there for the night. The rancher we went to see yesterday made up a party and there were four good-looking girls in his crowd, so we had company for the night. Ninth day—packed up and pulled out for Neihart; got in that night around 10 P.M. Tenth day—split up some wood for the Supervisor's house and the office, then rode down to Belt Creek for the night. Eleventh day—pulled out for Dry Wolf Station with Ranger Ensleth. Twelfth day—pulled out for Judith Station. When I arrived, I found about 100 head of cattle in the patch of oats I had planted for hay. Some ranger meeting!

Nor was the work they had to do any easier. There was no infrastructure within the agency, nor was there much support for the efforts of individual rangers. Most took their instructions and did the best they could, as R. L. Woesner of the Flathead National Forest recalled:

My own experience in the Forest Service [1909–1920] was after it was under the Department of Agriculture and "modernized" to some extent. Although there were still no telephone lines, there were a few more roads and trails, and the Forest Service built cabins for the rangers. That is, the Forest Service furnished the material for construction and as there were more rangers then, they were allowed to "gang up" some on improvement projects.

Salaries had also risen somewhat, as I started in with a salary of $75.00 per month and only had to furnish two horses of my own as the station in the District I was assigned to was only 30 miles from the Post Office. I only had 60 miles to go for supplies. The district I had was a small one, only about 250,000 acres. I was all alone in this district and had no way of communicating with the supervisor's office except by mail through an isolated post office 30 miles away that received and sent out mail twice a week.

My first winter assignment was on a timber sale in what is now Glacier National Park. There was a ranger who was on furlough throughout the winter staying at the station here and I batched with him during my assignment on this sale. Generally speaking, we got along fine. There was some difference, however, in our ideas on the handling of the sour-dough jar. He didn't believe it should ever be cleaned out. He said the "green" that formed around the edges wouldn't hurt anyone. He also objected to dumping out the tea grounds because it took too much tea for the next brew if there were no old grounds to start with, and I was advised not to wash the frying pans as washing wore them out. He said he had used them for twenty years without washing them. I had no reason to doubt this statement.

This was in a deep snow country where the wind blew a lot, and when we left the cabin we always set up a pole in order to be sure to find it when we returned, as we often had to dig down in the snow to find the cabin when we had been away any length of time.

One of the worst features of life in the Forest Service was the loneliness caused by long stretches alone or with one or two other rangers. Toward the end of the first decade of the twentieth century, life in the Forest Service had improved for rangers. There were more of them, their pay was slightly better, and the beginning of an infrastructure seemed to be in their immediate future. But their opportunities to find spouses remained limited.

There were women in the backcountry, but they often acted more like men of the time than as other turn-of-the-century women of any class were described. These women were valued for a set of skills much like those for which men won esteem, as Ralph Thayer of the Flathead National Forest pointed out:

I first went to work for the Forest Service in 1911. I helped move the office and files from Indian Creek Ranger Station which was in Glacier National Park, near what they call the Henshaw Ford. You could ford it when the water was low or Park Service [actually it was the General Land Office; the Park Service did not exist until 1916] had a boat above the ford about 1/2 mile. We hauled and carried some of the equipment to the boat landing about 1/4 mile from the Ranger station. The cabin was made out of big logs. It had two doors and two windows. Harry Vaught was the first Park Ranger. He and his wife were there for about two seasons. She was a real all-around woman. She homesteaded west of Belton, Montana, on the Middle Fork River. She had a trapline in the hills south of Belton on which she made her living until she

The Bull River Ranger Station in 1908. A transient worker stands with the family of ranger Granville Gordon. (Photo courtesy USDA Forest Service)

and Harry Vaught were married, then they moved to Indian Creek Ranger Station.

There were also women in the woods who were unusual for their time. These women had cast off the conventions of society or in some cases never known them. In a world that was overwhelmingly male, nearly every women who wanted to find a mate had little trouble. In fact, the scarcity of women sometimes led to tension, as Bert Cramer of the Flathead and Nezperce National Forests remembered:

While working as Commissary Clerk at the old Hungry Horse Ranger Station, during the latter part of the 1920 season, I met Supervisor Joe Warner and Deputy Supervisors Charles Hash, K. Wolfe, Eldon Myrick and, last but not least, "Smokey," the "bull-of-the-woods" packer, and Ruby, the lady packer. Ruby was an ex–doctor's-dude-wife from the East who fell in love with the big out-of-doors and bought and operated a 30-horse pack string between Coram and Big Prairie at that time. "Smokey" was the "Paul Bunyan he-man" type who packed and otherwise looked after the 30 head of pack horses owned by Ruby. Smokey, Ruby and their horses spent several winters at Big Prairie during and just prior to the early twenties. Ruby later became the wife of Ranger Ray Quiman who was District Ranger at Big Prairie at that time.

Joe Warner probably never knew how near he came to getting shot by Smokey on a number of occasions. You see, that big "bull of the woods" got heap mad over Joe meeting Ruby at Hungry Horse and escorting her to Coram a time or two—on official business, of course. Ruby's pack string was being used by the Forest Service for seasonal South Fork main-string packing, but Smokey just couldn't understand that official-business idea—or could he?

There were even more unusual women in the woods, rough individuals who could more than hold their own against men and even officials, as Leon L. Lake of the Helena, Deerlodge, and Kootenai National Forests recounted:

> Over on the Kootenai Forest we had a tough female character to deal with. She lived at the mouth of Dunn Creek just off the Kootenai River. She was reported to have been married four or five times, and it was alleged she had killed one husband, one or two had died mysteriously, and another had fled. She was an early day barroom type who, in her younger days, lived at Jennings, the lower port for steamboats that plied the Kootenai River from some point in Canada. These steamboats carried gold ore and other commodities for reloading on Great Northern freight cars at Jennings. No use in saying that this was a wild town in the early days. Our female character was given the nickname of "Dunn Creek Nell" and it still sticks with her. At last reports, she was living at Libby, Montana.
>
> "Dunn Creek Nell" hated Forest Officers or any others whom she considered prowlers around her abode. She had a homestead way up Dunn Creek and reached by trail until a logging road tapped that locality. However, she lived on an old cabin at the mouth of Dunn Creek. She wanted a special-use permit for this cabin so went to the Supervisor's Office at Libby to find out about it. She always carried a big long six-shooter. She got the office force into a near panic the way she yelled and talked with profane language. The outcome of it all was that I had to go down there and check things over. She was not at home, but by running out

lines we found her cabin to be on patented private land and she was so advised later on.

One day "Jack" Lilliveg, assistant supervisor of the Kootenai, was riding down Dunn Creek on his way to the Warland Ranger Station. The trail led fairly close to "Dunn Creek Nell's" cabin. All at once he looked up and saw a female character behind a stump with a gun leveled at him. She said to him (Jack's own story), "Don't you come any closer or I'll bore you center." Well, Jack being very coolheaded, told her who he was and where he was going, but it didn't make any difference. So he began to talk to her about guns and asked her what kind of a gun it was, advancing a little as he talked. He told her she ought to be more careful about pointing loaded guns at people, because she might accidentally kill someone. By this time he was getting rather close. He suddenly asked to see her gun as he thought perhaps he may have one like it. She gave him the gun, he looked it over, threw the shells out on the ground, mounted his horse, and told her that she would find her gun on yon stump and rode off. However, Jack went on to say that she had him guessing for a little bit.

Another episode that seemed funny to the perpetrators. Her last husband was a docile little man who was unable to hold his own or even dare to talk back to her. One day he was in a Libby barbershop getting a haircut. The barber told him that he should not take everything laying down, but to stand up to her and show her he was a man. Apparently he had been telling his troubles to the barber, who was trying to get him out of the doghouse.

They had finally convinced the husband that he should talk right up to her. Well, in stepped "Dunn Creek Nell" (I do not recall her real name) and she told her husband to do certain things and get to going. At that he stepped right up to her and said, "You are no longer going to boss me around as you have done. I'll get those things when I get ready." The story goes that she told him, "You dirty little cur, what are you up to?" and hauled off and knocked him down flat.

Incidents such as this certainly made any younger forester who sought a conventional relationship despair. Although his job might be satisfying, its conditions and location created limits

on the future of family life. Before foresters could really become
settled in the woods and be full-fledged members of local communities, the agency had to create the amenities to make their
personal lives mirror those of the people around them. Before
1910, the Forest Service had only begun to recognize that need.

This meant that flexibility, both personal and professional, became an important characteristic of early foresters. Those who
could not adapt simply failed, for no education could emulate
the conditions in the field. Foresters remained a close network,
adaptable and dependent on each other, as Albert Cole remarked:

> About the middle of June I took charge of the Elliston Ranger
> District. There was no ranger station there and I had to stay at a
> hotel, but was fortunate in getting very favorable terms. As my pay
> had been raised to $75 per month, I made out very well. About
> October 1, I moved from Elliston to the vicinity of the Bald Butte
> mine to look after a timber sale to that outfit. I stayed with the
> foreman of the cutting crew all winter and looked after the admin-
> istration of the sale, did all the marking, scaling, and supervised
> the brush disposal.
> Early in the spring of 1908 I moved back to Elliston, and about
> May 1 a Mr. Harris and a Mr. Holt came out from Helena to take a
> small crew to the head of the Little Blackfoot River to estimate
> dead standing and down timber for a sale to a man who was plan-
> ning on cutting it and shipping it into Butte for mining timber and
> fuel. I had orders to accompany them, so we rustled a pack outfit
> and went up the river. The weather was very bad—snow and rain
> every day. The river was high and we had extreme difficulty in ne-
> gotiating the way after we neared the head of the river. We nearly
> lost a pack horse that fell over a steep bank into the river, and we
> had great difficulty in rescuing him. We made camp in the Little
> Blackfoot meadows, and for about three weeks we tried to cruise
> this country under about the worst weather conditions imagin-
> able. A great fire had passed through here between 20 and 30
> years before and the down timber was lying from 5 to 15 feet
> above the ground. Reproduction in lodgepole pine covered this
> area, and it was from 10 to 20 feet high. It was hard enough to go

through stuff over the down timber in dry weather, but three or four times as tough to try to force your way through with wet snow clinging to it.

About June 22, 1908, Supervisor Bushnell came to the Elliston District and informed me that I was to be transferred to the Muskrat Ranger Station to take charge of the Boulder Ranger District. After cleaning up some work on the Elliston District, I went to Boulder and took over that district from the man there, who was leaving the Service. After a little over a year on the Muskrat Station I was again transferred to East Helena to look after the north end of the district which I had been handling, as the district had been divided on account of the heavy volume of the work on the north end. This new district was called the McClellan Creek District and was a very active district in regard to timber sales and large free use business for the ranchers of the Prickly Pear Valley.

One trip which I recall just before I left the Muskrat Station was a trip on "additions and eliminations" to the National Forest, which I made with Walter J. Derrick, who had transferred to the Helena from what is now a part of the Deerlodge Forest and what was then called the Hell Gate Forest Reserve. We made good progress around the north end of my district along the Forest boundary, and I expected to go back when we arrived in the vicinity of Radersburg, as another ranger was to go with Derrick from there. This man did not show up, due to some confusion in his orders or to some other cause, and Derrick got in touch with the Helena office and I was instructed to stay with him until he finished the job. We had a camp man who moved camp by team and who was a very good man for the job. This was the early part of October and while the weather had been fine the trip had been quite pleasant. We left camp early one morning and it started to rain about 10 P.M. This quickly changed to snow and by noon it was snowing very hard and visibility was almost zero. We had to keep moving as we had arranged to have the camp man meet us on Crow Creek some 15 or 20 miles from the place which we left. The weather got worse and a fog or mist came down, reducing the visibility much more. We left the timber and came down to open country and plodded on. Darkness came on, but we did not like to stop as we were afraid of getting chilled even though we could have built a fire. We had eaten our lunch and saw no gain in hovering around a fire all night, so we kept on, and on, and on. Neither of us had ever been in that part of the country, but we had a fairly good map and were confident that we could find our camp eventually. We got tired and weak, and our spirits were at very low ebb. We finally found a road and followed it for hours. Finally, as we were stumbling along and falling quite frequently, I, being slightly in the lead, tripped over what I thought was a tree limb and fell on my face. I heard someone say, "Who the hell are you," and when I recovered my wits I saw a dim shape. I yelled to Derrick and a voice much closer said, "Is that you, Cole?" I had stumbled over a tent rope (our tent rope), and Scotty, our camp man, told us to "come on in out of the wet." You bet we were mighty glad to see him and to see our beds. He explained that he was afraid we would miss him in the dark, so he had set the tent right on one side of the road and stretched one of the tent ropes across it. He said, "I did not think any other damn fools would be coming along this road on a night like this. Anybody but a poor dumb Forest Service man would stay in out of such weather."

Six

"See That the Company Complies"

Early Timber Management

During the early years of the Forest Service, its operatives had no more important job than the management of timber resources. The agency had been founded as the result of a sense that the natural resources of the North American continent were dwindling. The mission of the USFS was to promote wise use—use that would allow future generations to benefit from the natural attributes of the American land. Gifford Pinchot's commitment to local constituencies was at the core of this philosophy. Not only did the Forest Service want local economies in the West to prosper, its leaders insisted that the resources that sustained the growth of the moment had to be protected for the future. The agency sought a middle course between administration and restriction, but when it erred, it did so more often on the side of use, largely as a result of its regional emphasis. Timber existed to be cut, albeit in a wise and regulated manner.

For district supervisors and rangers, timber management highlighted the paradox of their profession. As professional managers and people with ties in the local community, they had responsibilities that necessarily caused conflict. Foresters had to determine which of the wide range of requests that crossed their desks were appropriate. When they approved a request, they faced the possibility that someone in the Washington office of the Forest Service might suggest that they had abdicated the public trust. When they denied a permit, a local insurrection against the policies of the Forest Service was likely. Forest rangers frequently faced situations in which someone with the ability to affect future decisions was unhappy with their choice. Maintaining both local peace and agency policy required a combination of skill, foresight, and tact.

From the inception of the agency well into the 1920s, timber management dominated every aspect of agency policy. In part this resulted from the orientation of Pinchot himself, who at the time believed wise use of natural resources was the apex of natural resource policy. It also emanated from the agency culture that Pinchot encouraged. He and his successor, Henry Graves, built an agency that revered its scientific and egalitarian principles as much as it did the ideas of its founders. In a pattern similar to that which occurred in antebellum American politics, the second generation of USFS leaders could not equal their predecessors. Instead they codified the policies that Pinchot developed into an inflexible dogma that worked less well in changing social, cultural, and economic circumstances. The result was an almost religious adherence to sciences-based timber management policies.

In heavily forested Region 1, with railroad lines running to important ports and industrial centers, the issue was aggravated. Timber companies sought to harvest the forests and send them to market. Railroad construction consumed immense amounts of timber; the original four thousand miles of track in the Inland Northwest required ten million ties. This demand established a relationship between federal agencies and timber companies that the Forest Service was loath to break. At least in Washington, D.C., foresters sought to protect the forests from timber producers with exceedingly voracious appetites. In the field, Forest Service officials often sided with the timber companies; in 1910, the Missoula office noted that it could not comply with a directive not to sell federal timber to companies that owned large quantities of timber because of "local conditions." In certain instances, it seemed that the Region 1 office had been captured by its constituency.

The needs of local ranchers and homesteaders also were an element in the administrative puzzle of the Inland Northwest. Although the population of the area was generally small and dispersed, occasional booms in mining, timber, and—at the onset of World War I—agriculture, brought transient populations that sometimes settled in the region. Many needed to find new ways of making a living after their particular boom ended. Others

Fir-logging chutes for transporting cut timber. (Photo by K. D. Swan courtesy USDA Forest Service)

sought to achieve the nineteenth-century American dream: ownership of their own little piece of the continent. These issues also took the time of USFS personnel.

As a result, timber, grazing, and people management dominated the workdays of foresters. Except in rare instances, issues like recreation, wildlife, and watershed management were only remote contenders for their attention. The small number of foresters and the vast acreage for which they were responsible limited opportunities for science and even for planning within the district. Before the 1920s in Region 1, the USFS and its staff managed a commodity at a breakneck pace. Invariably they had more requests for uses of forest land than they had people to perform the surveys and complete the paperwork. William Morris described the loose set of procedures that made up early agency policy:

At the time of which I write the Forest Service had few trails on the Coeur d'Alene Forest, and many regions were not only inaccessible in case of fire, but almost unknown. One of the first

"Doping" a chute with crude oil to make logs slide more easily. (Photo courtesy USDA Forest Service)

things we wanted to know in order to make a working plan for the forest was how much timber we had, what areas were timbered or burned, and what areas might be profitably planted or restocked. A working plan is a detailed plan of running a forest. In the plan a certain amount of timber is allotted to be cut each year on a certain area, or during a certain period, so arranged that the forest will not be overcut. The plans also show the areas to be restocked, and the improvements to be made.

But this set of goals ceased to be sufficient. By the end of the first decade of the twentieth century, the Forest Service was in

In a typical early timbering procedure, horses provided momentum to power logs down the chutes. (Photo by K. D. Swan courtesy USDA Forest Service)

the midst of a gradual change in the people who made up its personnel. In the first years of the agency, a significant number were hired through the kinds of testing so dramatically described by Elers Koch. By 1908, more and more of the new entrants to the agency were graduates of the growing number of forestry schools springing up in the wake of the credentials revolution sweeping American society. Those with degrees had different expectations of life in the agency and were expected to perform differently than those selected from local areas.

For people in the field this set up complex dichotomies. Initially the people who managed forests were of a place. By 1910, more and more had little allegiance to the place they served. As a result, the conflict formerly between foresters and the public became an intra-agency issue, as rangers with experience in the field had to work in concert with book-taught college graduates. The result for the old-time foresters was a kind of displacement that grandfathered them in but limited many of the higher-level administrative aspirations they might have. The new graduates, often called "Junior Foresters" (an obviously pejorative label), had to supervise people who knew the physical terrain and its attributes far better than the newcomers did. This complicated situation was only resolved with the passage of time.

Yet in 1908, foresters still had a seemingly pristine playground in which to learn their trade. John F. Preston remembered the early years of timber management:

> The real need for immediate help in the timber business was found to be on the Snowy Mountains. The office at Neihart had two National Forests under its direction—the Little Belt National Forest, which was the country immediately surrounding Neihart, and the Snowy Mountain National Forest.
>
> About April 15 in 1908 I was transferred to northern Idaho. Newport, Washington, was the headquarters of the Priest River National Forest, afterwards known as the Kaniksu. Rudo Fromme, a graduate of the Yale Forest School, was the Forest Supervisor in charge. Northern Idaho was a wonderful place in 1908—a veritable paradise of woods and lakes. That was before too much of the country had been laid waste by logging and fires. The Priest River Valley from the Great Northern Railroad to its northern extremity at the Canadian line was a dense, mostly mature forest of white pine, hemlock and white fir. The road from Priest River to Priest Lake was nothing but a winding trail through the woods, and the old stage coach operated from one chuck hole to the next. The distance was about 25 miles, and it was a long, hard day's trip.
>
> Timber sales had already begun in the Priest River Valley and the Forest Service was struggling even then with the problem of whether or not the cut-over land should be opened to settlement or should be retained for timber growth. In the years which followed, this problem was one of the most urgent. Soils men, tim-

ber men, and farmers struggled over it and in the end the farmers, as usually happens, won the battle. A great deal of that heavy timber land was opened to settlement under the Act of June 11, 1906. I have not been back in that country in recent years, but I am sure it was a mistake to try to make farms out of land like that. The cost of clearing was too high and the chances of livelihood from the products of the soil after clearing were too slim. It was wonderful timber producing land, but poor farm land.

In the fall of 1908, the inspection system was changed to field administration. Heretofore, the administrative line had been direct from the Supervisor to Washington. Field Districts (later called Regions) were instituted. District One took in the Montana–north Idaho country, and I was assigned to this District with headquarters at Missoula. Bill Greeley was the District Forester, with Gus Silcox as associate. Bert Cooper was in charge of the timber (I have forgotten whether it was called silviculture or management at that time). Dave Mason was his first assistant; Joe Warner, Joe Fitzwater and I were traveling representatives. Dick Rutledge was there in charge of lands, and C. H. Adams (locally known as "Cow-Horse Adams") was in charge of grazing. I soon realized that I was in a traveling job.

I was assigned to the forests of eastern Montana. My job was to look after the timber sales, particularly from the standpoint of the silvicultural systems and to see that the marking was brought up to standard. In practice I also had the job of running out sale boundaries, appraising the stumpage, and drawing up sale contracts.

The middle part of January in 1909 I reported to Mr. V. Giffert Lantry, Supervisor of the Absaroka National Forest at Livingston, who had requested some timber sale assistance. Livingston and the surrounding country in January of any year is not likely to be a very delightful place to do field work. This particular January I remember very vividly because of the penetrating cold. The particular sale which I was called upon to visit was located on the north end of the Crazy Mountains division which was about 40 or 50 miles due north of Livingston. After a few preliminary discussions with Mr. Lantry I went to the town of Big Timber, took the stage north, and walked 12 miles to Ranger Durgan's camp, then by saddle horse to the north end. The temperature during those two or three days' travel was at least 40 degrees below zero. Most of my route lay along exposed ranges but fortunately a part of the way I traveled through the timber. I alternated between walking and riding and thus succeeded in keeping up circulation so that no part of me froze completely. In due time I arrived at the mouth of Cottonwood Creek, got in touch with the Ranger, and together we rode some 5 or 6 miles up the canyon to the sale area. The Supervisor had been making 100-dollar sales to local sawmill men operating under the name of Mosback and Eicke. The snow was about four feet deep on the sale area. The sawmill was a little one-horse portable affair which would cut, when pushed, perhaps 3,000 feet in 10 hours. The camp was one of those combinations where one-half of the building was devoted to housing of the horses and the other half a combination bunkhouse and cookhouse. The door, I remember, was so small that one had to bend almost double before entering. When I found what the proposition was, my egotism, if I had any, was rapidly deflated. What Mosback and Eicke wanted was another 50,000-foot sale, which at the appraised stumpage price of $3.00 made it an advertised sale. The Supervisor had no Rangers sufficiently experienced to handle even so simple a proposition. My job was to lay out the sale boundaries, mark the timber, make out the sale contract, or rather the application, and then return to Livingston and help the Supervisor fix up the necessary papers for advertisement and arrange, as a rule, for the privilege of "advance cutting" since logging must proceed. All of this was a very simple process. I remember the sale application read something like this: "We, Peter Mosback and Peter Eicke, partners, doing business under the firm name and style of Mosback and Eicke, hereby apply for the privilege of cutting 50,000 feet of standing timber, alive and dead, . . . etc." All of this expedition to the sale area and return to Livingston required about 10 days.

The next two weeks were spent on the Little Belts again [then part of the Jefferson National Forest, later the Lewis & Clark] mostly marking timber on existing sales. This was interesting and worthwhile work. The Rangers of those days knew only a little about forestry, but they were anxious to learn. I worked with several different men. The temperature continued cold, but the woods is the best place in the world to work in the wintertime. No biting wind can penetrate the shelter of the trees and bodily activity keeps up the circulation. If one is properly dressed, there is no time of year so suitable as the winter for such activities of the forester as cruising, running lines, or marking timber for removal.

Upon my return to Livingston I found a letter from Missoula asking me to report to the Supervisor of the Helena National Forest for assistance with a timber sale on the Big Belt Division. My assignment, as contemplated, was to be for several months. I went to Helena and interviewed Supervisor Dwight Bushnell. The purchaser was a mining company which was cutting mining timbers; the Ranger was having difficulty making the company live up to the timber sale regulations. The company had refused to pile brush or to comply with the utilization requirements and were pretty slow in making their payments. Bushnell wanted me to go to the Big Belt, live in a tent on the sale area, take charge of the sale and see that the mining company complied with the Government regulations. Several months' assignment on a policemen's job, on work which could and should have been done by the local Ranger, was about the last straw. I told Mr. Bushnell that I wanted to consult with my superior officers in Missoula before accepting the assignment. I got on the train and went to Missoula and expressed myself rather forcibly to Mr. Cooper. This was about February 15. Mr. Cooper was, fortunately, sympathetic and after a conference with Mr. Greeley, I was assigned to the Bitterroot with headquarters at Missoula. The next several months I worked under the direction of W. W. White on various assignments, the most important of which was the old A. C. M. Lick Creek sale on the Bitterroot.

When the train left Missoula on Sunday afternoon bound for Hamilton, we were surprised to find that our party, in addition to myself and wife, consisted of Bert Cooper representing Silviculture at Missoula, E. E. "Nick" Carter representing the same office in Washington, and G. B. MacDonald then in charge of planting at Missoula, later and for years identified with the forest school at Ames, Iowa.

Hamilton boasted of only one hotel, the Ravalli, which was really first class; it was full, and it looked for a time as though we might have to get out our camp beds. Finally the manager turned over a child's bed to the one lady of our party and the men slept in a room above an adjoining saloon. We dined that evening in splen-

dor or rather amidst splendor. Our woods clothes very illy fitted
the grand furniture and decorations and white table linen of the
dining room in the Ravalli; we felt more at ease a little later, however, when a serious attempt to order a grand dinner from the imposing menu card disclosed the fact that there was nothing left
but veal stew, potatoes, and boiled onions. The difficulties and
the incongruity of our situation finally broke down all formali-
ties; the whole party became well acquainted and were highly en-
tertained.

Next morning (very early) the whole party left on the A. C. M.
logging train, bag, baggage, and passengers, on the empty flat cars
which were en route to camp to be loaded with logs—western
yellow pine. As an observation car, a "flat" can hardly be improved upon; there was plenty of scenery—the sunrise and the
fading starlight, snow and frost on pine and fir and the grand
spectacle of distant snow-covered mountains. No one became
seasick with the swaying motion of the cars on the uncertain
roadbed, and we arrived at the company's camp about 10 A.M.
That was the end of our transportation; the government cabin
(and timber) was about 2 miles further, but we had lots of help
with the baggage.

Mr. and Mrs. White were at the cabin when we arrived. Claget
Sanders was there too; he was the scaler; we became better acquainted with him later. He could tell many a weird tale of his experiences in the mountains. Just a short mile or so from that very
cabin he had (two years before) stumbled upon the skeleton of a
man and alongside him a note book which told of his last days
alone in the woods with a broken hip. The victim was within
sight of ranch houses below him; he could see the lights at night,
but he couldn't get word of his plight and he died a slow linger-
ing death as attested by his daily entries until oblivion captured
one more human being from life's stage.

Our visitors left next morning, but life presented never a dull
moment at the Lick Creek cabin. There was the daily occupation
of marking trees for cutting and studying the new system of logging being tried out on the company land and proposed for use
on the National Forest. C. H. Gregory, the big Forest Service lumberman, and Earl Tanner, then a Ranger but afterwards a lumber-

man, spent several days with us. Lumberjacks came and went and soon the sounds of "Timber!" rang out in the woods all around the cabin. The very first night, with not less than seven people sleeping in the bunks and on the floor of the small cabin, Mr. White became exasperated with the ravages of a pack rat and, in the middle of the night, blazed away at him with his sixshooter. As I remember now, he failed to hit the rat, but did succeed in rousing all the sleepers.

During the time I was in charge of this timber sale the company started donkey logging. The equipment had been set up, the company given permission to try the equipment, but without commitment by the Forest Service as to the conditions under which it would be permitted. The decision depended upon the amount of damage which the ground skidding of logs would entail. The company had previously been using donkey logging on their own lands and I had watched the results without being able to visualize how the method could be applied on the National Forest without ruining the growing stock which was being left. The machines were set up, the fallers went through the woods felling the trees; the system to be used was the dragging in of entire trees; limbing or bucking to be done at the landing. As the ranking officer in charge, I decided that limbing and bucking must be done in the woods before skidding. I reported to the logging superintendent (Mr. Blackmore) whom I found at the landing where the logs were being loaded on cars. I introduced myself, explained my responsibility and gave him my decision. Unfortunately, we had never previously met, and he sized me up as a young upstart who probably could be bluffed; he very coolly informed me that I would have to go to Hamilton and take up such matters with the main office, that he was there to carry out the logging as planned, not to change it. This had me stumped, but I recovered quickly and informed Mr. Blackmore that I was not going to Hamilton, that I was giving my instructions to him, and that tomorrow morning I would stop operations and seize all the logs if he failed to follow instructions. I had talked pretty big, but I was worried; that afternoon I walked 10 miles to get to a telephone to inform Supervisor White of the crisis which had been reached on the sale area. Fortunately, Mr. White backed me up. I returned to the cabin and waited with considerable anxiety to see what would happen. I did not then fully appreciate the power of the Federal Government. At daybreak next morning the fallers went through the woods and proceeded to limb the trees and buck them into log lengths. Evidently the logging superintendent had also telephoned to his superiors. Anyway, after that the logging proceeded without serious friction.

Toward the end of my assignment to the Bitterroot, which was along in June 1909, I learned that I had been acting in the capacity of deputy Forest Supervisor but I had not known it and so far as I was able to learn, Supervisor White also did not know it. Incidentally, I have never worked under more pleasant conditions than I encountered during the three or four months' assignment on the Bitterroot and never worked under a better Supervisor than W. W. White.

Conducting timber sales continued to be a difficult task for new rangers. David Lake of the Lewis & Clark National Forest found himself in such a circumstance:

In 1915 I was appointed as administrative guard for the North Snowies and was requested to pick up the office equipment at the Rodgers Ranger Station, a distance of about 10 miles from my place (the ranger was being transferred and had left everything behind). Well, to make it short, I did so, and then decided to write the forest ranger at Union Gap regarding the matter. In the outfit there was an old Oliver typewriter, the first one I had ever seen. I put in two sheets and wrote a full page letter, listing all the property. It took me about one-half day, and then I found I had put the carbon wrong side up. This was my first error.

My next error was as follows. I made an S-22 timber sale of 200 lodgepole pine poles and failed to mark them. And before they were cut I was appointed as forest ranger and had moved away to the South Belts, a new district. I turned everything over to my brother, Leon L. Lake, who was appointed as guard in my place. When the time came to close this sale, he inspected the cutting area, found that the cutting was done on private land, and so reported it. I was then asked why I had sold timber from private land and why I did not mark the timber. That took a lot of explaining, and I thought I was finished before I had gotten started. I was learning the hard way.

J. A. Fitzwater, who started on the Coconino National Forest in Arizona in 1908, faced a different kind of complicated situation. Following the establishment of the new district system in December 1908, he was transferred to Region 1 in Missoula. He found himself in a typical predicament for foresters as the Inland West became more open: Two railroads raced for the right to convey passengers to the soon-to-be-established Glacier National Park, and Fitzwater had to determine the merits of their claims to right-of-way lands:

When I got to Missoula I found that the job was to take a crew of rangers up on the North Fork of the Flathead, then on the Blackfoot National Forest, and estimate the timber on the proposed rights-of-way of the Great Northern and Milwaukee Railroads. The job had been given to one of the lumbermen but he had resigned rather than take it. The Glacier National Park had just been, or was just about to be, created and these two railroad crews were having a race to see which one could file its plats of survey first and thereby be granted a franchise. The railroad was to run from Columbia Falls to the Canadian line. My job was to get an estimate of the timber which would be removed in clearing the right-of-way. Mr. [F. N.] Haines (Roscoe Haines' father) was supervisor of the Blackfoot, with headquarters at Kalispell, Montana. My crew was made up of C. N. Whitney (now in Products in the Northern Rocky Mountain Experiment Station), Rangers Theo Christianson, Dad Reynolds, E. Clark and John Rice. Winter had set in before we got on the job, and it was pretty tough pickings. To complicate matters, apparently when one of the railroad survey crews got behind, it hopped over on to the other crew's right-of-way and used it until it caught up and then jumped off into the brush again. This made it almost impossible to follow the two separate survey lines. Sometimes the lines would end

abruptly and then pick up again 200 yards away. Only too often
the blueprints gave an entirely different picture from what we actually found on the ground. The snow got pretty deep and travel
was difficult, especially along the west side of the river above
Coal Creek where steep shale banks ran down to the river almost
perpendicularly—we slid into the river frequently.

We had a fellow by the name of Joe Crosly, a half-breed Indian,
as cook and packer. While Joe was an excellent cook, he was one
of the dirtiest men I have ever encountered and one was never
just sure what he was eating. He was a picturesque fellow—always wore a red sash for a belt. I can see him yet backed up to
the camp fire with his face lifted to the stars, reciting "The Wreck
of the Julie Plant."

Ranger Christianson had a station about half-way up the river
and had three or four very fat horses in his pasture. Our pack
string was rather ragged and we were constantly urging Christianson to let us use his horses, but to no avail. Those horses to him
were something sacred, and were to be gazed upon in all their ro-
tund beauty rather than used. One frosty morning while we were
packing up under the twinkling stars, Joe Crosly appeared on the
scene and said that our horses had disappeared. He had looked
everywhere for them but could find not a trace. Christianson had
official business calling him to Kalispell so Joe proposed that we
use his horses. I did not like to do this without Christianson's permission, but camp had to be moved, so we rounded them up.
The rest of the crew went out on line and I stayed with Joe that
morning to see that the moving of camp got under way. The new
camp site was on the other side of the river. We put five 50-
pound sacks of flour on one of Christianson's horses and lashed it
down good and tight. When in the middle of the river something
came loose and this horse started to kick. As a matter of fact,
these horses were so fat it was almost impossible to cinch a pack
on them. In kicking, the horse caught the back of his shoe in one
of the sacks of flour and in just a few minutes the whole river was
white. The flour spread out just like oil. By the time that horse
got through kicking and unloading, the flour was gone. To add to
the difficulties, the river was full of slush ice. Well, the move was

made and Theo got his horses back without injury, but he never forgave us.

Upon completion of this job I was sent to the Kaniksu to make a topographic map of the famous Section 26 in the lower West Branch River. The snow was between six and eight feet deep, and, of course, all work had to be done on snow shoes. It was the first time I had ever had webs on, and the first few days my antics were anything but graceful. Incidentally, I made a five-foot contour interval map of this section with an aneroid barometer— some stunt on eight feet of snow. Notwithstanding, I think I made a pretty good map. Anyway, it was reproduced in Colonel Graves' "Principles of Handling Woodlands."

Using the contours as a basis, we located the higher elevations of the section on the map and then went in the field and picked up these locations and established the boundaries to solid blocks of timber to be reserved for seeding purposes. The balance of the section was cut clean and the slash piled and burned. I have always regretted that it was not possible to carry to completion this proposed method of treatment, but before the cutting of the section was completed the land was classified as agricultural; eventually the balance of the timber on the blocks was removed. To my knowledge this section has burned over three times since then and the men who filed on the land have never even made an approach to a decent living. Much of this section ran 100,000 feet of white pine timber per acre.

I worked out of the Missoula district office on timber assignments to various National Forests until July 1909, when I was sent to the Absaroka National Forest as deputy supervisor. I entered the Forest Service at a salary of $1,000 and had had no promotion to date. I was really sent to the Absaroka to start off the boundary work and I always felt that the title of deputy was merely given to me in lieu of a pay increase—promotions were rare in those days, money was scarce.

When I stepped off the train at Livingston, [V. Giffert] Lantry, the supervisor, met me. Lantry was a very picturesque man of the old cowman type. I had never met him before but he greeted me, "Hello, Fitz, how are you?" Just as I reached the platform my hat blew off and I started after it. Lantry said, "Wait a minute. Don't chase that hat. Just stand still and another one will be along in a minute." Livingston has the reputation of being one of the windiest places out-of-doors. The supervisor and I had lunch together and he told me that he had two propositions to suggest to me. Either I would handle the office and he would take over the boundary work, or he would run the office and I would do the boundary work. I appreciated, of course, that he was merely trying to give me a cordial welcome and had really no intention of allowing me to make any such momentous decision. Lantry was of the old school and did business in a far different manner than it is done today. But with all his unorthodox procedures he was much respected and a good boss.

I had a boundary crew on the Absaroka made up of rangers and guards—Harry Coffman, Shoemaker, Ora B. Yates, Hank somebody, and Jack Crane. We started our work from the junction point of the southeast corner of the south division of the Absaroka, the Beartooth and the Yellowstone National Park and worked counter-clock-wise around to the southwest corner of the south division. The crew all had horses and the first two days there was lots of grief. All of these boys had on riding boots and believed that any place you couldn't take a horse wasn't a place where anyone should go. We struck lots of country where a horse simply could not hold his footing, and as a result those high-heeled boots caused much grief, but the boundary had to be run and we could not change the topography, so run it we did on run-over boots. In connection with the running of the boundary we surveyed all June 11 claims pending on streams which cut the boundary, dropping boundary work temporarily until we could complete the June 11 surveys in each drainage.

The new breed of foresters was also in evidence. William W. Morris, a college graduate, was typical. By 1910, forestry schools had become an important training ground for the Forest Service, and more and more of its new rangers had experience with the science of forestry as well as its practice. As is often the case, the lessons of the classroom were sometimes irrelevant in the field:

It was with a light heart that after five years of study at this university [which Morris neglected to name], I was able to pass the

Civil Service examination given by the Government for admission into the U.S. Forest Service.

Soon after taking this examination I was summoned by wire to report at the District Office of the Forest Service at Missoula, Montana. I arrived at Missoula July 3, 1909. Met Mr. Silcox, Mr. Rutledge, Mr. E. E. Carter, Mr. Greeley and many others. From Missoula I was soon detailed to the town of Wallace, Idaho. To be frank about it, I had never heard of the town of Wallace before, and as the train puffed up the beautiful valley of the Bitterroot River, over the summit of the Bitterroots, which marks the Montana-Idaho divide, then glided rapidly down into the Coeur d'Alene Valley, I wondered many times what kind of a town it was going to be my lot to strike. I was very agreeably surprised, for as the train sped into the station I saw a unique little city, set like a tiny jewel in the heart of the mountains, where five canyons meet.

It seemed like a toy city as I obtained better views of it later on from the high surrounding hills, but it was clean and spotless, and very much up to date, with fine homes and fine people. The hills on all sides of the town, coming down to the very doorsteps in fact, were covered with a beautiful young growth of timber. I had very little difficulty in locating the office of the Forest Service, as one can walk the entire length of the city in a few minutes. Here I met my supervisor, W. G. Weigle, under whom I worked for two years, and for whom I always had the greatest respect and regard.

A few days after arriving I was sent out on my first trip on the Coeur d'Alene National Forest. At that time this forest comprised about a million and one-half acres, and included the land drained by the St. Joe and Coeur d'Alene Rivers, in northern Idaho. As there were only a few rangers and forest officers on this forest at that time, it kept one constantly on the jump, attending to fires, timber sales, and other work that needed attention. Few were the trails in those days, and much of the forest was unknown. Most of the trips were taken on foot, with one's blankets and supplies in a large Duluth packsack carried on the back. A walk of twenty-five miles carrying from forty to eighty pounds was not uncommon and often the distance was even greater than this in a single day's trip.

My first trip on the forest was to look over some burned timber on the Little North Fork of the Coeur d'Alene River. A man had applied for this timber, as he thought it would still make good lumber. Our duty was to make a map of the area and an estimate of the amount, with recommendations as to the manner of cutting, and the proper price at which to sell it. From Wallace we went to Harrison by rail, down beautiful Coeur d'Alene Lake, to the town of the same name, which is ideally situated at the north end of the lake. From this point we made the walk into the river, the deputy supervisor, two rangers, and myself. At the river I saw for the first time beautiful stands of white pine timber, one of the most valuable timbers that the U.S. has produced. I soon learned that the main species growing on this forest were western white pine, Douglas fir, western larch or tamarack, western yellow pine, lowland fir, western hemlock and cedar, the order given showing about the relative importance. We were fortunate enough to find a settler's cabin the first night. The next day we went on up the river, located and mapped the burned timber. The following night we stayed at a cabin belonging to a small mining company.

At this mining cabin our host happened to be a man who had come in from the town of Wardner, Idaho, where the great Bunker Hill and Sullivan lead mine is located, one of the largest in the world. He had come into the river to tell the man who was working the claim, where we were staying, that his brother had just been killed in the mine at Wardner. Thus I got my first idea of the dangers attending this rough mountain life, in the mines and logging camps.

The rest of the summer, which was in the year 1909, I had the good fortune to be assigned on rough reconnaissance work, with an old lumber cruiser. In this manner I was able to get over a great deal of the forest, and become acquainted with the timber, and other conditions. At that time it was known what areas were timbered, and what were burned or bare, so our methods on this reconnaissance were to make a map of the watershed of timber, that we were estimating, showing by suitable colors on the map, timbered, burned, and bare areas. Then we would go into areas of timber that were good averages of the whole, and make a careful estimate of a small plot. After determining the amount per acre, the total acreage of timbered country was obtained from the map, and a rough estimate of the timber made. I considered it lucky to get out with a man trained in the woods all his life, and the experience proved valuable later on. Most of the summer we spent in a little tent, or sometimes in the open, doing this sort of work. You may be sure it was all most interesting to me. The country was new and almost unexplored.

It was my good fortune to spend a considerable part of the fall of that season, on stem analysis work. This is a detailed study of the growth of trees, and consists of a measurement of the diameter growth, usually at every sixteen foot section of the tree, for ten year periods, and other diameter and height measurements are also recorded. In this way the contents of the tree in board feet can be obtained for ten year periods, and from these figures yield tables, showing the average stand per acre at different ages, are obtained. These yield tables are of great value in determining what any piece of land, not now timbered, might be expected to grow in any given period of time. This work was done along the line of the new Chicago Milwaukee and Puget Sound Railway.

Morris also revealed a more aesthetic side when he talked of his winter experiences:

About the first of February 1910, I found the town of Wallace buried under snow, figuratively speaking, with more coming almost every day. At this time I was initiated into work in the mountains in the winter time. If it was hard to carry a forty pound pack in the summer, it was doubly hard when one had to wade through five feet or more of snow.

However after a little practice, I soon became adept with snowshoes. As there were several tracts waiting to be examined at the time, I was assigned to make these examinations and reports.

The Idaho woods in the winter are wonderful. In the month of February the snow fell quietly almost every day. Sometimes stumps and logs get covered to a height of six feet or more, as there is usually little wind to blow the snow off. The great boughs of the spruce, hemlock, and cedar bend almost to the breaking point with their white load. The silence is awesome but inspiring. I often thought, as I worked in these snow clad regions, how few people have the opportunity for the enjoyment of such absolute solitude and quiet as are afforded by these mountain vastnesses in the winter time. Frequently we saw the large round tracks of the mountain lion, or the smaller ones of the lynx, the dog like track of the coyote, the deep hoof like marks of the deer, and down by river streams the claw marks of the marten and mink. None of these animals will molest one unless they are cornered. The snow often came so wet that it would cause great branches to be broken off of the trees. I remember one night a young fellow (Wilfred Willey) just graduated from Yale University and I had turned in early after a hard day's work. A wet snow had been falling heavily for some time. We were camped in a little log cabin, built by some prospector who evidently had an eye out for the timber, but it had been abandoned. I was dreaming peacefully when a great roar awakened me, and then all was silent. Thoughts of snow slides went into my head, but I was soon asleep again. In the morning we saw that a mighty branch of a giant old fir tree, standing near the cabin, had been broken off by the weight of the wet snow. The fact that the snow would pile up so high on stumps and logs, often caused us a great deal of annoyance if not of danger. The only means of crossing the small streams where we were working was over foot logs covered high with snow. One day, crossing on the top of one of these snow laden logs on snowshoes, the snow suddenly gave way, and I found myself holding wildly onto the foot-log face upward, gradually slipping into the water. I called to my companion to come to my assistance, but before he could do so, I was forced to let go my hold, and found myself lying back down in the icy waters. Fortunately the stream at this point was not very deep, and the discomfiture of a cold bath in the winter time, several miles away from dry clothes, was the only bad result.

March of that year [1910] was a beautiful month. One perfect day followed another. Along about the first part of the month we started out on our trip to estimate and report on a large area of timber lying on Big Creek, tributary to the St. Joe River. Our route lay from Wallace up Placer Creek of the Coeur d'Alene over the divide to Big Creek on the St. Joe. It was a beautiful March morning when a party of six of us (Weigle, Gregory, Willey, Halm, Pulaski, Morris) started out with our toboggan. Ropes were attached from the front and two from either side. Several feet of snow lay on the level in Wallace, and grew deeper as we increased our elevation. It was easy work at the start, and we were all feeling our oats, and lighthearted with the beautiful day, the crisp mountain air, and the ease with which our equipment was moving along on the toboggan. We felt that it was going to be a success. It was after leaving the road, however, and turning up the West Fork trail, that we began to experience trouble. Here the trail had been built in some parts on a thirty degree slope, and with about five feet of snow on the level no sign of it was visible. It was necessary for us to go ahead and break a level place in the snow for the toboggan to travel on. Moreover we were somewhat fearful of snow slides as a result of this, for the slopes above us were all bare of timber, and we had already passed over a large slide that had vent its fury on the few trees that had been in its path. These were strewn promiscuously in the gulch below. None of us felt that we would like to be substituted for one of these trees.

By night we had traveled about three miles. We sought shelter in a small cabin, where I taxed my culinary ability by baking a loaf of baking powder bread. The roof of this cabin was covered with about six feet of snow. We saw several cabins that had been completely broken down by their weight of snow. The following day was when our hard work really began. Our trail now lay up a steep hogsback, which led to a large ridge running to the main divide. By hard work, which involved packing some of the things on our back, we succeeded finally in getting the toboggan to the main ridge. Before starting this climb, we took a drink of water in the creek, and filled a canteen which however did not go far among several perspiring men. Soon we began to suffer quite severely from thirst. Eating snow only aggravated the situation. The going was somewhat easier on the ridge, as it extended for a mile or more at an easy grade. We sat down in the snow at noon, and snatched a bit to eat, but without water our food stuck in our throats. Slowly and with increasing labor we continued on. About four o'clock we suddenly came to the divide, the highest point of our trip. The top was covered with an enormous snowdrift which ended in a sheer drop on our side of about ten feet.

There was no other way than to cut steps up this, and by putting a stout cruiser's stick deep into the snow on the top, we were enabled to pull ourselves up. We now saw that the usefulness of the toboggan had come to an end, and with great reluctance we hid it in some bushes near by, where it finally burned in the great fires that swept the country the following summer. We had left some of our things behind, and one of my companions (Wilfred Willey) and myself went back to get these, while Halm and Pulaski returned to Wallace. The things which we went back for were mostly blankets, and putting a large supply of these in our pack-sacks we started again for the summit. It was a wild scene that lay before us. Darkness was coming on and to add to our discomfi-ture, it began to snow, so hard at times that it was hard to see many feet in advance of us. The wind too was blowing a gale as we neared the exposed summit. At this point, the ridge narrowed to a sharp edge, with steep slopes on either side covered with frozen snow. The footing was difficult and my companion lost his snow-shoe, which slid for about a hundred feet down the mountain side and fortunately stopped by striking a tree. He had to cut steps down to it, which took considerable time. We finally made our way to the summit up the steps cut in the frozen snow by our two companions in advance. It was quite dark now, but the ridge was level and the walking good. Weigle and Gregory had constructed a rough shelter in the snow in the most secluded place they could find. They had dug a hole in the snow, covered a portion of the top of it with boughs, from a nearby tree. After spreading a "tarp" on the snow under the boughs, we put the blankets we had brought on top, and then built a large fire in front. We would have been very comfortable, had we not suffered so from thirst. We ate our supper of boiled beef, bread and some preserves with great relish. We tried to melt some snow in the preserve can, but with-out success. We estimated that there were twenty or thirty feet of snow beneath us, and it made a soft and feathery couch. Shortly after turning in a heavy blizzard struck us, the wind howled, the air was thick with hard pellets of snow which came even through our roof of boughs. The storm stopped as quickly as it came upon us, the wind ceased, the stars came out, nature was at rest again, and I knew no more until morning.

The sight that greeted our eyes on arising was one that only a few people get a chance to behold. The sun was just appearing. The air was exceptionally clear, and the bare mountain sides glis-tened as if set with myriads of diamonds. Miles and miles of the rough mountain country lay before us, with shining snow clad peaks and ridges as far as the eye could see. Even the Cabinet range was visible in far away Montana. I did not wonder at the remarks that I had so often heard that if Idaho could be leveled off and pressed out it would make some state. I longed for a camera, but on a trip of this kind it is hard enough to pack necessities. That day we made our way down to Big Creek in the St. Joe watershed, where we were to do our work. Water never tasted better to me than that morning when we first struck a mountain stream. Weigle and Pulaski returned to Wallace, while Gregory, Willey and I stayed to make the estimate.

We remained in this watershed almost two weeks, estimating the timber and making maps. Some of our trips were hard, but most of our work was enjoyable. I know at one time we were troubled with snow blindness, and used to rub our faces with the burnt bark of the red fir, which is quite corky. This apparently gave some relief, but we presented ridiculous appearances. I remember one evening a companion of mine and I had wandered on our snowshoes many miles from our cabin in our estimating work. We were in another fork of Big Creek at a place where in the following summer eighteen men, fire fighters, were to lose their lives in the great forest fire. We could not reach our camp that evening and were contemplating sleeping out in the snow, when we came in sight of a neat little cabin. Nobody was at home and we took the liberty of staying for the night. We found flour and I made some cakes and tea, and altogether made out very well. The cabin was as neat as a pin. In one end was a crucifix and a folding bed. We were indeed fortunate to strike such a place in this wilderness. The next day we returned to our camp, and a few days later went down the creek to the St. Joe River, where we returned home by rail and boat to Wallace.

Forest management continued to be a process that combined the skills of nineteenth-century woodsmen and the principles of twentieth-century forestry. Foresters still performed the same kinds of activities under similar circumstances, but they did so with different goals and objectives. The vague sense of regulating the forest had been replaced by a set of standards and measurements that defined timber management. The future of the agency was in scientific management, a reality reflected in the growing number of new rangers in the agency who were trained in American forestry schools. These men had knowledge of techniques, but they also needed the skills of the outsdoorsmen possessed by the first generation of foresters. Nowhere were these more important than in fighting forest fires.

Seven

"A Fight against Nature from the Beginning"

The Fires of 1910

F ire was the nemesis of early foresters. Foresters and their agency embodied control of the physical environment, and nothing destroyed that illusion of control so much as a major forest fire. With the limited technology and infrastructure available at the turn of the century, foresters faced any large conflagration with extreme trepidation. Fire destroyed property, took lives, ruined homesteads, and threatened the rudimentary structures of the peripheral societies of the Inland Northwest. It was a volatile enemy, one to fear and hate.

Although forest fires were frequent even before the turn of the century, there was little institutional structure within the Forest Service to combat them. Response to fire was the most local of local phenomena, the responsibility of the person who first saw it. Most fires were manageable with local resources and the help of weather; those that were not were often so far from the limited corridors of access that a comprehensive response by the Forest Service was impossible. Despite bad fire years in 1902 and 1905, foresters felt that they had some measure of control over the threat of fire in the northern region.

The situation began to change during the summer of 1910, when dry conditions contributed to the more than seventeen hundred fires that burned three million acres of forests in the Inland Northwest. A massive and widespread conflagration, the fires of 1910 compelled a range of reaction that superseded existing mechanisms of the Forest Service. The scale of destruction was vast and dramatic. More than eighty firefighters lost their lives, as did numerous homesteaders, trappers, miners, and others. Flames engulfed entire towns. For many in the Northwest, foresters and others, 1910 was the most significant year of their lives.

The ominous signs of a calamitous fire season were evident throughout the summer. The beginnings of fire suppression more than two decades before had built up a significant accumulation of brush, called a fire load, and combined with a dry season, this accumulation had severe implications. Foresters took note, as Clarence B. Swim of the Kaniksu National Forest—now called the Idaho Panhandle National Forest—recalled:

> The late summer of 1910 approached with ominous, sinister and threatening portents. Dire catastrophe seemed to permeate the very atmosphere. Through the first weeks of August the sun arose a coppery red ball and passed overhead red and threatening as if announcing an impending disaster. This fiery red sun continued day after day. The air felt close, oppressive and explosive, drift smoke clouded the sky day after day. District Forester W. B. Greeley, en route to Missoula on the Great Northern, wired from the train to be met at the depot. His first question was, "Where are the fires?" He was very much surprised when told that there were no fires of serious proportions on the Kaniksu and that most of the smoke in the air was reported to be drift smoke from Canada. Shortly thereafter fires began springing up seemingly from no cause. The town of Newport and locality had been cleaned of men and fire-fighting tools. About August 18 or 19 so many fires appeared along and within sight of the railroad that trainmen in alarm reported the condition to the depot agent at Newport. The agent, sensing that a conflagration was inevitable, called a hasty meeting of townspeople at his office. Mr. Millar was absent in the field. I attended the meeting. The critical situation was discussed and the nucleus of an organization started. Later during the same day the mayor called a hasty meeting to further discuss the best means to protect the town and adjacent property. It now seemed inevitable that the numerous fires burning within and outside of the Forest boundary could no longer be controlled, especially in the event of a high wind. Groups of citizens were organized, and arrangements made, with what little there was to work with, to keep the fire as far from the

town as possible. Every available tool was placed in service, even garden hoes, rakes and pitchforks. August 20 arrived more ominous and threatening than the days preceding. Reports of so many fires came in that it was impossible, with means at hand, to even begin to cope with the situation. The wind began to increase in velocity from the west. Small fires were fanned into large ones. The air was rapidly becoming filled with smoke more dense than previously. From the window of the office we could see for several miles along the timbered bench lands northeasterly from the river. These yellow pine slopes were occupied by several ranchers. We could see fires break out from these ranch locations and sweep up the slope beyond. It was clearly evident from location of these new fires that the ranchers were starting what they thought to be back fires as a protection to their own property. There is not anything more dangerous than a back fire started by hands of the inexperienced. These fires spread with great rapidity. Finally the expected hurricane broke in all its fury. Local fires burned together and swept through the forest as one vast conflagration. The flames swept across the Pend Oreille River as if it had not been there. The mid-afternoon became dark. The roar of the flames and crash of falling timber could plainly be heard in town. Newport was entirely spared. The flames cut a straight swath to the northward.

The hurricane passed, leaving death and destruction in its wake. Telephone lines were down, and only fragmentary reports were received. No deaths were reported among the Forest personnel or firefighters on the Kaniksu. [Other accounts suggest three homesteaders perished near Newport, Washington.] On the following morning I saddled and rode north through the smoldering burn to the summit of the Priest River divide. Only blackened waste could be seen. I returned and started down the river on the west side. The burned area was a tangled mass. The road was completely blocked. I was forced to turn back. All that remained was to salvage what material that could be salvaged from the disaster, and reorganize for a new start.

William W. Morris of the Coeur d'Alene National Forest faced the beginning of the great fires in somewhat unusual circumstances:

Never within the memory of all the old-timers did the Coeur d'Alene [National Forest] experience such a dry spell as occurred during the summer of 1910. Even as early as April the south slopes were quickly relieved of their snow burdens, and became quite dry. A fire was reported to the office on one of these slopes the latter part of that month. A few scattered showers in May and June about completed the sum total of the rainfall for the summer.

Returning from another hard trip up the Coeur d'Alene River by pole boat in early July, I was taking a somewhat needed rest in the office, by writing up reports, etc. when Professor Kirkwood from the University of Montana made us a visit. As he wanted to make a study of the flora found upon our forest, I was very much pleased when the supervisor asked me to accompany him on his trip, and show him some of our more accessible timbered areas. July 13, 1910, saw us climbing the top of Striped Peak, about five miles from the city of Wallace, and reached by what is known as the West Fork trail. It was a beautiful day, but quite hot and dry with a stiff southwest wind. We arrived at the top of Striped Peak, which has an elevation of over six thousand three hundred feet, about lunch time. We had hardly sat down on the top of the peak to eat our lunch when I noticed smoke in the southwest. I took a compass shot in the direction of this smoke and then sat down to finish our lunch. As we were eating smoke suddenly appeared in the southeast, and fanned by the gale that was blowing quickly developed into what looked to be a stiff fire. Looking carefully in the direction of the other fire we also detected smoke, a thin narrow band of it, in the southwest but nearer than the first one we had seen. This was too much. It was necessary to report these fires at once and postpone, for a time at least, our trip. Hastily taking a compass shot on the three fires and estimating their distance as near as possible, I plotted them approximately, without the aid of a protractor, on my map, and we started on the return trip to Wallace.

At that time no telephones connected this peak with the office, as is now the case with all of the mountain peaks that command a good view of the country. Before descending we took a look at the fire in the southeast. It was coming our way rapidly, and although possibly twenty miles away, it seemed as if it might be at our mountain peak in a short time. Little did I think as we left that high point that day, a point commanding a view of timbered slopes and canyons, bare peaks and green ridges, stretching away as far as the eye could reach, that it would be my last view of this beautiful panorama of green clad hills. The next time I was to behold it was with a feeling of great sorrow, sorrow for a fallen race whose scattered and broken remains lay spread out before me. The greenness had vanished. The canyons and hillsides were covered with a twisted mass of broken blackened trees, in some places five trees deep. It reminded me of jackstraws more than anything else. Great pines almost two hundred feet long were there, broken, twisted and fallen, the product of hundreds of years of slow but sure accumulation of food from the earth and air. What a sad sight it all was for one who had viewed the same country from this spot only a few months before.

We reached the forest office in Wallace in the afternoon. The stenographer said that the supervisor had already gone out on a fire. The fires we had seen had all been reported, and action taken. From then on until about eleven o'clock that night, the telephone was going continually, either the same or other fires being reported from various sources. Thus the fires had caught us all at once, and from then on until the middle of September it was one continual fight, though at that time we did not know it was to be. The next day I was sent out to one of the fires that we had sighted the day before from Striped Peak. This fire was on the North Fork of the Coeur d'Alene river about thirty two miles from Wallace by rail. Professor Kirkwood was to accompany me. I was to stay until the fire was under control, then go on up the river with Professor Kirkwood. It was thought it would probably take a day or two to control this fire. It took just fifty-five days and nights.

Edward G. Stahl of the Cabinet National Forest (now called the Kootenai National Forest) had a similar experience with the start of the great fires:

On August 20, 1910, a forest fire raced unchecked for one hundred miles in two days, to devastate one million acres of wilderness in the Idaho Panhandle and northwestern Montana. Eighty-seven persons perished in the flames and countless numbers of forest creatures were destroyed.

If you could see a little black bear clinging, high in a blazing tree and crying like a frightened child you could perceive on a very small scale what happened to the forest creatures.

At twelve o'clock noon on August 10, 1910, Supervisor J. E. Barton at Sandpoint, Idaho, received a telegram from Fire Guard William Brashear at Cabinet: "Send a man to relieve me, fires out of control, men should be withdrawn to safety." Brashear was in charge of several firefighting crews located south of Cabinet near the northern foothills of the Bitterroot Range. [Cabinet was a small town on the Clark Fork River near the Idaho-Montana line.] He had been a logging contractor with a background of experience that well qualified him for the job ahead.

Since this was before the time of autos and good roads, no action could be taken until the train went east at 5:00 P.M. Supervisor Barton asked me go to Cabinet and take charge, since I was deputy Supervisor at the time. But before I left we received a second wire, this time from Brashear's cook: "Brashear and ten men trapped in the fire, all assumed to be dead."

John Keefe, Forest Ranger from Clark Fork, met me at Cabinet. We proceeded to the fire front, now within one mile of Cabinet. John was a tall, lanky lad of twenty from the Idaho State School of Forestry. He was quite an athlete and held the track record for his college.

We learned that Brashear, after sending the wire, decided that immediate action was urgent since the wind had increased to a gale. He returned to camp, turned his horse over to the cook with instructions to warn distant crews. Brashear then hurried up the mountainside on foot to warn an isolated crew of ten men.

The cook and about thirty men who were working east of Brashear's party reached Cabinet safely after a mad race ahead of the flames. They had met a boy taking lunches on a pack horse to Brashear's party, threw the boy on the pack horse, and turned him about to lead the race toward Cabinet. None of the men who had been in the big stampede would return to the fire front with Keefe and me, but we got six Finlanders who lived in the vicinity to volunteer.

We selected the intersection of two skid roads as a strategic location to try and check the fire. It had spent some of its force and slowed down at nightfall. I was acquainted with this locality and knew that one skid road led to the firefighters' camp.

It was 2:00 A.M. when Keefe and I decided we could venture through the fire front in a race to the trapped men although the fire was still dangerous, burning intermittently through the tree tops. I had left an automatic pistol on the skid road with the Finns. Days later it was found with the breech clip blown out, cocked and locked solid, a souvenir of the fire. One man asked us to watch for his abandoned suitcase. All that remained of it was the metal rim.

We would run awhile, then lie down at intervals to get fresh air. Continued exertion in the smoke and heat will cause a person to faint. We passed a dead porcupine in the road as we traversed a blackened area of death and destruction where no living animal or bird remained. I was reminded of a vast graveyard. The small fires flickering dimly in the darkness high in the blackened snags could be candles burning for the dead.

Upon reaching the spring near where the camp was located we shouted until our parched throats were hoarse but got no reply. Then we climbed out of the burned timber upon the ridge to the clearing. There in the darkness we saw the huddled forms. We thought they were all dead, but to our relief we found they were sleeping the sleep of exhaustion after their ordeal. Some had their heads covered with the charred remnants of coats and blankets.

Brashear's dog lay dead in the clearing. Two men crazed with fear had bolted and perished in the flames.

The race with the fire had been hopeless and Brashear had led the men to the clearing, warning each man to soak his bedding in the spring and lie down under the wet covering. He knew this was their best chance to survive. Brashear was the only man to soak his blanket at the spring. Nothing could live at the spring since it was in a ravine in the timber. The spring was boiled dry when Keefe and I reached it.

Brashear had made a futile attempt to stop the two men who ran off. The rest of the crew were about to panic and run when he knocked a man down with a mattock handle and threatened to brain the first man to try and run. They lay down, heads toward the wind, as the fire raged past on each side of the clearing, flames hundreds of feet high fanned by a tornadic wind so violent that the flames flattened out ahead, swooping to earth in great darting curves, truly a veritable red demon from hell.

At daybreak we found the charred bodies of the two men. Brashear's eyesight was temporarily impaired. Several men were sent to the hospital for minor burns.

John Keefe remained to guide the men out by the best route while I returned in haste to Cabinet to reorganize the firefighting. This was quite a problem since tools, supplies and records had been destroyed in the fire.

This fire before being checked burned to the outskirts of Cabinet and fired the timbers in the railroad tunnel nearby.

The Forest Supervisor of the Coeur d'Alene Forest had lost all contact with a large party of firefighters located about seventy miles north of Wallace, Idaho. This area was accessible from Cabinet by a journey south of about twenty-five miles across the summit of the Bitterroot Range. I was delegated to go and investigate their fate.

A husky young graduate from Michigan University, named Gillis, accompanied me on this trip. We were about to start when a woman came to our camp asking for help. Her husband, during a drunken spree, had beaten up the family and smashed the furniture. We went to her home but the place was deserted. The doors were open and a little old pack pony had wandered into the house. We found him with his nose in the flour barrel. He was brown color and looked comical with his face decorated with flour. We appropriated the horse and a pack saddle, then with a light pack we started for the North Fork.

We stopped that night at a sheep camp just over the summit of the range. There was no trail beyond so we left the pony there. As we descended into the valley we both suffered violent headaches from smoke. We were approaching the northern limit of a fire that had burned an area forty miles wide and seventy miles in length.

We found the abandoned campsite of the missing men and tracked them westward until we were assured that they had safely crossed the Coeur d'Alene Range to Lake Pend Oreille. We were not acquainted with this area and did not carry enough food for such an extended journey. As darkness overtook us on the mountainside we stopped, made two fires and lay down between them. I had shot a blue grouse on the way. We cooked it on sharpened sticks and picked the bones clean. At first dawn, we went on, picked up the pony and returned to Cabinet.

By the time we had returned to Cabinet, the great fire was declared a national emergency. All efforts were directed to the protection of homes, towns and private property. Guards were placed at the entrance to mountain valleys and no unauthorized persons were allowed to pass.

After organizing the firefighting at Cabinet, I joined a party of forty laborers who were en route from Spokane by train and guided them to a fire near Noxon, Montana. Men worked in relays all night, shoveling dirt to check the flames, and save a homesteader's buildings. His pasture fence had burned down and the calf was removed into the house.

I carried a small canvas tarp and got a little sleep that night for the first time in over fifty hours. This fire was in the Cabinet National Forest.

I returned to Cabinet to find a desperate appeal for help from a settler located across the Clark Fork River. I summoned the faithful Finns and started but the boat was on the wrong side of the river. The Finns carried a cedar telephone pole to the river for me and riding astride the pole I paddled across and got the boat. My feet and legs in the water acted as a stabilizer to keep the log from rolling.

We found the settler in desperate straits. The Finns worked all night and checked the advancing flames.

The Cabinet Gorge is now a noted scenic attraction where the river is compressed to rush through a rock crevice so narrow that the river virtually runs on edge. It was here at the mouth of

the gorge in a big eddy that I crossed the river [the Cabinet
Gorge Dam was constructed at this site on the Idaho-Montana
state line].

Albert Cole of the Helena National Forest found that not
everyone took the situation as seriously as he did:

One of the worst situations that I have ever been in contact
with occurred during August of 1910 on part of the Forest. The
Forest Service has good cause to remember the fire season of
1910, and that portion of the Helena had its troubles as well as the
rest of the country. The smoke from the fires in the West was so
thick that visibility was confined, even in the middle of the day, to
a radius of only a few miles, and I spent a great deal of my time on
patrol watching for telltale smokes. I discovered what I was sure
was a new fire on the district adjoining mine, and as there was no
telephone connection between these two districts I rode over to
the adjoining headquarters to tell the ranger what I suspicioned or
to see if he was aware of this danger. When I got to his headquarters his wife said that he was helping some ranchers do their
threshing and would not be home until night. I insisted on going
on, and she finally directed me so that I could find him. I told him
of my fears and he laughed and said that he had been up there a
day or two before and that things were all right. There had been a
small lightning storm the day before and I was sure it had set
things going. We had quite an argument and he finally agreed to
go up there with me after dinner. We returned to his headquarters
and had dinner. After dinner we started up the creek. I suggested
we take a mattock and shovel apiece, but he said it would not be
necessary as he knew there was no fire, and although I pleaded
that it was no trouble to take them along he refused to take any
tools or to let me take any out of the cache. We rode up the creek
about five miles and came to a point where we could see the head
of the creek and it was plain that the smoke was much denser
there. He had a small monocular [telescope] and after some time
let me take it, and I immediately saw where the smoke was boiling
up from a good-sized blaze.

I finally showed it to him, and he admitted there must be a fire there. I then told him to go back to his headquarters and get some men and tools and I would go on up and see what I could do. He flatly refused to do this and said we could handle it and that he could get a couple of shovels from an old prospector up near the fire. Well, we went on up and did get the shovels which the ranger said he could get, but they were old and dull and the handles were none too good. When we reached the fire it was very plain to me at least that we could never control it with the manpower and tools that we had and I again pleaded with this obdurate man to return to his headquarters and get help and some decent tools, but as usual he refused, saying we could control it by morning and that then he would go down and send up some man to watch it. We worked until midnight, then this ranger said we would go back to the place where we got the shovels and have the old man and his wife get us some supper.

When we were ready to come back I again proposed that either he or I go to his headquarters and procure men and equipment so that we could hold the fire in the morning, but as usual my pleas fell on deaf ears, and we returned to the unequal battle. About five o'clock the next morning the ranger broke his shovel handle and finally agreed to go back to his headquarters and send some men and equipment up to the fire. I told him to make it as quickly as possible, as I knew that it would be a miracle if the fire did not go out of control when the sun got hot.

He left, and I continued to work, trying to complete the fire line before it got too hot. About eight o'clock, however, a strong wind came up and the fire started jumping our poorly constructed trench, and in less than fifteen minutes it was out of control and sweeping up the slope at an appalling rate. There was a large stand of big fir just above the fire line and when the fire hit this timber it sprang to the crowns and went faster than a horse could travel on up the slope. I managed to get up on the ridge on one side of the fire and while standing there in despair I heard someone yell and met a man who said that he was from the Helena office, that the fire had been reported from the other side of the mountain and he was to take charge of this fire. I told him that men were coming as far as I knew, but that I was going back to my own district. He said for me to go, but to send the ranger back up there as soon as he could get there.

I returned to the ranger's headquarters, found him asleep, but met some men going up to the fire. I woke the ranger up and made my report, and rode back home.

This fire cost the Forest Service some $2,000 and was not put out until the last of August, when a light snow put the finishing touches to it. Why this ranger was so chary of taking tools and men to that fire, I have never been able to find out. It could have been controlled that night, I fully believe, if we had had two more men and the proper tools. This ranger had been a Supervisor of the then extinct Elkhorn Forest, and he evidently did not believe in taking the advice of a mere ranger who had such a small district to handle or who was practically under his orders.

The threat of fire reached every area of USFS operations in the Inland Northwest that summer, for the risk was great. Precautionary measures often failed, requiring reinforcements, as R. L. Woesner of the Blackfeet National Forest (now the Kootenai National Forest) recounted:

> The year 1910 was a bad fire season. There were still no telephone lines or no regular established lookout points in the area where I was located, which was on the Great Northern Railroad. There was, however, a telegraph station within five miles of my headquarters, which was a decided improvement in communications over what I had been accustomed to.
>
> The district I was assigned to had a considerable mileage of railroad in it of fairly heavy grades, and in those days they burned a poor grade of coal in their freight engines. The firemen usually punched the spark arresters full of big holes in order to make the engines steam better, with the result that a large number of railroad fires were set along the right-of-way.
>
> Early in the season I was advised by the Supervisor to try and handle the situation alone if possible, but to hire help in case of dire necessity, as there was a small appropriation for fire fighting, but it was to be used sparingly. I got by with the help of the sec-

tion crew for a while by working day and night as there was fire every day. I was finally allowed a couple of extra patrolmen to assist me. Then one day in August, the wind came up and one of our fires made a run of about five miles out away from the track. I wired the Supervisor for a hundred men with tools and supplies. He wired back, "Are you sure you need that many?" I wired back, "Yes."

Well, I got about 60 men within the next two or three days and a few days later a company of soldiers from Fort Harrison arrived. By this time I had decided to put in a fire camp near a lake about five miles from the railroad, but had only two old Government pack horses to move the necessary camp equipment in with. These horses had seen better days some ten years or so prior to 1910, and were somewhat string-halted and knee-sprung at the time. They were also broke to the harness and it was decided we would hitch them to an old wagon we borrowed as they were at least able to hold up the neck yoke and tongue. We loaded up the wagon with camp equipment, tools and supplies, tied a long rope to the end of the wagon tongue, hitched 60 of the soldiers to the rope and away we went over the hill to camp by combined horse and man power. After camp was once established, it was supplied by J. W. Whilt, later known as "Rimes of the Rockies," now of Kalispell, Montana, and the two old knee-sprung horses.

The soldiers turned out to be just as good at taking the place of a fire fighter as they were at pinch hitting for a draft horse and we soon had things under control and kept them so throughout the rest of the season. This was on the old "Blackfeet" Forest near Stryker, Montana.

Roy A. Phillips of the Lolo National Forest also had to expand his fire-fighting efforts as a result of the railroad:

Perhaps to those who went through the 1910 fire season that experience is the highlight of their Forest Service experience. It was so to me, and I had had very little training and experience along that line, other than that I had handled small crews of men since I was 15 years old. When I went in to see Elers Koch about a job, he blinked a few times and said I could have a job at $75 a month if I would provide two horses and equipment. I would, of course, have to subsist myself. I went to work on a timber survey crew April 4, and about June 1 at the Savenac Nursery. I helped put in the first seed bed there. We also did some experimental planting with corn planters and in seed spots.

After June 15 the fire situation became critical and [Frank] Haun sent me to a flag stop called Borax on the Coeur d'Alene branch of the Northern Pacific Railroad for fire patrol duty. The job consisted of patrolling the territory from Saltese to the Montana-Idaho state line and particularly the Northern Pacific and Chicago, Milwaukee & St. Paul Railroads. As coal was the fuel used by all locomotives and the rights-of-way were highly inflammable, the job was not an easy one. I had no previous training whatever in fighting forest fires and only instructions from Ranger Haun to put out any fires that might occur on my district. Also, none of the railroad section crews, of which there were three on my district, had fire training; so, as fires occurred I proceeded to train them on the job. About the only directive given me by Haun was that results were all that he was after, and that the guard the previous year had not gotten them so he had had to fire him.

Many and varied were the experiences of that 1910 season, performed at first on foot and later on a railroad speeder. The crucial test perhaps came on the first fire, a 10-acre blaze near Drexel on the Chicago, Milwaukee & St. Paul Railroad on a hot June afternoon. Seeing it was beyond one-man stage I went to the nearest section gang and got them into action. These men were Bulgarians under an elderly Irish foreman. The crew was recently from the old country and could speak very little if any English. The foreman turned the crew over to me and immediately found a spot in the shade. Two big black [probably inferring a swarthy complexion] fellows, the cream of the crew, had selected the names of George Washington and Abraham Lincoln. I gave Abe my ax, informed him that he was the crew boss and that the job was to trench the fire. He sure "poured it on" to the other Bulgarians. We got in front of the fire and tried to stop the forward run, which was bad tactics as it repeatedly jumped over our heads, when we would back up and make a fresh start.

At sundown we were still frantically battling the fire, which had not gained appreciably in size but had caused a lot of sweat and blisters. About that time Ranger Haun appeared on the scene, having seen the smoke from down the river. When he observed how worn out we were, he suspended operations for the day, took me back to Saltese with him and the next morning detailed Ranger Jack Breen to assist me. With the Bulgarians again on the job we quickly got the fire corralled and Breen gave me some valuable pointers in fire fighting.

This section gang, as well as the others, became efficient fire-fighting units, as circumstances required that I train them since I could not hope to do the job alone. One of the crews, however, persisted in burning tie piles and caused me considerable trouble. One day one of these fires occurred just west of Saltese on the edge of town. Thinking to give old Tom a lesson, I trenched the upstream spread of the fire and left the town end untended. As there was a slough on one side and the railroad track on the other, there seemed only a remote possibility of the fire spreading except in the one direction. This it did, and by late afternoon had spread into the limits of Saltese and burned one building. This made a "good Indian" of Tom Hanlon and years afterward, when he had a section on my older ranger district, he would go long distances from the railroad to put out lightning fires and never charged the Forest Service one red cent for his services.

Some 30 fires along the two railroads were suppressed during the summer and none of these fires exceeded 10 acres in size. Many and varied were the experiences in that connection but success was dictated entirely by force of circumstances. When I left my cabin there was no certainty that I would return that night or perhaps for several days. Hoboes cleaned me out of most of my worldly possessions so I boarded up the windows and put a sign on the door, "Look out for the gun." This was a bluff but it worked. When lumberman John Baird and Ranger Charles Vealey later came into camp en route with a fire crew for the Bullion fire on the Coeur d'Alene Forest, they got a long pole and shoved the door open after unlocking the Forest Service padlock.

A lightning fire occurred on Denna Mora Creek and Guard L. H. Foote was given charge. It burned an area of about 40 acres and Harvey Polleys, of the Polleys Lumber Company of Missoula, was killed on that fire by a falling snag. I reached the fire at about the time this happened and assisted in removing the body. At that time

Polleys had started operation on Randolph Creek and had purchased the timber in the upper St. Regis drainage. This was the timber we had cruised that spring on 6 feet of snow.

E. A. Woods of the Lewis and Clark National Forest remembered how frightening fighting the fires could be:

The Two Medicine fire was scattered from Summit to the Blackfeet Reservation. At the time about forty of us were camped on a gravel bar on the edge of the Two Medicine River. To the rear of us was an overmature growth of spruce.

The fire in this spruce swamp was divided in two parts. One fire was burning up the river and another was burning down the river. It was very evident that these two fires would come together.

Among my several duties of foreman, bookkeeper, and assistant cook, I was also the packer, using my own string of four pack horses and my saddle horse. Confronted with all these duties, it was obvious that the days were far too short to accomplish everything. So I did the packing at night.

On one particular evening I approached the camp at about eleven o'clock. Suddenly the heavens lit up. The two fires had met. When I rode into camp every man was on his feet. An atmosphere of fright was apparent. Even the horses seemed to sense that danger was near. The whimpering of my dog didn't lessen the tension. Pretending not to sense the danger, I began to unpack and made a few wisecracks.

The main fire had died down and hundreds of woodpecker-drilled spruce snags were shooting their varicolored columns of flames a hundred feet or more into the air. It was an awe-inspiring scene. The tension in camp had died down somewhat when suddenly a new outburst of flames shot skyward. A small patch of overmature timber close by was going up in flames. I had hardly had time to look around when I saw two young chaps heading across the creek, on the high jump, carrying a large kettle of beans between them which they had snatched off the stove as they made their getaway.

I was never able to account for it, and neither was the young fellow when questioned later, but every time he had covered fifty feet or more he discharged the six-shooter he was carrying in his hand. The uncomfortable part of it was that he was shooting toward camp, never once looking back to see what was what. I was standing on the bank of the river cussing them for all I was worth when I felt a grasp on my shoulder. Turning around, I faced a powerful railroader from Havre. Fear was written all over his face.

"How about this," he roared, "are we all going to burn up here? I've got a wife and two kids in Havre."

Instead of answering his question, I reached into my watch pocket and pulled out a ten-dollar bill. "I'll bet you this at the rate of two to one that you are just as safe here as you would be in Havre."

The tension on his face relaxed.

"All right, boss, if you say so, it's a go with me."

I don't recall at what hour the men with the bean pot returned or the six men who had started down the creek, but the next morning all hands were on the job.

John F. Preston was on the Beartooth National Forest when the fires began. He found fighting fires less difficult than administering their aftermath:

Passing over most of the events which altogether form a very happy chapter in my life, we come to the summer of 1910 when the sky was filled with smoke from the fires which increased in intensity in western Montana and Idaho. I must recite one experience in firefighting on the Beartooth. I remember during July the smoke was so dense in Red Lodge that frequently we could hardly see across the street. But the Beartooth escaped until on August 21 some careless camper up the west fork of Rock Creek let his fire get away. In a few hours we had fire from the creek almost to the top of the mountain. The next few days was a period of excitement and intense activity. I have forgotten how many men we finally put on this fire, but I think it was about 50. I can't say that the organization was very good or that the technique of firefighting was all that it should have been. I remember mostly the difficulties which surrounded firefighting activities of that period. I

know that we did not have the fire under complete control when
the fight ended on August 24 when about 6 inches of snow covered the fire. Then our difficulties really began. The firefighters
had to be paid and there were no facilities for meeting such an
emergency, at least on an eastern Montana Forest. Payrolls could
be made out and sent to Missoula and checks would come back to
the firefighters but a large number of firefighters demanded cash
and the cash had to be advanced by the Supervisor. I threw into it
what cash I could muster, added to it what I could borrow from
the bank, borrowed about $200 from Sam Dana [Samuel T. Dana
later became the leading figure in American academic forestry and
the author of the major text in the field, *Forest and Range Policy*],
who happened to visit my headquarters about that time, and finally paid off all of those firefighters. I suspect a good many of
them never did 15 cents worth of work, but our time records were
not the best and in order to avoid trouble and perhaps personal injury, we gave a good many of them the benefit of the doubt and
paid them for firefighting when we were almost certain they had
been loafing on the job. Later the firefighting was organized so
that such difficulties were not encountered and Supervisors were
not called upon to advance the money. But in 1910 I know that
my experience on the Beartooth was repeated on many National
Forests further west where the problem of firefighting was multi-
plied manyfold.

Eugene R. (Gene) Grush of the Kootenai National Forest remembered the administrative complications of hiring all kinds of
temporary fire fighters:

> In the early spring of 1910 I decided to take Horace Greeley's
> advice and go West, so I left Pittsburgh and worked my way across
> the country, arriving in Spokane in August. Men were being hired
> to fight fires, so I decided to take that on. A crew of us was sent to
> Troy, Montana. We arrived there early in the morning, had break-
> fast at the old Doonan Hotel which at that time included a bar, and
> some of the boys got pretty well tuned-up.
>   A wagon pulled up to the hotel partly loaded with grub, and we
> added our bedrolls to the load. When we got down to the ferry on

The remains of the town of Wallace, Idaho, after the fires of 1910. The house on the hill was the only one left in that part of town. (Photo courtesy USDA Forest Service)

the Kootenai, the wagon and some of the men were part way across the river. A well-liquored Irishman named Kelly, anxious to get to the fire apparently, stripped off and jumped in the river with the intention of swimming across. We fished him out and dressed him. At O'Brien Springs the cook prepared a lunch for us of bacon, eggs, fried spuds, bread, and coffee. I can still smell the aroma of that bacon and coffee.

We made camp that night at the spring on the east side of Yaak Falls. Next day part of the crew was sent up to the Bob Holmes homestead camp about three miles above the town of Sylvanite which had just been completely burned out. The Forest Service had built a bridge across the Yaak at the falls that spring. The fire was closing in on us so the team and wagon were moved across the river "just in case."

One of my duties was to keep the fire crew supplied with water. Water bags were either nonexistent or we didn't rate any as I was given a 12–quart pail and a tin cup for this duty. When we were trying to head the fire off up Arbo Creek I had to go down a very steep side hill to the creek. Before I got very far up from the creek the contents of the pail included not only water but twigs and leaves from the thick brush through which I traveled. I dumped it, refilled the bucket, tied my red bandanna over the top and returned to camp with clean water.

When the rains came and doused the fire we moved down to Charlie Dennis' homestead below Kilbrennan Lake (at that time, Dennis was Ranger of the Troy District). We were assigned to build trail up O'Brien Creek and got quite a little way before the fire money was cut off. We were paid in cash at Troy—no checks at that time.

Thomas G. Myers of the Coeur d'Alene National Forest missed most of the excitement:

I had a little experience in the fires of 1910 on the Coeur d'Alene Forest. I had just got back to the Judith Station [in the Lewis & Clark National Forest] from my honeymoon trip when I got orders to report to the District Office in Missoula for assignment for fire duty, and was sent to Wallace, Idaho, to report. I got in there on Friday night and was sent out to the fire at the head of Boulder Creek out of Mullan to size up the fire and report to the office Saturday night. I walked from Mullan up to fire camp nine miles; arrived at the fire camp about one in the afternoon. Put in all afternoon going over fire, and when I got back to camp at 7:30 P.M., I was too tired to make the hike back to Mullan so stayed at camp. This was the night of the big blow-up and we had fire all around us. All of us were burned quite badly and one boy lost his life. I was only on the fire a half day when the blow-up came; spent the rest of the season in the hospital and reported for duty after the first of January 1911.

Eight

"Our Drenched Clothing Steamed and Smoked"

In the Middle of the Conflagration

There was no experience like a major forest fire to separate those with heart, character, and commitment from those who lacked such qualities. Many of the first generation of forestry found out much about themselves in the big fires; they learned their strengths and weaknesses, their resilience and creativity, and they came in touch with their innermost fears and feelings. Even two or more decades later, no event shaped these people like their experiences in the summer of 1910.

Many years later, some stopped to recount their experiences for popular audiences. Of these, Joseph B. Halm of the Coeur d'Alene National Forest was one of the most talented. His story of the fires of 1910 was first published in *American Forests and Forest Life* in July 1930:

> Out of the underbrush dashed a man—grimy, breathless, hat in hand. At his heels came another. Then a whole crew, all casting fearful glances behind them.
>
> "She's coming! The whole country's afire! Grab your stuff, ranger, and let's get outa here!" gasped the leader.
>
> This scene, on the afternoon of August 20, 1910, stands out vividly in my memory. The place was a tiny, timbered flat along a small creek in the headwaters of the St. Joe River, in Idaho. The little flat, cleared of undergrowth to accommodate our small camp, seemed dwarfed beneath the great pines and spruce. The little stream swirled and gurgled beneath the dense growth and windfall, and feebly lent moisture to the thirsting trees along its banks.

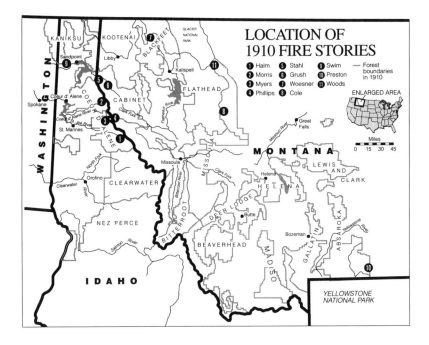

LOCATION OF 1910 FIRE STORIES

1 Halm 5 Stahl 9 Swim
2 Morris 6 Grush 10 Preston
3 Myers 7 Woesner 11 Woods
4 Phillips 8 Cole

— Forest boundaries in 1910

ENLARGED AREA

Miles
0 15 30 45

For weeks forest rangers with crews of men had been fighting in a vain endeavor to hold in check the numerous fires which threatened the very heart of the great white-pine belt in the forests of Idaho and Montana. For days an ominous, stifling pall of smoke had hung over the valleys and mountains. Crews of men, silent and grim, worked along the encircling fire trenches. Bear, deer, elk and mountain lions stalked starry-eyed [glazed-eyed] and restless through the camps, their fear of man overcome by a greater terror. Birds, bewildered, hopped about in the thickets, their song subdued, choked by the stifling smoke and oppressive heat. No rain had fallen since May. All vegetation stood crisp and brown, seared and withered by the long drought, as if by blight. The fragrance of summer flowers had given way to the tang of dead smoke. The withered ferns and grasses were covered by a hoar-frost of gray ashes. Men, red-eyed and sore of lung, panted for a breath of un-tainted air. The sun rose and set beyond the pall of smoke. All nature seemed tense, unnatural and ominous.

It had taken days to slash a way through the miles of tangled wilderness to our fire, sixty-five miles from a railroad. On August 18, this fire was confined within trenches; all seemed well; a day or two more and all would have been considered safe. Difficulties in transportation developed which necessitated reducing our crew from eighty-five to eighteen men.

I had just returned after guiding our remaining packers with their stock to one of our supply camps, when our demoralized crew dashed in. Incoherently, the men told how the fire had sprung up everywhere about them as they worked. The resinous smoke had become darker, the air even more oppressive and quiet. As if by magic, sparks were fanned to flames which licked the trees into one great conflagration. They had dropped their tools and fled for their lives. A great wall of fire was coming out of the northwest. Even at that moment small, charred twigs came sifting out of the ever-darkening sky. The foreman, still carrying his ax, was the last to arrive. "Looks bad," he said. Together we tried to calm the men. The cook hurried the preparation of an early supper. A slight wind now stirred the treetops overhead; a faint, distant roar was wafted to my ears. The men heard it; a sound as of heavy wind, or a distant waterfall. Three men, believing safety lay in flight, refused to stay. "We're not going to stay here and be roasted alive. We're going."

Things looked bad. Drastic steps were necessary. Supper was forgotten. I slipped into my tent and strapped on my gun. As I stepped out a red glow was already lighting the sky. The men were pointing excitedly to the north.

"She's jumped a mile across the canyon," said the foreman, who had been talking quietly to the men. Stepping before them, I carelessly touched the holster of the gun and delivered an ultimatum with outward confidence, which I by no means felt.

"Not a man leaves this camp. We'll stay by this creek and live to tell about it. I'll see you through. Every man hold out some grub, a blanket, and a tool. Chuck the rest into that tent, drop the poles and bury it."

The men did not hesitate. The supplies, bedding, and equipment were dumped into the tent, the poles jerked out, and sand shoveled over it. Some ran with armloads of canned goods to the small bar in the creek, an open space scarcely thirty feet across.

Frying pans, pails, and one blanket for each man were moved there. Meanwhile the wind had risen to hurricane velocity. Fire was now all around us, banners of incandescent flames licked the sky. Showers of large, flaming brands were falling everywhere. The quiet of a few minutes before had become a horrible din. The hissing, roaring flames, the terrific crashing and rending of falling timber was deafening, terrifying. Men rushed back and forth trying to help. One young giant, crazed with fear, broke and ran. I dashed after him. He came back, wild-eyed, crying, hysterical. The fire had closed in; the heat became intolerable.

All our trust and hope was in the little stream and the friendly gravel bar. Some crept beneath wet blankets, but falling snags drove them out. There was yet air over the water. Armed with buckets, we splashed back and forth in the shallow stream throwing water as high as our strength would permit, drenching the burning trees. A great tree crashed across our bar; one man went down, but came up unhurt. A few yards below, a great log jam, an acre or more in extent, the deposit of a cloudburst in years gone by, became a roaring furnace, a threatening hell. If the wind changed, a single blast from this inferno would wipe us out. Our drenched clothing steamed and smoked; still the men fought. Another giant tree crashed, cutting deep into the little bar, blinding and showering us with sparks and spray. But again the men nimbly side-stepped the hideous meteoric monster.

After what seemed hours, the screaming, hissing, and snapping of millions of doomed trees, and the shower of sparks and burning brands grew less. The fire gradually subsided. Words were spoken. The drenched, begrimed men became more hopeful. Some even sought tobacco in their water-soaked clothing. Another hour and we began to feel the chill of the night. The hideous, red glare of the inferno still lighted everything; trees still fell by the thousands. Wearily, the men began to drag the water-soaked blankets from the creek and dry them; some scraped places beneath the fallen trees where they might crawl with their weary, tortured bodies out of reach of the falling snags. The wind subsided. Through that long night beside a man-made fire, guards sat, a wet blanket around their chilled bodies.

Dawn broke almost clear of smoke, the first in weeks. Men began to crawl stiffly out from their burrows and look about. Such a scene! The green, standing forest of yesterday was gone; in its place a charred and smoking mass of melancholy wreckage. The virgin trees, as far as the eye could see, were broken or down, devoid of a single sprig of green. Miles of trees—sturdy, forest giants—were laid prone. Only the smaller trees stood, stripped and broken. The great log jam still burned. Save for the minor burns and injuries, all were safe. Inwardly, I gave thanks for being alive. A big fellow, a Swede, the one who had refused to stay, slapped me on the back and handed me my gun. I had not missed it.

"You lost her in the creek last night. You save me my life," he said, simply. His lip trembled as he walked away.

The cook had already salvaged a breakfast from the trampled cache in the creek. Frying ham and steaming coffee drove away the last trace of discomfort.

"What are your plans?" asked the foreman, after several cups of coffee.

"First we'll dig out our tent, salvage the grub, and then look the fire over. We'll order more men and equipment and hit the fire again."

Little did I know as I spoke that our fire that morning was but a dot on the blackened map of Idaho and Montana. After breakfast we picked our way through the fire to our camp of yesterday. All was safe. We moved the remaining equipment to the little bar. Our first thought was for the safety of our two packers and the pack stock at our supply camp. The foreman and I set out through the fire over the route of the old trail, now so changed and unnatural. With ever-increasing apprehension we reached the first supply camp where I had left the packers. Only a charred, smoking mass of cans and equipment marked the spot.

What had become of the men? Not a sign of life could we find. They must have gone to the next supply camp. We hurried on, unmindful of the choking smoke and our burned shoes. We came upon our last supply camp; this, too, was a charred, smoldering mass. Still no signs of the men. A half mile beyond we suddenly came upon the remains of a pack saddle; then, another; the girths had been cut. Soon we found the blackened remains of a horse. Feverishly we searched farther. Next we found a riding saddle. With sinking heart we hastened on. More horses and more sad-

A burnt-over tract in the St. Joe National Forest in Idaho. (Photo by Joe Halm courtesy USDA Forest Service)

dles. The fire was growing hotter. We halted, unable to go farther. We must go back for help and return when the heat had subsided.

Smoke darkened the sky; the wind had again risen to a gale; trees were once more falling all about us. We took shelter in a small cave in a rock ledge where the fire had burned itself out. Here we sat, parched, almost blind with smoke and ashes. Once the foreman voiced my thoughts: "The wind will die down toward night, then we can go back to camp." This fury of the wind, however, increased steadily. Fires roared again, and across the canyon trees fell by the hundreds.

After what seemed like hours, we crept out of our cramped quarters and retraced our steps. The storm had subsided slightly. If the remains of the trail had been littered that morning, it was completely filled now. We came to a bend in the creek where the trail passed over a sharp hogback. As we neared the top, we again came into the full fury of the wind. Unable to stand, pelted by gravel and brands and blinded by ashes, we crawled across the exposed rocky ledges. I had never before, nor have I since, faced such a gale. On the ridges and slopes every tree was now uprooted and down. We passed the grim remains of the horses and supply camps. In the darkness we worked our way back over and under the blackened, fallen trees. Fanned by the wind, the fire still burned fiercely in places. Torn and bleeding, we hurried on, hatless—in the darkness, lighted only by the myriads of fires—[me] picking the way, the foreman watching for falling trees. While passing along a ledge a great tree tottered above us and rent its way to earth, rolling crazily down the slope. We ran for our lives, but the whirling trunk broke and lodged a few feet above. So absorbed were we with our plight that we nearly passed our camp on the little [sand]bar in the creek bottom.

By firelight we ate and related our fears as to the fate of the packers. As we talked, one of the men, pointing to the eastern sky, cried, "Look, she's coming again!" The sky in the east had taken on a hideous, reddish glow which became lighter and lighter. To the nerve-racked men it looked like another great fire bearing down upon us. Silently the men watched the phenomenon which lasted perhaps ten minutes. Then the realization came that the sky was clearing of smoke. In another brief space of time the sun shone. Not until then did I know that it was only 4 o'clock. A change in wind had shifted the smoke toward the northwest. We later found that the burn extended but a mile or two to the south of us.

Daylight next morning found us chopping and sawing a route back through the now cooled burn toward civilization, searching for our packers. That day I visited a prospector's cabin on a small side creek, a mile from the trail, to learn the fate of the man, a cripple. His earth-covered dugout by some miracle had withstood the fire. There were no signs of life about. Whether the man had gone out earlier in the week, or had suffered the same fate as our packers, I did not then know. Evening found our little party many miles from camp. We saw the remains of an elk and several deer; also, a grouse, hopping about with feet and feathers burned off—a pitiful sight. Men who quenched their thirst from small streams immediately became deathly sick. The clear, pure water running through miles of ashes had become a strong, alkaline solution, polluted by dead fish, killed by the lye. Thereafter we drank only spring water.

A burned-over area from the fires of 1910 in the St. Joe National Forest, Idaho. (Photo by Joe Halm courtesy USDA Forest Service)

Late that night, weary and silent, the men returned to camp and crept into their blankets. Daylight again found us on the trail equipped with packs and food and blankets. About noon we came upon an old white horse, one of our pack string, badly singed, but very much alive, foraging in the creek.

Late one day, the sixth since the great fire, a messenger, be-

Cutting a new trail after the fire. Joe B. Halm, the author of one of the best fire stories, is on the right. Government photographer R. H. Mackay holds the camera. (Photo courtesy USDA Forest Service)

smudged and exhausted, reached us. From him we learned that Wallace and many other towns and villages had burned; that at least a hundred men had lost their lives and that scores were still missing. He had seen many of the dead brought in.

Our crew had been given up as lost. Several parties were still endeavoring to reach us from different points. Ranger Haines with his crew was then several miles back and would cut the trail to take us out. Our packers, he said, had reached safety. The crippled prospector was still among the missing, and we were to search for him. For three days we combed the burned mountains and creeks for the missing man. On the third afternoon, weary and discouraged, we stumbled upon the ghastly remains, burned beyond recognition. His glasses and cane, which we found near, told the mute story of the last, great struggle of the unfortunate man who, had he but known it, would have been safe in his little shack. In a blanket we bore the shapeless thing out to the relief crew.

From Ranger Haines I heard the story of our packers. Shortly after I had left them they had become alarmed. Hastily saddling the fourteen head of horses, they had left the supply camp for Iron Mountain, sixty miles away. Before a mile was covered they realized the fire was coming and that, encumbered with the slow-moving stock, escape would be impossible. They cut the girths and freed the horses, hoping they might follow. Taking a gentle little saddle mare between them, they fled for their lives, one ahead, the other holding the animal by the tail, switching her along. The fire was already roaring behind. On they ran, the panting animal pulling first one, then the other. Hundreds of spark-set fires sprang up beside the trail; these grew into crown fires, becoming the forerunner of the great conflagration. By superhuman effort they reached the summit on the Idaho-Montana state line. Here the fire in the sparse timber lost ground. On sped the men down the other side until the fire was left behind. Ten miles farther, completely exhausted, they reached a small cabin, where they unsaddled their jaded, faithful little horse, threw themselves into a bunk and fell asleep.

Two hours later the whinny of the horse awoke them. A glare lighted the cabin. They rushed out; the fire was again all around them! They rescued the little horse from the already burning barn and dashed down the gulch. It was a desperate race for life. Trees falling above shot down the steep slopes and cut off their trail. The now saddleless, frightened little beast, driven by the men, jumped over and crawled beneath these logs like a dog. Two miles of this brought them to some old placer workings and safety. Exhausted, they fell. The fire swept on.

They had crossed a mountain range and covered a distance of nearly forty miles in a little over six hours, including their stay at the cabin—almost a superhuman feat.

Like nearly everyone else in District 1, William W. Morris of the Coeur d'Alene National Forest spent most of that summer fighting fire:

The one daily combination freight and passenger train took us up the river quite near the scene of the fire where the Graham Creek Ranger Station was, and is still located. A small stream emptied into the river at this point, and it was up this stream the fire was burning. With the ranger from the station we started for the scene immediately. A road led for about two miles up the canyon along this little stream. Three settlers had taken up claims in this canyon some time before. The fire originated probably from burning brush from the furthermost claim, about two to three miles up the stream. It had started the day before we arrived, and conditions were just right to give the fire a great start up the mountainside. At the first cabin about one mile up, some young ladies from Spokane had been visiting. Their suitcases full of clothing were still in the stream where they had thrown them the day before, in their hurry to leave the place. As it happened it was not until about fifteen days later that anybody on this little road would have been in any great peril. The fire was burning quite near the second cabin, and that afternoon we confined our efforts to stopping it at that point, which we did temporarily. Only a few men were working, and we all had to turn to with axes and mattocks. Professor Kirkwood proved himself to be an expert with the mattock, as well as in the classification of plants. A camp down the river had promised to send up a big gang of men, but they did not arrive until the following day. When they finally came I divided them up into two groups, one going up to the head of the fire, another group working to head it off in some valuable timber on the slope just over the ridge from the second cabin. These fire lines eventually met. Most of the men were foreigners and not highly satisfactory. We had a crew of about sixty all told. In making a fire line axes and crosscut saws are first employed to clear away all windfall and dead stubs, and these are followed up by men with mattocks who clear a trail exposing the mineral soil, about three feet wide. Patrol men are sent back on this trail as it is increased in length, to keep sparks and fire brands from blowing over it, or to put out fires caused by these being blown over the line, before they have developed into a large fire. Usually these fire lines are constructed a little to the lee side of a ridge, as it offers a favorable place to fight a fire, and it will run down hill on the lee side much slower than it comes up on the other.

Everything was going along favorably except the weather. It seemed as if it could not rain. Several times clouds appeared that under ordinary circumstances would have poured rain copiously, but not so this year. After getting a fire line around the fire on the east slope of the canyon we tackled the west slope, where a fire had been burning lightly in some small timber. That day the wind came up strongly, and scattered fire everywhere. However, we were enabled by working several nights to get a fire line up to the top of the divide, on the west side of the creek, so it was kept for the time being from going down towards the mouth. Many of the men had left or were unsatisfactory, so I went about the last part of July to Wallace to get hold of some more men. I returned with twenty-nine. Conditions were then bad in Wallace. The air was filled with smoke and fires were raging everywhere in the mountains. Our supervisor was almost exhausted with the strenuous work, both night and day. I met a man on the train when going to Wallace, an old-timer, with whom I conversed. He said, "We will be all right as long as we don't get one of those 'Palousers' lasting about three days, which would scatter our fires everywhere now that it is so dry." Now a "Palouser" this time referred to a gale of wind from the Palouse country [the hilly agricultural area of southeastern Washington] which strikes the whole region occasionally. The Palouse country is famous for its wheat, and the wind picks up the fine red soil and carries it for miles, filling one's throat and nose and covering everything with a fine powder. Fortunately these are rare and the country is usually calm, with very few violent storms. But this year one of these was to come along with many other things. The wind is one of the chief factors in fire fighting. When the wind blows hard and other conditions are right, the fire leaps up into the crowns of the trees, and travels along at a great pace, by brands blowing ahead of it and starting new fires. When it is quiet one may work quite close to a fire, but let the wind blow, and it is necessary to keep a respectful distance. It is also well to get on a fire early in the morning for this is usually the coolest and quietest time of the day, and the dew has a tendency to check the fire.

At this time we had only one small fire that was not under control. This was burning in a small area of rather poor timber on the east side of Graham Creek but nearer its mouth than we had been before. But this fire was to be our downfall, for it was in an old slashing, and a wind came up strongly the day we attacked it, and soon it was leaping and rushing over our fire line in all directions, but mainly towards the mouth of the stream. We could do nothing with it. Bringing down the men we put forth all our endeavors keeping it on the east side of the stream. Here for the first time we had a chance to use water, its natural enemy. But it was no use. Looking up on the west slope we suddenly saw smoke, and in a short time this side was a roaring furnace, traveling rapidly down towards the mouth of the creek, and threatening to shut off our escape in this direction. Men worked like heroes that day. I remember one man, a "lumberjack," who had come to the camp drunk. I had hesitated to employ him, but being short of men at the time took him. I will always remember how that man dashed into the fire with buckets of water or shovels of earth, as cool as a cucumber, doing everything that human power could do and much more than most human power. The men called him Patsy, and I will always be grateful to Patsy for his strenuous endeavors against such great odds, as well as to many other faithful ones. It was necessary for us to get out of the canyon now in a hurry, and running through some fire that was already before us we reached the railroad. At the mouth of the stream just before coming to the railroad track was a small schoolhouse [Graham Creek School near the Prichard Ranger Station]. The fire was there as quick as we were. As we lay down on the track exhausted I remember hearing the school bell give a final clang as it fell to the ground, its supports being eaten away by the tongues of fire. As the fire came down the west side of the stream toward the mouth of the river the timber was uprooted at just about the time the flame struck it. The falling trees caused a continual roar, and in some places were thrown in rough whirls, resembling the work of a tornado. Arriving at the mouth of the stream, the fire jumped the railroad tracks and river, and started burning in a flat on the opposite side about an eighth of a mile from the mouth of the stream where we had heretofore confined it. On this flat was a cabin belonging to a logging camp, and in this cabin were several boxes of giant powder. This we buried in the river, so that no sparks could get at it.

Taking a much needed rest that night, we began early the next morning to fight the fire on the flat. Had it gotten away from here the whole upper river would have been threatened. The fire jumped the main Coeur d'Alene River and threatened the Grizzlies. Fortunately we were able to get a fire line around it the first day. Once it jumped the fire line, and for a moment the upper river seemed doomed, but by quick work this danger was avoided. The next few days our efforts were confined to stopping the fire on the west side on the river slope. After building several miles of fire line, only to have the fire jump over it in spite of all efforts, we finally succeeded in running a fire line to the summit of the slope, taking advantage of a rock slide part of the way. Here we stopped it completely on the western front. The watershed in which we had been fighting the fire was now almost burned over. So far however we had confined this fire within it, with the exception of some small areas on the main river. It was away up at the head of this watershed on the east side that the danger now threatened, for the fire had jumped over our lines, and was threatening the large watershed of beautiful timber to the east. We established a camp on this high ridge, separating the two watersheds, and cut a fire line along it. This camp was not in a very desirable place as far as water and provisions were concerned, for everything had to be packed in with horses, and for a time it was necessary to carry the water on our backs with five-gallon water bags that we had for that purpose. A logging camp was situated in the watershed below us, and possibly three miles away to the east, nearer the main Coeur d'Alene river. From here our supplies were packed by pack horses coming to camp every two or three days. It was necessary for us first to build a "shotgun" trail as they call a very rough trail in that country, and this was so steep in some parts it was hard for a pack horses to get over it, even with a moderate load.

About this time a man appeared for work who said he had been a cook. We had been bothered a great deal heretofore by not being able to get a man who knew the art of cooking for a crew of men in the "open." Formerly we had done a good deal of the cooking at the ranger station, and at one of the cabins in the watershed below. I determined therefore to give this man a try, and he proved to be a wonder, and soon had order out of former chaos. He had a place for everything, and built a fireplace with stone he found on the mountain top. He had the men line up for their meals, and dished it out to them in a lordly manner as they passed in review.

He could turn out some dishes that would make some of our fine hotel chefs take notice, and with very little in the line of provisions or dishes to do it with and under the most trying circumstances.

We were situated on a bare ridge, with a lodgepole thicket a little way below us. The men built Indian "tepees" with this young lodgepole, and we looked for all the world like an Indian village stuck away up there on the top of a high ridge.

There were a great many bears on this ridge, attracted there probably by the huckleberries that grew in great profusion, and which sometime stayed our thirst, when water was not obtainable. One of the boys in his spare moments made a bear trap of logs. This was made in the nature of a figure four, the bear having to crawl under a heavy log to get the bait. On eating this bait, the stick holding the heavy log would release, and allow it to fall on the unfortunate bear. But we were destined not to have any bear meat, much as we wanted fresh meat, for although Mr. Bruin got into the trap one time, he managed to pull himself out.

Thus passed the first stage of operations at this camp, days of most strenuous toil on the part of everyone, but days which I can now look back to with somewhat of a feeling of pleasure, for the fire at that time was under control, and the life in the camp went along smoothly. But this was the calm before the storm. It had been a fight against nature from the beginning, and so far it looked as if we were getting the best of it. But soon nature was to show us what she was capable of doing when in her rougher moods.

It was near the twentieth of August and our fires had been surrounded by well made fire lines and things looked fairly favorable. But it was extremely dry, so much so that the soil was like powder, and a spark dropped at any point would quickly start a conflagration.

On the afternoon of the nineteenth of August I walked down to the ranger station, to talk over the situation with Ranger Schneider. Our fires were smoldering, but I felt they were under control. The following morning the ranger and I started for the fire camp. The wind was fresh in the early morning and strengthening every minute. When we reached the camp it was blowing a gale. Our "Palouser" had arrived. With great rapidity the smoldering fires below began to gather headway, and in a few minutes had gone over our ridge below the camp with a mighty roar, and down into the watershed we had been working all the summer to protect. But it was necessary for us to get busy now to protect our camp and ourselves. We cleared a place on the ridge where we placed all the provisions. We made a fire line below in the lodgepole thicket, but while doing this the fire jumped up into the crowns of the trees, and the head axeman was almost suffocated. We had to abandon this fire line and confine our attention to work on the ridge above our camp, where the fire was threatening to come over.

It was getting late and I was strongly hoping the wind would die down with the coming of night as it so often does. But there was no let up this time. It was blowing about sixty miles an hour now from the southwest. Our work on the ridge above us was in vain, for with a rush the fire was upon us at this point, then over. No human means could stop it now. Over the ridge it went into our precious timber below. The work of the summer was undone, at least I thought so then. We were in a serious predicament. Fire had gone over our ridge below us in the morning, and above us in the evening. Trees were falling and burning on these areas contin- ually. Our food supply was covered with sand and dirt. The men were called in. We sat down and ate what we could.

Never had any of us seen such a wild sight. In the direction of the city of Wallace great masses of smoke were blowing wildly up the valley of the South Fork. Southward toward the St. Joe River stood a great white cloud pillar, apparently still, looking like a great thunder cap, or the steam cloud that attends the eruption of a volcano. Many of the men thought it was a cloud and predicted rain at last. Westward the sun was setting in a flying black mass, looking like a great red ball of fire. Our high ridge gave us a won- derful view. The weird scene greatly impressed them, and one could not help having the feeling of fear and awe which the scene produced, as if a great tragedy was about to happen. Many fire fighters from other parts spoke of this later. They said the very air was afire. And tragedy was taking place in all these regions.

At Wallace at this time women and children and the sick from the hospitals were crowding the cars to escape the wall of flame that rolled down the mountainside that same afternoon and burned almost a third of the town. Where the great white pillar of smoke hung, townships of timber were being consumed, great trees were being uprooted and snapped in pieces by the thousands with a mighty roar that could be heard for miles, and many a brave fire fighter met his doom on that fateful day and the day following.

The wind continued to blow all night. Most of the men, dead tired, turned into their lodgepole shacks. The situation however looked too serious to make me think of sleep. At nine o'clock it was apparent that something must be done. The men were awakened, and each one told to take his blankets and other belongings, and start off down the ridge. Two of us buried all the tools we could find. Our provisions had already been put together in an open space.

It was rather dangerous work going through the fire in the dark on the ridge below, where trees were still burning and falling, from the fire that had passed over in the morning. The trail was completely obliterated by fallen trees, and in the darkness was hard to follow. We made it all right and after walking several miles, lay down on the ground and slept until morning. I was awakened by one of the night patrol men coming in. "Say," he said, "you ought to see our old camp, there is nothing left of her." I went back and took a look. The lodgepole shacks, provisions and all tools that had been left were completely gone, and the ridge was swept bare. A few tools had been left near the provisions, in the cleared open space, yet only the iron parts were left, showing with what heat this fire had rushed over our camp.

We were indeed fortunate to have escaped so well. It was necessary that something be done at once. The men had had very little supper, no breakfast, and no dinner was in sight. They were worn out from overwork, and lack of water both for drinking and washing purposes. Sending some men down to the logging camp for provisions, I went to the ranger station to see what I could get and report the situation to the Wallace office, and try and get some more men to tackle the fire again. Supervisor Weigle answered my telephone call. He said, "The situation is serious. A great deal of Wallace has been burned, and our ranger here [the famed Edward Pulaski] has lost six men in a tunnel. I can't send any more men. You will have to do the best you can without them." I got several loaves of bread at the ranger station, and hastened back to camp. It was a dark day and the sun was hidden, as it was for many days following.

When I arrived at camp, I found most of the men leaving. I was unable to make them stay by either persuasion or force. However some of the faithful few stuck, among whom was my cook, fortunately. We made arrangements with the foreman of the logging camp to get a line around the lower part of the fire, which was now burning in the watershed where the logging was being done, and we attacked the fire at the top and finally connected up with their fire lines. A patrol was established on these new lines, which formed a circle four or five miles long, and on completion of their trip around the circle the patrol man would report at the camp. The wind continued to blow for four days, gradually slacking on the last day and getting colder, so that the fire went down greatly. It was traveling down hill, and protected from the wind, as well as being on the more moist eastern slope, so we soon had it under control again.

The last few days on the fire in camp on the high ridge I look back to with somewhat of a feeling of pleasure. The weather had changed. It was getting colder and a feeling of approaching autumn was in the air. Everybody seemed to feel that their hard work was nearly over, and their spirits rose accordingly. Around the campfire at night I had a chance to size up my crew. A number of men who had been with me all through the fire were there. One was a young Englishman who had fought in the Boer war. He could tell many exciting stories of his experiences, and also was quite a poet and singer. Often he held the attention of the whole camp as he recited bits of poetry of his own composition, or sang some old English airs. There were also two Montenegrins [immigrants from Montenegro, which was later to become one of the provinces of Yugoslavia] who were the best workers I had, and they had been with me from the first. They were very faithful and never seemed to get tired. One time one of these men was carrying water for the camp in two five-gallon water bags. He had a hard climb up a steep trail, but there was not water enough for all the men to wash. "That all right, I get some more," he said, and though it was late and he had been working hard since early morning, back he went for more water. We also had two southern boys with us from South Carolina. They were a different type from most of the others, but good workers. They were out for a trip to get adventure and experience in the West, and I believe they went home satisfied.

Another young fellow who had been one of the foremen throughout the fire was with us (Guard Burk, later a ranger). He was the wag of the camp, and always making the men laugh with his jokes. I remember he said in regard to our first cook, "He was so greasy that every morning he had to roll in the ashes of the fire to keep from sliding down the hill."

On the night of September 4th raindrops on our faces awakened us. First only a few fell, and then, increasing, it soon began to come down quite heavily. We lay there and enjoyed it. We were glad to get wet, for we knew our long fight was over. The next day the rain continued, so we broke up our camp, and I bid an affectionate farewell to the faithful crew, the men going on their various ways, most of them never to see each other again. I returned to Wallace, where the people were just recovering from the effects of the fire. The hills surrounding the city, which formerly had been so green and beautiful, were now bare and black.

One of the first things that we found it necessary to do after the fire was to clear out our old trails. Most of these were absolutely impassable, and not an easy matter. Gangs of men were out on this work all the fall. Great tree trunks were piled across the trails in twisted and broken tangles, often five trees high, and it was necessary to cut through all this with axe and saw. This work took much time and money.

Nine

"Put Them Dead Out as Quickly as Possible"

What the Fires Wrought

The fires of 1910 transformed forestry in the Inland Northwest. The scope and scale of the fires and the need for response dramatically reshaped the way foresters assessed their obligations. The culture of the agency, the way in which foresters saw themselves, and nearly everything else about the agency at the grass roots changed in the aftermath of the fires of 1910. The foresters faced a different world after the fires. More than three million acres burned in the 1,736 fires, destroying communities, farmland, and barren land as well as timber. At least eighty-five deaths were recorded; of the dead, seventy-eight were firefighters.

The fires of 1910 reminded foresters of their own mortality and forced the agency to face its ineffectuality. Despite knowledge of earlier large-scale fires in the United States and significant management experience in the north woods, the Forest Service was unprepared to fight massive conflagration. It lacked the resources to support even a forestwide protection scheme, much less a regional disaster. Beyond the very few foresters, the personnel available to fight fire were largely undisciplined and inexperienced. The summer of 1910 taught hard lessons.

As much as thirty years later, the jolt to standard ways of operating that the fires of 1910 caused was still the pivotal force in the cosmology of the Forest Service, not only in the Northwest but throughout the nation. Federal foresters were as scarred by their ineffectiveness as the forests were by fire. USFS leaders began a systematic campaign to acquire the resources necessary to prevent such fires from ever reoccurring. In the thirty years that followed the fires, the agency invested what resources it received based on its collective memories of that summer.

The immediate aftermath of the summer of 1910 was a change in the way foresters saw the world around them. Their previous view had been of a pristine and benign world—dangerous, but only to those who did not respect it. That naive sense was replaced by a more guarded response as well as a mechanistic approach that involved re-creating the disappeared forests by means of a blueprint based in the values and technology of an industrial society with a yen for efficiency, an emphasis on management, and faith in credentials that certified expertise. In a reflective essay, T. Shoemaker tried to make sense of the experience from both a temporal and spiritual perspective. His defense of his agency and analysis of the problems it faced were prescient, if skewed to its mainstream perspective:

> The awful holocaust of August 1910 snuffed out the lives of more than 80 fire fighters and laid waste half a million acres of timber. This was not just a single fire at its beginning, but a sudden breaking away of many fires that had been burning for days. Men were on these fires or cutting their way to them when a gale of tornado-like force struck and sent them roaring and spotting ahead, fanning sparks into blazes and blazes into crown fires that joined other fires to form an almost solid front as it crossed the Bitterroot Mountains into Montana. It consisted of overheated air that swept up from the desert-like plains of central Washington and was almost entirely lacking in humidity. It was unforeseen because the weather-forecasting system that plays such a vital part in present-day fire fighting was not then in force.
>
> On it swept, its progress greatly accelerated by burning fagots hurtling from exposed ridgetops out across intervening canyons to set new fires. These in turn quickly became crown fires that swept up to the next ridgetops to repeat the process. Entire wooded slopes and the headwaters of many branches of the Clearwater, St. Joe and Coeur d'Alene Rivers were blackened.
>
> Where the wind got a clear sweep it pushed fingers out ahead of the main fire. One of these pointed toward the city of Missoula and came near enough to shower its streets with ashes and

burned-out embers. Missoula is about 100 miles, air line, east of Wallace, Idaho, which being hemmed in between very steep, heavily wooded slopes, caught fire and suffered heavy damage.

It is but natural to ask why this happened and to wonder whether it will ever happen again. This resolves itself into many specific questions, among which the one that bears most directly on the subject of progress in fire control is this: Why were so many fires still burning several days after the storm which set them? Before answering this question, let us try to frame a question so comprehensive that a single answer will cover its many elements, at least in a general way.

Why did those men have to die, literally burned at the stake, and all that valuable timber have to go up in smoke? The answer is that our Government waited too long before putting the forest lands of the West under protection. It waited too long because of the apathy or unawareness of the Members of Congress and of the people at large. The people of the West were too busy getting title to the land and exploiting the timber and other resources, and the people of the East were too far away to care or even know about problems in the West.

To an extent, and in a very general way, this answers the specific question as to why so many fires were still burning when the gale hit, but because of its bearing on the progress that has been made toward adequate fire control, this question should be answered in more detail.

At that time few lookout stations had been established, due to lack of funds and time for building the trails and telephone lines to connect them, hence some fires doubtless had not even been discovered, and certainly others had not been discovered until they had spread to large size. Some of the known fires were remote from trails and the crews sent to them had to fight their way through thick timber and undergrowth with their tools, food and beds on their backs. This meant delay.

Few men had had experience in fighting fires up to that time, and doubtless poor strategy and techniques accounted for delay in gaining control in some cases. Fighting forest fires is a science, and there had not been time enough to develop it when these men were confronted with the problem of where to begin and what kind of line it takes to hold fire from crossing it. They would, in most instances, have arrived at the fire tired out, the less hardy ones exhausted even, with food not well adapted to the purpose and insufficient in quantity, and the location of water and a safe place to camp unknown to them. With a hundred or more fires widely distributed, it is not hard to explain why many of them would still be burning for days after the storm struck.

Other factors, chiefly that of morale of the men so hastily gathered, had their effect on the output of line built and held. The fact that fires were destroying the forest meant little or nothing to most people in those days. There had always been fires and always would be, they thought. Anyway, it was just a job to most of them, and unless there was the best of leadership—foremen who knew how to handle men—they would not deliver even a reasonable amount of fireline.

Regardless of the reasons, the fact that many fires were burning when the wind hit was the crux of the situation. Winds do not start fires, they only make them spread faster, and in forest fires the spread is often augmented greatly when flames reach the crowns where the wind has a clear sweep.

The lesson taught is that any time fires are burning out of control they are a hazard. In terms of action, this means simply that men must get to fires in the shortest possible time and put them dead out as quickly as possible. Back of that, of course, are many things—prompt discovery and reporting; fast travel and transportation of equipment; preparedness in all its details; and most important of all, men with the determination and know-how to make every fire a dead fire in the shortest possible time.

This concept of fire suppression dominated the subsequent sixty years of federal fire management policy, long after scientists and others recognized that natural fires had regenerative and transformative characteristics that benefited timbered land. Full-fledged fire suppression grew out of the fires of 1910 and became the most rigid of dogmas. Since the Forest Service became the lead agency for fire management in the federal system, its values were transmitted across a range of bureaus, administrations, and generations. It was not until the 1970s that advances in science and the hard realities of dramatically increased fuel loads, which caused increasingly fierce conflagrations, led to the development of new alternatives.

The fires of 1910 created a deep-seeded and sometimes irrational kind of fear in the people who experienced them. Uncontrolled fire became an emotional enemy that could and did take the lives of friends, threaten all that individual foresters held dear, and challenge the very basis of activities of the Forest Service. After 1910, no forester ever took distant smoke lightly.

The experience of the fires made people profoundly reflective, forcing them to recognize their personal shortcomings along with those of their agency. Roy A. Phillips of the Lolo National Forest offered a postfire view of the agency before the fires:

> The year 1910 was pretty much a one-man show and that will be as I will always remember it. Foresters as a class had very little if any training as fire fighters. Trails were few and those that did exist had been blazed out by trappers, prospectors, miners, and others having some interest or investment in forested areas. Discovery of fires was the result of patrols, often seen only after fires had burned several days and columns of smoke had drifted high into the sky. Patrol men tried to make some high point immediately after lightning storms but this often meant fighting dense brush up a steep mountain for hours at a time. Often when men reached a fire they were too worn out to fight it and had no food supplies or effective tools to work with.

T. Shoemaker had observations about the fate of those thought lost who managed to survive the debacle as well as those who did not:

> A few lines about the men who, from day to day, came straggling in out of the blackened waste, weak and emaciated from lack of food, feet burned and skin blistered, clothing in shreds, and faces bewhiskered and begrimed to the point of making them unrecognizable. The strong helped the weak up the steep slopes, over the down logs and through the roughest spots, but even they were scratched, bruised and limping at the finish.

With each new arrival came renewed hope for those still missing, but finally all hope had to be abandoned, and in its stead the most grueling task of all was faced—the search for and recovery of the bodies of those who perished.

Bodies were found widely separated—one here, two or three there, several close together elsewhere. Mostly they were along trails which they vainly hoped would lead them to safety, or in the beds of streams where they had submerged their bodies as the only chance of survival, only to be suffocated or scalded in the sizzling water as the burning embers dropped in around them.

Heroically, and methodically, the search went on until all were accounted for. But not all could be identified and some were not claimed by anyone, since they were transients with no next of kin known. It is gratifying to know that a sightly plot of ground was set aside for the burial of all the men whose relatives preferred it, as well as the unidentified, in the cemetery at St. Maries, Idaho. It was appropriately monumented and is scrupulously tended as a mark of respect to the men who, in life, essayed to save the forest from destruction by fire but were themselves destroyed by it.

Among the bodies recovered were those of 5 men taken from the shallow tunnel into which the heroic Ranger Pulaski took his crew of 40 men as the only chance of survival. The tunnel's entrance was at the bottom of a canyon whose slopes on either side were very steep and heavily wooded. As the fire passed over, great trees, uprooted or broken off by the gale, tumbled or slid down, creating a veritable furnace around the mouth of the tunnel that exhausted all the oxygen. As breathing became difficult the men instinctively fought to get out. That would have meant certain death, but Pulaski held them back at gunpoint and commanded them to lie down and suck air from the damp floor of the tunnel. Finally, quiet reigned and Pulaski lay down in the most exposed position, the last he remembered until several hours later when the fire had pretty well burned itself out. He was awakened by men crawling out over his body and heard one of them say, "Too damned bad, the ranger is dead."

As might be guessed, all the men became unconscious. All regained consciousness but 5, and after all efforts to revive them failed and it became light enough to see to find his way, Pulaski led and helped the others down over or under the charred timbers and around the boulders that had tumbled down to obstruct the trail. At

The mouth of War Eagle tunnel, where Pulaski and his crew took cover during the fires of 1910. (Photo courtesy USDA Forest Service)

last they reached Wallace, and to its citizens who knew their approximate whereabouts and had given up all hope of their escape, it was like seeing them rise from the dead. Pulaski nearly lost his sight from exposure to the heat and glare as he stood guard at the mouth of that tunnel, and carried other ill effects to the day of his death.

How were the awful 1910 fires put out? It certainly was not by anything men did, or could have done. Those fires were stopped dead in their tracks by a change in the weather as sudden as was that which started them on the rampage. It rained for days, and although the break came some 10 days earlier than normal, the fuels never became dry enough to let them start up again. As a consequence, little was learned about the strategy and technique of fighting fires in times of high fire danger.

Joseph B. Halm of the Coeur d'Alene National Forest emerged from the fire to offer heartfelt sentiments about the experience and those it claimed:

Returning to Wallace from the St. Joe River fires, I learned that the outside world had suffered far more than we. Eighty-nine men had given up their lives in the great holocaust. The hospitals were overflowing with sick and injured. Hundreds had become homeless refugees.

Assigned the task of photographing the scene of the many casualties, I had an opportunity to observe the extent of the appalling disaster and to reconstruct the scene of the last, hopeless stand taken by those heroic, unselfish men who gave their lives that others might live. Still, not all those heroic efforts were hopeless or vain. Ranger Pulaski, who so valiantly saved all but six of a large crew, has become a national hero, an outstanding figure in the annals of forest history.

Forest Supervisor Weigle, who for weeks had so tirelessly worked day and night, unselfishly and alone plunged through the very face of the tempest of fire in an attempt to warn the citizens of Wallace of their danger. At last hopelessly trapped, he rushed through a burning mining mill into a tunnel. As the building fell the tunnel caved, threatening to bury him alive. Covering his head with his coat, he crawled out, plunging through the burning wreckage into a tiny creek. In a few hours he had worked his way through the fire to Wallace, there directing and assisting with the dead and injured.

Ranger Danielson, who so courageously led his little crew into an open mining cut on a mountain-side, will bear the horrible, purple scars on neck and hands to his grave, as will all those who were with him. Rangers Phillips, Watson, Vandyke, Rock, Bell, and many others saved the lives of hundreds by their cool, timely judgment. Scores of other unsung heroes still live and work among us, their fortitude a bright and lasting example.

On Big Creek, thirty men lost their lives while others lay prone for hours in the chilling waters of a tiny stream, great forest giants falling around and across them. Here three men were crushed by a falling tree. One of these unfortunates was caught only by the foot. Men a few feet away heard his cries and prayers, but were powerless to assist. He dug and fought to tear away, but the thing which he had come to save held him fast until coma and finally death relieved his sufferings. On Seltzer Creek the ghastly human

Ranger Edward Pulaski, one of the heroes of the fires of 1910. Note the burns on his face. (Photo courtesy National Archives)

toll was twenty-nine. An entire crew was annihilated. The men fell as they ran before the merciless fire.

Each scene is a gripping story of almost unparalleled heroism and sacrifice. Our experience as compared with these was tame, indeed, insignificant.

More than three decades have passed through the hour-glass of

Cleaning up the damage after the fires of 1910 in the Coeur d'Alene National Forest. (Photo courtesy USDA Forest Service)

time and nature has long since reclothed the naked landscape with grass, shrubs and trees, but the great sacrifice of human life is not, and can never be, replaced or forgotten.

Edward G. Stahl of the Kootenai National Forest reflected on the way in which the fire affected animals in the forests:

The destruction of animal life in the forest fires, as noted by the writer, is not pleasant to contemplate. The clowning bear, the chattering squirrel, even the fleet-footed deer, all suffer death in the forest fire. The animals that escaped the flames and were seen near our camp were dazed. Squirrels and chipmunks could be picked up, deer fed near the camp.

John F. Preston of the Flathead National Forest commented on the limitations of the response of the Forest Service to the fires:

> Bill (W. C.) McCormick was Ranger (or was it guard?) on the North Fork of the Flathead during the 1910 fires. His system of firefighting in 1910 was to put out all the fires that he could by himself or with the few guards assigned to his district and then when the fires got too big, ride to Belton, which was the nearest telephone and source of supplies, some 40 miles away, for help, gather a crew and equipment together, go back over the trail and to the fires. It is no wonder that the 1910 fires spread all over the country.

Destructive as the fires were, they were also a great advantage for the nascent regional timber industry. The fires destroyed much timber but left much salvageable downed timber in their wake. The fires also made access to some previously remote timbered areas much easier, as C. S. Webb of the St. Joe National Forest recalled:

> The 1910 fires burned large areas of the St. Joe, Coeur d'Alene and Cabinet Forests. By 1913 logging was brisk in these areas. The Wintons built a mill at Rose Lake, Idaho, and started cutting on Independence Creek in 1911, driving the logs all the way to Rose Lake. Herrick built the Milwaukee Lumber Company mill at St. Maries in 1911, and St. Maries Lumber Company—a Michigan concern—built one there in 1912. This is the present Pugh Mill. Coeur d'Alene had the Coeur d'Alene Mill Company, Largey Estate interests, the Stack Gibbs Lumber Company—presently Browns Mill—and the William and David Dollar interests. McGoldrick Lumber Company was established at Spokane, the Export Lumber Company and Grant Lumber Company were at Harrison, and I believe Russell and Pugh were there. The Mann Lumber Company had a large mill at the west end of St. Regis cutoff.
>
> Timber in the white pine belt swept by 1910 fires was mostly large old growth, quite sound, choice white pine. Logging was somewhat difficult, with big horses furnishing the skidding power. Horse-skidding, chutes, flumes, railroads and river-driving

were the means of transportation. There were no "cats," no trucks. Sleigh haul was employed a lot on Priest River, Pack River and the Kootenai. Big river drives were the order of the day each spring on the Kootenai, Pack, Priest, Coeur d'Alene and St. Joe Rivers. The "river pigs" had considerable leeway in moving about. The Milwaukee [rail]road had been completed through St. Maries in 1910, so by 1913 the plants there that were logging by rail hauled their logs clear to the mill by rail. Milwaukee trains at that time did not run through Spokane. Early in 1915 the Union Station at Spokane was completed and the Milwaukee started routing its passenger trains through that city.

The damage to the vast forests of the Inland Northwest changed the needs of management in Region 1. Instead of having millions of acres of timber to administer, the domain included more than one million acres denuded of trees. Forest science was in its infancy, and the Forest Service regarded timber production and management as its primary if not sole obligation. Lacking an understanding of the nature of forest regeneration, the Forest Service faced what its leaders perceived as an imperative: the need to replenish the necessarily diminished stock of timber with seedlings that would mature into board feet of lumber.

This was a tremendous job for which the Forest Service was only marginally prepared. It had inherited vast forested land at its founding and had never been faced with the need for comprehensive management. The changed sense of responsibilities took two major forms: better training, particularly in fire suppression and firefighting, and a massive planting effort. But the Forest Service lacked an infrastructure capable of supporting a widespread fire-suppression program as well as of creating and distributing the vast number of seedlings to the many locations where they were necessary.

To fulfill this new and urgent responsibility, the Forest Service broadened the structure of its operation in Montana and Idaho. The establishment of communication systems, such as telephone lines to speed the spread of news, was crucial. Smoke-jumping schools, such as one described by Ralph Thayer, became common:

A 1920s smokechaser starting for a fire. (Photo courtesy USDA Forest Service)

The last part of June 1911, we had smokechaser school at Indian Creek in Glacier National Park. Supervisor R. P. McLaughlin was there. Along with Ranger W. C. McCormick I helped build Moran Ranger Station, skidded the logs into where we put up the Ranger Station. George Grubb was an old timer from eastern Montana. He was a blacksmith at Zortman, Montana, in his early days. In 1908 he settled on a homestead in what is now Glacier National Park. He was a real good broad-axe man. A fellow by the name of Ben Mace and myself sawed logs for George. Between cooking times and chasing smoke we hung an emergency wire telephone line. It was something in those days to keep the telephone lines up.

Telephone.lines remained a problem for the Forest Service, particularly in the aftermath of the fire. Joseph B. Halm recounted his experiences hanging wire:

> The spring of 1910 I was assigned the job of building telephone lines. The first line was between Taft, Montana, and Avery, Idaho, via the summit of St. Paul Pass over the C. M. P. S. tunnel to Grand Forks, to St. Joe Ranger Station and down the North Fork to Avery. The crew consisted of Ed Holcomb, Harvey Fearn, Tom Robinson (acting cook), John Winnington and myself. We also built a line from Kellogg, Idaho, to Montgomery Creek Ranger Station and that fall after the great fire, we rebuilt the line between Wallace and the St. Joe Ranger Station near Grand Forks. These lines were mostly grounded lines and hung on topped trees. The trees were climbed and the tops cut out similar to spar trees on the coast but of course were not as high.

Technological innovations also occurred in the wake of the fires. Those who fought the fires of 1910 often found themselves without the tools to do the job, a fact that Halm was instrumental in remedying:

> During the winter of 1910 the first Pulaski tool came into being. Supervisor Weigle requested Ed Holcomb and me to design and make a model of a shovel, axe and mattock combination tool suitable for patrolman's use.
>
> I took a double-bitted ax and with Mr. Holcomb's help cut off one blade leaving a spike. To this spike I welded the cut-off portion of the ax blade which, when drawn out and shaped, became the mattock blade. The shovel attachment was made from an old burned-out shovel cut down. The shovel sleeve was flattened and shaped to fit over the ax head. A hole was drilled through the ax head and sleeve for a bolt with a wing nut. The model was exhibited at the supervisors' meeting in Missoula the spring of 1911 but apparently nothing was done about it at that time. The shovel at-

tachment never was practical for obvious reasons, but years later the same ax-mattock combination with minor improvements was adopted as standard equipment and is now known as the Pulaski Tool.

In reforestation, the Forest Service quickly transformed its operations to meet the vast need created by the fires. The forests benefited from both natural conditions and increased planning. Ryle Teed recalled the gathering of seeds in units called "squirrel camps," which began to become important in 1911:

> I took a string of horses into a camp where Ralph was cooking for one of the "squirrel camps." Yes, I know. "Squirrel camp" sounds like maybe a field party from a nuthouse. That wasn't it, though. The year 1911 was a wonderful seed year and the Service really stocked up on western white pine seed. Several camps were organized and worked the area between Priest Lake and the Pend Oreille River. All available labor from the forest and farm communities was used, and in addition many laborers from the Spokane market—and they weren't all woodsmen. The camps were squirrel camps because the principal method of gathering was to prowl more or less aimlessly through the woods watching for squirrels. The squirrels would lead you to their caches, which you would rob, not without objection from the rightful owners. The cones were sacked and stood along the trail for pickup by the pack trains which were covering the country being worked. I believe the pickers were paid $1.50 per sack. The payoff was finding all the pickers at the end of the day. Some were lost nearly every day and had to be rounded up. Most of the nonwoodsmen would lose their heads and then trails and telephone lines meant nothing to them whatever. A pair of them actually waded across Priest River, although they couldn't help knowing that they were all camped west of the river.

The Savenac Nursery at Haugan, Montana, played a critical role in the reseeding and replanting effort and came to supply most of the seedlings in the region. David S. Olson of the Lolo

National Forest recounted the origin and development of what became known as Uncle Sam's Biggest Nursery:

> On a honeymoon trip by horseback, Elers Koch spotted a small clearing abandoned by a German homesteader named Savennach [this spelling may be incorrect, but it was not Savenac as Olson spelled the name of the nursery] that impressed him as an ideal site for a small tree nursery to serve the needs of his forest. That was the beginning of Savenac Nursery.
>
> Seed beds were prepared on this small patch in 1908. Three similar nurseries were under development in the Region at this time: Trapper Creek to serve the Bitterroot, Camp Crook, South Dakota, to serve the Dakota National Forest, and the Boulder Nursery for the Helena. These small nurseries were operated by District Rangers and called Ranger nurseries. The disastrous fires of 1910 changed all this. Now a tremendous job of reforesting the 1910 burns faced the Region. Savenac Nursery was wiped out by these fires before the first crop of seedlings was ready for planting but it was decided to rebuild and enlarge this nursery to serve all the western forests of the Region and particularly the planting needs on the three million acres burned over in 1910. The Boulder Nursery continued operations until 1916; the other two nurseries were abandoned earlier.
>
> Land clearing of the thirty-one acres of benchland along Savenac Creek started immediately. By 1915 it was fully stocked with about ten million trees of various age classes and ready to maintain an annual output of three million trees [this amount would plant about 5,000 acres annually]. It had become the largest tree nursery in the Forest Service.
>
> During this early period of development, Savenac Nursery remained under the administration of the Lolo Forest. Supervisor Koch spent much of his time directing the work, with Ranger Frank Haun and Assistant Ranger Will Simons supervising operations. Research to aid in developing nursery practices was being carried on at the Priest River Experiment Station.
>
> I went to Savenac Nursery to work several weeks before returning to school. This time Jim Brooks and I were used on time studies being made of the transplanting operation. Some members of

These screened enclosures protected seed beds at the Savenac Nursery in Haugen, Montana. (Photo courtesy USDA Forest Service)

the Regional Office—Regional Forester F. A. Silcox, Assistant Regional Foresters Dave Mason and Roy Headley and Chief of Planting H. H. Farquhar—had become interested in the principles of scientific management as practiced in the Franklin auto factories at that time. Savenac Nursery seemed to be a good place to apply these principles. As a result of the time studies that fall Savenac developed a transplanting operation that was by far the cheapest in the United States. In a two-hour period, Jim Brooks and I, as a team, transplanted 9,000 seedlings, a record that still stands. It probably was my interest in these studies that was instrumental in my being offered the job as nurseryman the following year.

Since the nursery was now serving many forests of the Region and the work there was looked upon as highly specialized, it was decided in late 1914 to place it under the direct supervision of the Regional Office. In the spring of 1915 it assumed this new status and I was offered the job as nurseryman, at a salary of $1,100 per annum. At the same time E. C. Rogers was transferred from the Priest River Experiment Station to Savenac to continue research on the propagation of planting stock for this region. Rogers wanted to carry his nursery studies into the field for final determination of results and for this purpose established what we called the Wallace Experimental Area, about three miles south of Wallace on Placer Creek. Today this is an interesting study area.

If ever a guy was plopped squarely in the middle of things to work his way out, that was me when I landed at Savenac March 1, 1915, fresh out of school. I think the biggest break I got that difficult first year was an unseasonably early spring. We were able to put the plow in the ground the day I arrived and there were no setbacks due to unfavorable weather that year.

Of course, there was no clerk at the nursery and I was completely ignorant of fiscal and administrative procedures so I soon encountered trouble. In those days we hired and fired at will. Most of the 40–man crew consisted of transients "riding the rails" and dropping off at Haugan for a short period of work at the nursery. When they quit or were fired, I paid them with personal checks and obtained "cash receipts" for the payments. These receipts were then submitted on expense accounts for reimbursement. Thus, it seemed, my slim capital would serve as a revolving fund and take care of the situation ad infinitum. That is, I thought I could send in my expense account and have the expense check back in a day or two for deposit. Hah! I didn't know how many errors the fiscal office could find in an expense account. As a result, the three saloonkeepers in Haugan were soon waving fists full of checks in my face—checks that had been returned for lack of sufficient funds. I knew nothing of the $50.00 limit on purchases without bids until the fiscal agent began firing back the vouchers. Nor did I know that laborers for the Federal Government could not be paid on a piece-rate basis such as we were using on some of the nursery operations for speeding up performance. I was told to adjust the men's earnings to an hourly basis on the payrolls and this resulted in some fantastic rates, such as 28 and 39/61sts cents an hour. Incidentally, the base rate of pay for labor was 25 cents an hour plus board, which cost the Government about 25 cents per meal.

The total planting allotment for Region One was about $40,000 at this time. This was enough to pay all the costs related to producing the stock and planting about 4,000 acres annually. At Savenac, every effort was concentrated in producing as much good stock as possible on the thirty-one acres at the lowest possible cost. Development work went into research, devising new methods and equipment, and time studies to improve efficiency in nursery operations. Buildings and grounds lacked much to be desired and our standard equipment and watering systems were "haywire." We got along somehow.

In a few years the work at this hustling young nursery was getting some attention from the outside. Research was paying dividends in reduced losses and high-quality stock. Cost of tree production was the lowest in the Service. Some of the new developments in methods and equipment were aimed at meeting problems peculiar to the Region but found wider application and were adopted elsewhere. For example, the cylindrical burlap-covered tree bale was developed for pack mule transportation. In those days, nearly all tree shipments left Savenac by railroad express. From the nearest railroad point the trees were taken by pack train to the planting camps. The dead weight of the wooden crates formerly used was about equal to the weight of the trees. Material used for the bales was much cheaper and its weight only a few pounds, and this cut transportation costs just about in half. The bale is in general use today even though transportation of trees from the nurseries to the planting sites is largely by truck.

Another change made in these early days that was receiving wide acceptance was the use of shingle tow (the shreddy sawdust from shingle mills) instead of sphagnum moss for packing material to keep the roots of the seedlings moist en transit. Shingle tow was available at a local mill for the cost of hauling, whereas sphagnum moss cost $20.00 per ton plus freight from Wisconsin. In addition, the moss had to be fumigated when it reached Savenac to avoid the danger of introducing the eastern larch saw fly to this region. The bales of moss were placed in a tent and subjected to potassium cyanide fumes for 24 hours. A guard was stationed outside the tent during this period so no one would accidentally stick his head in the "gas chamber." Today, nurseries all over the country

Planting seedlings at the Savenac Nursery. (Photo courtesy USDA Forest Service)

use shingle tow in preference to sphagnum moss when they can obtain it at competitive costs.

We were beginning to have visitors. Foresters from here and abroad were calling at the nursery to see our operations and tourists were stopping in increasing numbers. E. E. Carter, Chief of Timber Management in the Washington Office, was showing unusual interest in the developments at Savenac and talking about them to other Regions. Savenac Nursery was beginning to ride the crest.

E. F. White, who had succeeded Farquhar as Chief of Planting about the time I took over the nursery, now saw a chance to go after the other phase of developments for Savenac—improvements in buildings, grounds, and other major facilities for operating the nursery. He brought Regional Forester Silcox out to the nursery and convinced him that Savenac should be made a showplace for the Region. Silcox was enthusiastic and immediately sent an engineer to the nursery to develop a 20-year improvement plan including detailed design and specifications. The plan provided facilities for regional meetings—especially during the winter—as well as improvements for the operation of the nursery. We had no idea where the money would come from for these improvements but it developed that by having the plan, money came from an unexpected source. Carter, in Washington, saw to it that unexpended planting balances in other Regions were transferred to Savenac. These balances were never available until about June 1, so for three years there were hectic times during June to make the most of these windfalls. The original 20-year plan was completed in three years. Today that would be simple with the many servicing divisions in the Region, but we had to do our own purchasing and our own construction work. For example, I had never laid a brick but I learned and by the time I left the Region I had built 16 chimneys and a stone fireplace for the Forest Service. Our greatest obstacle at this time was the $650.00 statutory limitation placed on all Forest Service buildings. There was no limit to water systems, septic tanks and the like, but building costs were thus limited, including the cost of labor.

In 1920 I was promoted to chief of planting. Instead of moving to Missoula, I transferred the planting office to Savenac. Savenac was now a little community of residences and yearlong inhabitants. The building limitation had been increased to about $2,000.00 per structure, so we were able to erect several nice cottages for the increased personnel. G. Willard Jones succeeded me as nurseryman, W. G. Wahlenberg handled research (after the death of C. E. Rogers), C. E. Knutson did the planting survey work, and we had a clerk. Frank Haun remained as Ranger for the Savenac District until his retirement 20 years later.

Other changes followed in the wake of the fires. The increase in management meant that the Forest Service had more to offer local people. Jobs planting trees became available seasonally, and the Forest Service came to be seen an asset rather than an intrusion in local life. K. D. Swan of the Dakota National Forest (now the Little Missouri National Grasslands on Custer National Forest), who displayed an intense passion for the scientific side of tree-planting, recalled some of the ways in which the spread of technology and infrastructure changed life in the Forest Service:

Automobiles were not in general use for prairie travel when I first rode out to the Dakota Forest from Bowman, North Dakota, in the latter part of April, 1912. Horses were considered a most dependable means of transportation, and forest officers thought nothing of making daily rides of fifty miles or more in the performance of their official duties. To an eastern-bred boy, recently graduated from the Harvard Forest School, this means of getting around seemed fascinating indeed, and it was with elation that I learned the Supervisor had left his saddle horse in a livery barn in Bowman for me to ride out to the Ranger Station. Later I was to ride from there to Camp Crook, the headquarters town of the old Sioux National Forest, from which the Dakota Forest was administered. I became well acquainted later with this Supervisor, Charles Ballinger, a kindly and able man who had the love and loyalty of those with whom he worked.

Spring had touched the prairies as I rode north from Bowman on that bright April morning. There was a shimmer of green on the rolling hills, and shrubs and trees showed signs of leafing out along the coulees. It was an era of homesteading. Many fields had been fenced and planted to grain or flax. I noticed the homes that these newcomers had built—some of them made of sod, others covered with tarpaper. I soon learned to detect the pungent smell of burning lignite coal, a fuel which did much to make the settlement of this prairie country possible. I remember seeing a homesteader digging coal from a bank near a coulee bottom. We had a little talk before I rode on.

Before leaving the Regional Office in Missoula (then called the District Office), I was given rather complete instructions as to what my duties would be as Forest Assistant on the Sioux and Dakota Forests. I was to become thoroughly acquainted with the far-flung divisions of the Sioux—the Long Pines, the Short Pines, the Ekalaka, the Cave Hills, and the Slim Buttes, for the purpose of preparing a silvical [silviculture] report and an economic plan for the best use of their resources. My duties on the Dakota Forest would deal primarily with planting projects. I was to assist the Ranger in expanding the forest nursery and selecting suitable sites for planting the young trees. I had gained considerable experience the previous fall on planting projects in the Big Snowies of central Montana, and R. Y. Stuart, then chief of Silviculture in District

One [and later U.S. Forester] felt that this experience might prove helpful in getting a planting program under way on the Dakota and Sioux Forests.

The Logging Camp Ranger Station was on Deep Creek, a tributary of the Little Missouri River. One saw it first from the head of a broad swale which led down from the higher prairie. It seemed an oasis among scoria buttes and badland bluffs on which were growing scattered ponderosa pines and junipers. There was a long one-room building, with a screened-in porch the entire length of the south side, and a substantial gambrel roof barn across the yard at the rear. The small nursery was near the creek south and west of the buildings. This nursery was irrigated by water pumped from the creek, which, as I remember, never ran dry. Green ash and other small trees grew along the stream and provided welcome shade on hot days.

Ralph Sheriff was Ranger in charge at the station. My first meeting with him came as I entered the building and found him taking a siesta on the bed, surrounded by several cats. Ralph was a graduate of the University of Illinois and had come to the western Dakotas with one of his college chums named Haines. The boys had worked for some time building sod houses for homesteaders in the country around Lemmon and Hettinger, and then decided to take the Civil Service examination for the position of Forest Ranger in the United States Forest Service. Both passed. Haines was appointed to help Supervisor Ballinger in the Camp Crook office of the Sioux—Sheriff got the job on the Dakota.

Sheriff was a very capable man, practical and able to do many things well. He was good at handling men and was well liked by all that worked with him. In dress he was quite unconventional, but he was a man of cleanly habits. He was always smiling and nothing ever disturbed him much—a good quality for a forest officer in those days. He was of medium height and rather stocky.

Work in the nursery was in full swing shortly after my arrival. Seedlings of ponderosa pine had to be transplanted from the beds where they had been grown from seed to other beds where they would be evenly spaced and have room to develop until they were three or four years old and ready to be set out in the field. A device known as the Yale planting board was used for transplanting. This consisted of a narrow board with notches in which the seedlings were placed so that the roots extended beyond the edge of the board. Another board of corresponding size was hinged so that it could be closed down on the crowns of the seedlings. When lifted, the evenly spaced seedlings were held securely in place with their roots hanging down so that they could be placed in a trench made ready for them. After the earth was firmed around them, the planting board was opened and removed for another loading of seedlings. The roots of coniferous species are very easily damaged by exposure to drying wind or sunlight and must be kept in the shade during the transplanting operations. For this purpose a rough booth was constructed of canvas tarps.

Homesteaders, known locally as "honyocks" (the meaning of the term remains obscure), jumped at the chance to pick up some badly needed cash by working in the nursery. There were several young couples whom I remember well, although I cannot recall all their names. One tall boy, Harry Roberts, was at the time courting the girl he afterwards married. I also remember Joe Miller, and his sister Marjorie, who later became Mrs. Ralph Sheriff. Several older folks also took part.

Travel home at night for most of these people was impossible, so they camped at the nursery. Well do I remember the happy evenings spent around the campfire exchanging stories or listening to music played on the violin and guitar by two of the talented persons of our little group.

After transplanting was finished, considerable field planting was done on various areas in the vicinity of the Ranger Station. I believe one of these areas was on Sand Creek. Planting was done by two-man crews. One man would dig a hole with a mattock; the other would place the seedling and press the dirt firmly around the roots. Many of the seedlings were set in the loose soil on the slopes of the scoria buttes. Rattlesnakes were a menace, and one had to be on constant alert when planting in these locations.

Much of the stock set out in these operations came from the Savenac Nursery in the Lolo Forest of western Montana. It was shipped by rail to Bowman in bales protected by burlap and transported to the Ranger Station by wagon. It is believed that a good deal of this stock was from seed collected in the Black Hills (*Pinus ponderosa,* var. scopulorum). Eventually, young trees from the

Dakota nursery would be used for planting, but at this time no stock of the right age was available from this source.

We felt at the time that the best planting sites were on slopes where some tree growth was already established rather than on areas which were more or less flat and where the seedlings would have strong competition from the prairie grass. I believe that where planting was done on grassy land, the trees were set in furrows made by a sod-breaking plow. In the more rolling terrain where pines of considerable age and size were growing were sites which seemed well adapted for successful planting. There were north slopes which were partially protected from the hot sun and also from the drying winds that swept across the prairie from the south and west. The soil in these locations was more or less loose and seemed capable of soaking up moisture readily. Here, in contrast to the heavily sodded areas, there would be much less grass competition. Whether or not our surmises were correct, I do not know. Studies were never carried to completion, to my knowledge.

But one region could only support a single major nursery, and the Dakota National Forest nursery was abandoned after only a few years.

In the aftermath of the fires, means of reseeding other than planting seedlings were attempted. William W. Morris of the Coeur d'Alene National Forest participated in experiments in direct seeding:

> After the 1910 fires much more attention was given to planting and restocking denuded areas. The tremendous loss through the non-use of vast areas of waste land began to make itself felt. In the fall of 1912 almost 2,400 acres on the Coeur d'Alene National Forest were seeded to white and yellow pine, the seeding being done with corn planters. This area was rather inaccessible, and it was necessary to build three miles of trail over a high ridge to get to it.
>
> Many a farmer's boy has used a corn planter all day where the fields are level and free from obstructions, but it is quite another thing to work steadily all day long, climbing steep hills and rockslides, and jumping over windfalls [trees previously felled by the

wind], all the time trying to keep a straight line, and an even distance apart. A small strip of western yellow pine plants was planted, this strip running clear across the seeding area, including all slopes. This was done in order to get comparisons on planting and sowing, and comparisons on the rate of growth on various slopes. At this camp our supplies were first shipped by rail to the town of Prichard, Idaho, from Wallace, a distance of about thirty-eight miles. From Prichard they were hauled by a wagon a distance of six miles up the Coeur d'Alene river, much of the road being in the river bottom, to the mouth of Lost Creek. From the mouth of Lost Creek, they were packed on horses, and taken about five miles over the temporary trail, which we had built. The difficulty of getting supplies to these inaccessible places is one of the chief factors for a logging company to consider, when undertaking a logging operation in these regions.

The area that we were attempting to restock was almost completely denuded of tree growth. Several fires had run over it and the last one in 1910 had almost cleaned it up. Hardly a seed tree was left which might in time restock the area. It was an ideal place for such work.

One night at this camp we had a very heavy windstorm. There were several burnt snags standing near our tents, and we were much afraid one of these might go over. These old snags are one of the most dangerous things with which a woodsman has to contend, and they are always careful to pitch their tents away from the reach of one. In our case we had chosen as clear a place as it was possible for us to find. On the ridge above us we could hear almost a continual roar, as tree after tree went over. Fortunately being between two ridges we were not exposed to the wind, and few trees near us went down. The only mishap we had was when a tent blew down in the middle of the night. Although this was a large tent and had quite a number of occupants, all slept soundly until morning, in spite of the fact that the canvas was lying directly upon them.

We had quite a character in that camp. He had been a circus performer, gave balloon ascensions, was a vaudeville actor and a singer, and could turn his hand to most anything. He used to get out in the evenings and in his old boots do stunts on the slack wire which he had found in camp, and strung up between two trees. One time he told me his greatest ambition was to invent a parachute, in which he could safely drop from an aeroplane.

The following year I read in a Spokane paper where a man of the same name, Francis Thayer, had attempted to drop from an aeroplane in a parachute near Seattle, and was drowned in Puget Sound. The wrist strap had broken or become released which attached him to the parachute.

The work on this area lasted about a month. The following spring a large area was planted on Placer Creek near Wallace. This was planted with western yellow pine, Douglas fir, and some western white pine. In order to get to it, so that our planting could be done in the month of May, it was necessary to cut through a snowslide which completely blocked the road at one point. In all about 500,000 young trees, mostly two years old, were planted at this place. This covered an area of approximately six hundred acres. The trees were sent to Wallace from the Savenac Nursery at Haugan, Montana, and from the Boulder Nursery at Helena, Montana. They came done up in bundles of one hundred each, all packed in wet moss, and placed in large strong boxes. Some of the fastest men on the work would plant as many as a thousand trees a day. Our camp at this place reminded me of a young army, for at one time over a hundred men were employed here. At this planting camp I suggested to Pulaski the value of a tool that a man could dig holes with and plant trees also. Pulaski produced one.

Possibly it may be seen to some degree, from what has been said above, something of the nature of what the National Forests are endeavoring to accomplish, in selling their mature timber, in restocking their waste lands, and possibly above all things in giving these lands adequate fire protection. Experience along these lines has improved the methods used wonderfully and the Service is every day becoming more efficient.

After 1910, the Forest Service became dramatically different than it had been at its founding in 1905. Gone were the inefficient patronage recipients, replaced first with tested local people and later with graduates of the forestry schools blossoming around the nation. A new professionalism, of which Gifford Pinchot would have been proud, was emerging. The fires accelerated the process of implementing such trends in the Inland Northwest as well as throughout the Forest Service, simultaneously highlighting the importance of a strong agency infrastructure both on the ground and in personnel. The fires also reinforced the cosmology in which foresters believed and gave the agency vast political clout. Its leaders had only to argue that similar conflagrations would become common if agency requests for personnel and funding were not met. The tragedy of the summer of 1910 also completed the work of building a constituency for the Forest Service among westerners. After 1910, foresters were heroes, and western legislators and their constituents increasingly appreciated the Forest Service and recognized the merit in its claims.

Yet even the vast infrastructural and attitudinal changes within the agency did not change its perception of its values. Foresters clearly recognized the objectives of their agency, as C. W. Webb recounted:

> The Forest Service was a pretty small outfit in 1916 and for sometime thereafter. I recall a detail to Timber Management in 1917, when the complete district office, except for the fiscal agent, had its quarters in the old federal building over the present post office space at Missoula. The aims, objectives and purposes were few in comparison to those of recent years. Principally, the job was visualized to be (a) manage and conserve the timber and range resource, (b) protect timber and range from fire, and (c) get listed and patented all lands which were classified as agricultural in character. Water resources, erosion control, training programs, personnel management, recreational use, information and education, road construction, and many other present-day concerns were never mentioned in those days. There were no motor vehicle accidents to investigate and report on. Yes, life was simple.

Forestry as practiced in the USFS was still a commodity science. Timber management remained the primary objective of the agency and its leadership, and as late as the end of World War I, there was little emphasis on any other kind of value for the forests. Conspicuously absent in the accounts of pre-1915 foresters is any emphasis on watershed, recreation, or wildlife habitat as important considerations. Fire, timber, and occasionally grazing occupied the early Forest Service to an even greater degree after 1910 than before.

By this time, an agency had been formed, developed, and tested. Its resources taxed by a natural disaster, the Forest Service embraced wholeheartedly the ethos of utilitarian conservation to the exclusion of other approaches. There was little room for countercurrents, new ideas, or different methods in the decade that followed.

Ten

"Fresh Challenges
Developed the Fellows"

Creating an Agency from Its Components

By the end of 1910, the Forest Service in the Inland North-west had passed from its initial stages into a more comprehensive kind of management. Much of the reserved land in the region had been surveyed. Large pockets of uncharted land remained, but the Forest Service had a general idea of the nature if not the quantity of its resources in its northernmost domain in the contiguous United States. A rudimentary infrastructure had begun to be developed and the roots of what would become the network of the Forest Service existed. What remained was to develop a system of administration and professional management.

Significant obstacles stood in the way as they had since the inception of the agency. One of the most important of these was political. Early in 1910, the Forest Service underwent major changes at the national level. Its founder and leader, Gifford Pinchot, was forced out in a complicated dispute that revolved around bureau autonomy, the role of the leader of a federal agency, and sheer "turf battles" and politics. Pinchot was replaced by Henry Graves, a close associate from the 1890s who had become dean of the forestry school at Yale University. Although a peer of Pinchot, Graves was less inspiring to the rank and file; after all, he was not the founder of their agency. As a result, agency culture and values hardened, reflecting Pinchot's policies and directives. Its leader figuratively beheaded, the agency began the process of turning Pinchot's policies into dogma.

In places like Region 1, Pinchot was revered. He shaped its direction as much by personal influence as by executive directive. The men and women of the region felt a kinship to Pinchot and his ideas; they had all attempted to execute his policies, and many of their leaders had worked in Pinchot's office. They appreciated the autonomy allowed in the Forest Service, recognized the efficacy of its decentralized strategy, and supported their chief vigorously.

Pinchot's forced departure increased the resolve of the people of his agency to carry out his policies. Most perceived the firing from the perspective of cultural westerners, sensing the intrusive hand of central government and recognizing that slothful bureaucracy—according to their cosmology—had temporarily triumphed over enthusiastic reform. In defiance of changing reality, they clung even more closely to the value system Pinchot established for his agency. There were villains afoot, they thought, as John W. Lowell, a longtime veteran of the agency recalled:

> Looking back over the years, there are certain facts and convictions that stand out prominently in my mind for these early days of the Service.
>
> Beginning with the time when the National Forest Administration was transferred from the Department of the Interior to the Department of Agriculture, there was a jealousy of the growing Forest Service by the Department of the Interior. It began to dawn on people generally, and particularly [Richard A.] Ballinger, who was Secretary of the Interior, that there was an extremely important Governmental Bureau that was destined to affect materially the lives and happiness of the majority of the people in the United States.
>
> This situation led up to the eventual conflict in 1910 between the two departments that resulted in the discharge of Gifford Pinchot in 1910 as head of the Forest Service. Ballinger, the Secretary of the Interior, and [Louis] Glavis, as head of the [General] Land Office, apparently had two particular motives in mind: (1) the discrediting of Pinchot; (2) the dismemberment of the Forest Service and eventual return of this Service to the Department of the Interior.

During this period, I knew from my own responsibilities and activities that the Forest Service was fully cooperating with the Department of the Interior without bias of any kind. This was particularly so in reporting after examination on mining claims and easements within the Forest boundaries, as well as fire cooperation and general land matters and jurisdiction of the Interior Department outside the boundaries of the National Forests.

Gifford Pinchot, in an attempt to save the integrity of the Administration of the Forests, violated what was then a steadfast administrative rule: that Bureau Chiefs must not appear before Congressional Committees to give testimony in behalf of their particular interests. [By the 1990s, agency heads routinely testified in front of Congress and had for decades.]

President Taft, either because of lack of knowledge of the real situation, or being incensed at Pinchot's taking the matter in his own hands with the Congressional Committees, together with his belief that Ballinger and Glavis had more political pull than Pinchot and the Secretary of Agriculture, removed Pinchot—or required the Secretary of the Department of Agriculture to do so.

The esprit d'corps of the Forest Service suffered a severe blow in Pinchot's removal. He was followed by Henry S. Graves, an old classmate of Pinchot's, but he was never able to put the punch and loyalty into the Service that had been initiated by Pinchot.

As the Forest Service grew to be an outstanding, efficient organization in the handling of national resources, the jealousy of the Department of the Interior increased and still exists to this day in 1940.

Lowell can be forgiven his evident bias. Like many of the people of the Forest Service, he was a believer in the near sanctity of its cause. In his time, the Department of the Interior was considered the most corrupt division of the government. Agencies such as the General Land Office were among the worst offenders, and with Lowell's range of knowledge, there were few other conclusions at which he could arrive.

Yet the battles between the Department of the Interior and the Forest Service were rooted in genuine administrative conflicts. They were the natural outgrowth of the creation of entities with overlapping constituencies and conflicting missions. The Forest Service was designated the agency in charge of the national forests, whereas Department of the Interior officials perceived domestic federal resources—including the national forests—as their domain. Particularly under the aggressive Pinchot, it seemed to officials in the Interior Department that the USFS sought to fulfill the duties of Interior bureaus such as the General Land Office. The competition that resulted was not surprising and was actually good for both agencies until it descended to the kind of territoriality that led to Pinchot's dismissal.

Despite any decline in morale that Lowell perceived, foresters remained fiercely loyal to the cosmology of their agency. Pinchot's dismissal renewed a tenacious vigor within an agency made strong by its decentralized management policies, and in the aftermath of Pinchot's departure, regional officials clung even more thoroughly to the doctrines their fallen leader had established. It was as if Forest Service personnel believed they could keep Pinchot in control by reflexively implementing the policies he advocated.

In this manner, policy became doctrine. In a decentralized agency, such a view spread only with the force of the people at the regional level behind it. In Region 1, the ties to Pinchot were strong. From Elers Koch to William Greeley, the leaders in the region had worked closely with Pinchot and had great respect for him and his ideas. The summer of 1910 only added to their determination.

The fires of 1910 became a watershed in District 1. They transformed the way agency officials and operatives saw their job. The response to the conflagration and the need for more sophisticated management expanded the vision of responsibility of regional officials and accelerated trends that were already underway. The fires demanded response; they also provided an overwhelming rationale for more comprehensive implementation of agency policies, the ideas of Gifford Pinchot.

The fires had revealed major structural problems in the way the Forest Service operated in the Inland Northwest. Not only were infrastructure and personnel in District 1 inadequate for catastrophe, they were also insufficient to meet the changing demands created by the fires. Although a process of institutionalization and professionalization had begun before 1910, the fires and the response to them reinforced the need for greater flexibility and better planning in support of management objectives. K. D. Swan of the Clearwater National Forest recalled:

> The year was 1913. District One of the Forest Service had tightened its belt and gone to work with renewed vigor after the great fires of 1910 which took such a heavy toll of human lives and timber in the Northwest. Fire-killed trees were being salvaged. Foresters were busy with planting projects which would help reforest the burns. New ideas in forest fire control were being worked out. We were just beginning to hear of the Pulaski, the Koch tool, the Jack Clack pack frame—gadgets which were to become standard equipment in the district.
>
> And with all this activity came a growing awareness of the timber resources of the forests, and a realization that as more accessible stands were depleted in providing for the expanding economy of the Northwest, reservoirs of potential lumber farther back in the hills would be drawn on.
>
> Just where were these stands, and how much timber did they contain that could be made accessible to the logger? Silcox, Stuart, Mason and others were seeking data to answer these questions. And so were launched a series of timber reconnaissance projects which, in the passing years, have become almost fabulous in the annals of the region. One tries to imagine how much material connected with these jobs has gone into the files of the regional office—material gathered with blood and sweat (a timber cruiser had to be too tough for tears), but imagination fails. Though the notes and maps have passed into oblivion via the closed files, it is safe to say that the homely details of those jobs still live in the memories of the men who took part in them. I was one of those men.

The world they encountered had not changed much. Even after the fires, the foresters administered millions of acres to which humans had not yet applied values, technology, and the power of their institutions. Loyd Rupe of the Nezperce National Forest told of this time. Carl A. Weholt, the son of one of Rupe's coworkers, recounted one of Rupe's stories:

In 1911, five men brought a bit of civilization to the Elk Summit and Hoodoo Lake region in the Bitterroots. They had been preceded by a few trappers and prospectors, but the only signs of their having been there were a few blazes on trees, marking the way they had traveled.

Major Fenn, Supervisor of the Selway Forest, assigned Adolph Weholt and his crew consisting of Loyd Rupe, Sam Weholt, Lou Lisne, and George Eckel, all of Harpster, to build a cabin and open trails in the Elk Summit area. Hoodoo Lake was a black gem, nestled in the heart of a miniature meadow, rimmed about with miniature lodgepole pine.

Number One was a ranger station 15 miles up the Middle Fork of the Clearwater. The semblance of a road had been scratched out that far. From #1, crude trails led to some of the most accessible back country.

Weholt had chosen his crew from husky mountain kids from 18 to 20 years of age. The wages were $75 per month. The workers furnished their own riding horses, and boarded themselves. After a tryout in the corral full of half wild horses, Loyd Rupe was judged the most adept at handling stock and throwing the diamond hitch, so he was chosen as the official packer.

The Lochsa was still swollen from the spring runoff when the crew reached the forks of the Selway and Lochsa at Lowell. Lou Lisne, Sam Weholt, George Eckel and Adolph Weholt crossed without incident. The pack string also swam across nicely. Loyd, however, was just breaking in a colt. He finally spurred the critter into the water. Three times the colt and Loyd went under. Loyd said later, "I choked that saddle horn till it turned black." He finally made it across, white wooly chaps and all.

It took seven days to make the trip from #1 to Elk Summit. When they reached Moose Creek they had to swim the stock across the rushing ice cold stream. When they forded East Moose, the salmon were so thick they splashed around the horses' legs and bellies. Up Moose Creek they followed blazes left by trappers.

Up to 6 feet of snow lay in sheltered spots near where they were to build the Elk Summit cabin.

Grass grew deep to a tall bronco. Deer were fat and plentiful. Moose fed on the tangled mass of vegetation on the bottom of the lake. To the south, Diablo Peak stood sentinel over the primitive area, while kid goats romped over its precipitous face, and billies and nannies lay unconcerned on ledges.

There were grizzlies, too. Unaccustomed to humans, and curious, they reared on their hind legs, and with their weak eyes got as good a look as possible at the intruders they were seeing for the first time. On returning from a fishing trip on East Moose, Sam and Loyd met a grizzly in the game trail. It stood on its hind legs for some time, while the boys fingered their Colt .45's determined to make a good account of themselves in case the old boy was hungry. Its curiosity satisfied, it moved off the path and allowed the fishermen to proceed.

This backcountry vision suggests the character of remote places in the region well into the 1910s. Human impact in these vast and forbidding mountains was limited to corridors of access; along roads and to a lesser degree trails, activity announced the human presence. But at the highest elevations, where snow could be found eleven and sometimes twelve months of the year in shaded places, that presence lessened greatly. To young foresters, this pristine world they entered offered a picture of a natural paradise. As Rupe's account suggests, they appreciated this world even as they hastened its demise.

By the 1910s, finding competent people for the ranks of the Forest Service had become easier. As the number of people in the region grew, more candidates appeared at the field tests. The quality of such applicants continued to vary greatly. The significance of professional forestry and the proliferation of college and university programs in the discipline enhanced the pool of potential foresters. The era of exclusively local foresters was coming to an end. More and more of the people who joined the agency understood the concepts of scientific forestry, and many had either college training or other experiences, as Albert J. (Bert) Cramer of the Lolo National Forest recalled:

I was born and raised on my father's homestead on the west shore of Flathead Lake and received my grade and high school education in the public schools of Flathead Lake and Sanders Counties, Montana. I graduated from high school in the spring of 1918. Immediately after graduation my younger brother Art and I went to Missoula and volunteered enlistment in the U.S. Marine Corps. Art passed the physical and was sworn in and left immediately for Mare Island training camp, leaving me behind because I had failed to pass the rigid eye test required. This was a great disappointment to both of us because our parents had talked me into staying in school until Art became 18 on June 5, 1918, so we could enlist in some branch of the military service together. However, I was accepted for enlistment in the Students Army Training Corps a few days later and assigned to the University of Montana unit at Missoula.

While I was in the "Trick Army," as we called it, I met up with Chic Joy, Monk DeJarnette, Ralph Crowell and a number of other young bucks who later entered the Forest Service. We talked about what we were going to do if and when we got out of Uncle Sam's Army. That is where I first became interested in forestry as a profession. Our Army barracks was just a stone's throw from the little old "shack" at the Montana Forest School. It was here that I first met Dorr Skeels, Charlie Farmer, Tom Spaulding, Peg Lansing, Dick Fenska and other early day Montana Forest School professors who taught Army courses and who built up my first interest in "Forestry" as a college education.

An intra-agency structure for disseminating knowledge also began to come together, as John F. Preston of the Flathead National Forest and the Regional Office recalled:

Early in 1910, a Supervisor's meeting was held at Missoula. Gathered at the meeting was a mixture of the old and new regime. There were young foresters who had gone through forest schools and had been made Forest Supervisors, but there was a good sprinkling of old-timers who were more or less hold-overs from the land office days. Such men as Haines from the Blackfeet, V. Giffert Lantry from the Absaroka, and Ballinger from those wild hills in South Dakota and extreme eastern Montana, the Slim Buttes, the Ekalaka, the Short Pines known as the Sioux National Forest. The meeting, which was held amidst howling blizzards which bore down upon us from Hellgate Canyon, was highly successful. I remember a rump session in which V. Giffert Lantry was the chief speaker. The subject of discussion was the necessity for a raise in salaries for Supervisors. Lantry and a number of others were in the habit of reinforcing their courage by frequent resort to strong drink. After a heated discussion at this rump session Lantry proposed that they go to Mr. [William] Greeley [District Forester in Missoula until 1910, when Graves summoned him to Washington, D.C., to be assistant chief in charge of timber policy] and make a proposition to him to this effect: Mr. Greeley could either arrange for an increase in salaries or "use his influence to take the tax off of liquor." Needless to say, such a proposition was never made to Mr. Greeley. The rump session and all its good intentions died when the influence of the courage-giving liquor died out the morning after.

I find in my notes that James T. Jardine talked at this meeting about the new system of "blanket herding of sheep." Afterwards, at a Ranger meeting at Hunters Hot Springs in eastern Montana April 1910, he talked on the same subject.

Along with Dr. Frederick V. Coville and Arthur W. Sampson, who later became known as the father of range science, Jardine was one of the first to develop scientific methods for grazing management.

At a meeting in Kalispell on May 11, 1911, the Northern Montana Forestry Association was founded. Bob McLaughlin and Richard H. Rutledge [who later became Regional Forester in Region 4, the intermountain region] were present at the meeting and Bob was the real motive force. Greeley had gone to Washington to take charge of timber management and Gus Silcox was installed as District Forester. Bert Cooper had left in the meantime and Dave Mason was running timber management. A vacancy existed in the position of assistant District Forester in charge of operations, which was the job of fire protection, improvements and control of finances on the National Forests. I took up these new duties on July 15 and moved my family, consisting now of a wife and a young baby, to Missoula.

Of the events at Missoula during the balance of 1911, only one is perhaps worth recording as out of the ordinary. That was the organization of a section of the Society of American Foresters at Missoula on December 11. It was organized as the Missoula Section and now is known as the Northern Rocky Mountain Section. It has always been a source of pride to me that I can class myself as one of the charter members of one of the first of the organized sections of the Society.

The process of institutionalization was critical to the future of the Forest Service in District 1. Despite the agency's federal mandate, foresters needed ties to the communities in which they lived. Even though their presence in times of crisis such as fires helped, an organizational structure and a personal presence that bound the foresters to the people they served became crucial.

With the influx of new foresters from universities, the agency needed to adapt to what was a new professional class among its employees. Such people had different expectations than those recruited from among locals. Stable living conditions were more important to them than to the individuals of the generation before, who had been trappers and woodsmen before they became foresters. To accommodate these newcomers as well as to enhance the status of their agency in the woods, the Forest Service needed to change in particular the way in which it provided for the families of its employees.

Introducing the families of foresters into the backcountry became one of the most important components of the system foresters were building in the woods. Prior to the fires of 1910, foresters had generally bached it in the woods. Those who were married left their families for most of the summer season. The fires indicated that a permanent human presence in the woods required more than infrastructure. Along the roads and trails it was necessary to have a presence that made local people believe in the commitment of the Forest Service to individual welfare.

The presence of Forest Service families offered strong proof of the sincerity of the agency and its ties to the region.

The increasing professionalization of the Forest Service and the broadened sense of agency obligations in the aftermath of the fires made conditions easier for foresters and their families. After the 1910 fires, regional administrators recognized the value of keeping foresters in close contact with the physical world as well as with the people they served by stationing rangers in some of the more remote stations through the winter. To accomplish this, families had to be accommodated.

As the world of the woods became less remote, the presence of families in general became more common. The Forest Homestead Act of June 11, 1906, had been the initial catalyst, bringing more people to the hinterlands and changing the composition of the population from prospectors and lumber camps to sedentary families attempting agriculture. This made the presence of the wives of foresters even more important. They joined a burgeoning community in the woods.

The appearance of these families changed the nature of foresters' responsibilities. Much of the land in the Inland Northwest was marginal, and a visible percentage of the families were inexperienced in agriculture. Foresters became sustainers of marginal communities through the seasonal work they could offer, the permits for timber and grazing they could issue, and not in the least, through the way in which foresters' wives helped neighbors in emotional and physical distress.

The changes in the Forest Service also offered new opportunities for rangers. The increase in people in the woods meant that many of the bachelors among the foresters had the opportunity to think about finding a mate. Some of the rough character of life in the woods began to be alleviated, as the combination of access, technology, and the presence of families allowed the woods to begin to take on the character of the larger world.

But finding suitable marriage partners could be problematic for foresters. Although a good job with the government gave foresters relatively high status, men still significantly outnumbered women in the woods. Occupations such as mining or timber-cutting were overwhelmingly male. In remote communities, there were few eligible women, for the populations were largely made up of older men and young families. Nearby cities such as Missoula and Butte, Montana, and Lewiston, Idaho, offered potential, but as often as not, a courtship depended on whether a ranger could get to town with any frequency. Rural school teachers provided another source of potential mates, as did the female clerical staff of the Forest Service, as Hank Peterson recalled:

> The Forest organization had been enlarged by many young men, mostly from college. Among these [was] Meyer H. Wolff, a Forest agent recently from the Gallatin Forest. Mr. Wolff was of Russian descent and was yet to become naturalized, hence his title Forest Agent. Mr. Wolff became naturalized the following year. I was present at the hearing in Spokane as a witness. He married our very competent office clerk, Miss Merle Jackson. I was present at a presentation at their little house boat on the lake a few days after the wedding, at Coolin, Idaho, and twenty-five years later had the honor and pleasure of attending their silver wedding at Missoula.

Such romances appear to have none of the negative connotation of such activity in the modern era, when it is considered unprofessional at best and harassment at worst. In a time when suitable mates were a valued commodity for either gender, proximity in the workplace created a kind of opportunity that might not be repeated for a number of years. Courtships followed easily from workplace familiarity.

Once married, the wives of foresters took on new roles and responsibilities. They took care of their families, managed the affairs of the small quarters they called a house, and generally coped with unenviable living conditions. When their men were away, these women served as rangers-in-absentia; when their husbands were present, they functioned as a female version of the ranger, with much of the authority and status attached to the federal job. When the forester was present, the labor of both husband and wife was necessary to make the forest station function. This led to a respect for the work, forbearance, and fortitude of the wives as well as deep personal respect. In this, USFS families were much like the pioneer families of homesteaders a generation before. They faced many of the same kinds of privation and

A typical ranger station circa 1920. (Photo courtesy USDA Forest Service)

experienced similar fears and anxieties, as G. I. Porter noted in this characterization of the life of a ranger's wife:

From some stories and from other sources, and particularly from my own experience, I have gained some knowledge of the part played by the wife of the early forest ranger. Many such wives made history; many more by their courage, initiative and steadfastness enabled the ranger-husbands to achieve a measure of fame they could not have accomplished alone.

Unlike the modern housing conditions available to fieldmen, the wife was often (most often) required to inhabit a decrepit, inadequately furnished remote cabin or shack, lacking in all facilities of sanitation and convenience; frequently located on side roads, unpaved-mud, ruts, dust, snow-year-round conditions, all nonconductive to neighborly or social contacts, miles from town; no telephone, no motorcar, no radio, no anything to take the curse off loneliness and household cares.

Alone, or with only the children for company, while husband-ranger was away on his travels through the remote portions of his district, sometimes for weeks without means of communication with home. All this, with the further hazards to him due to bad winds, waters, an occasional bad actor of a horse, [and] more unusual (but still to be considered)—bad men. This for the ranger.

For his wife, the uncertainty as to his safety, the ever-dreaded illness or accident to the children, the labor incident to procuring water from perhaps a distant well or stream, the handling of wood and building of fires, the care of horses and perhaps a cow. Another worry was the absence of medical facilities; sometimes even of neighbors. Also to vex the wife, the long-range shopping by catalog, the dearth of culinary accessories, the shortage of supplies, sometimes through carelessness in laying in long-term supplies. But above all, the anxiety about her husband away from home for how long or to what distant places.

Like Gilbert and Sullivan's constabulary in the "Pirates of Penzance" her lot was "not a happy one." Such, in the early years of the century, was the life of one wife—that of the narrator. Some wives had a happier lot, some a worse, but all were pioneers in a life that has continued to become easier and more liveable. Sometimes she took over the duties of the ranger in his absence. She hired and fed fire fighters and other employees, routed these to their jobs and stations, and, after telephones became available, transmitted orders and messages. In fact, when the ranger was absent the wife acted as unpaid able assistant and was often required to assume responsibilities and act with initiative and discretion. Tell me, what other helpmate of a worker with the responsibilities of a ranger, inadequately (at that time) remunerated, could or would assume or accomplish such duties? But they all did this, and more.

More power to the ranger's wife!

The closeness that this life created among foresters and their wives was reminiscent of some kinds of preindustrial families. Foresters and their wives were necessary complements, and the contribution of each made the life of the other easier. In this respect, the world of the periphery offered these women opportunities for status not necessarily available to them in the urban middle class. Their roles were more malleable, and their contributions had economic and social significance in ways that were not common in middle-class, turn-of-the-century society.

But women also maintained traditional roles in the woods. The administration of behavior, both of the ranger and the couple's children, also fell within the wife's purview, as Ryle Teed recounted:

Gleason Ranger Station, God knows why, was named for a filthy old hermit who was shacked up a couple or three miles away. The district ranger was Martin Murray, who had a jug cached in a hollow log not far from the station. Allie, his wife, was a strict one. If she'd known where the jug was, it would have been smashed right now.

But the life of a forester did not always accommodate his family. In many instances, long separations occurred, as families stayed in communities with schools and foresters did their job from a faraway location. The smaller the posting station, the less likely that a family could live there, as C. W. Webb of the St. Joe National Forest, remembered:

Up to 1916 no living quarters were furnished for anyone except the district rangers. Their quarters were pretty rough, usually of log construction without any modern conveniences. Stations such as Avery, on a road or railroad, were usually fixed up well enough for a man to keep a wife and family there if they were willing to rough it. The back country stations usually consisted of a hut and a bunkhouse, both small and of logs, which would provide shelter for the ranger and a small crew. At these stations women were taboo. If a ranger was married, his family stayed behind in town during the summer. In winter he might sometimes be home, but usually not for very long.

The initial quarters constructed for families were also limited, as Webb recounted:

If and when a ranger station dwelling was authorized, the district office would allot the forest $600, which usually was credited to the district ranger with instructions to go ahead and build a dwelling. Usually quite a lot of contributed time was provided him and the carpentry and other workmanship was a bit on the rough side. Even so, it was sometimes surprising how much the $600 produced.

At Avery I needed a place to live. [Roscoe] Haines sent up enough lumber to build two tent frames having 4-foot walls. He

A ranger's family at a backcountry station, circa 1920. (Photo courtesy USDA Forest Service)

provided a 14 × 16 tent and fly for living quarters and a 10 × 12 with fly for the culinary equipment. We had a wood-burning heating stove in the big tent and a little wood-burning cook stove in the other. The tents were set on one platform, end to end, with a breezeway between—and, believe me, it was breezy—the whole thing. We carried our water from a pump about 50 yards distant, and took our baths in an oversized galvanized washtub. A couple of gasoline lanterns provided good light. Such were the conditions that young brides put up with in 1916 and earlier, and even much later in some places.

We lived in a small tarpaper-covered shack at Bogle Spur; in a two-room, rough-board shack at Adair; and now in two tents at Avery, with water at some distance from the shacks in every instance. Our boys and girls today wouldn't do it, and I doubt if they could, since never having experienced such conditions, it seems doubtful if they would be able to manage it. But, the advancements and improvements made since those days certainly have increased efficiency immensely and have made for a comfort we had not known up to this time.

Children who grew up in the woods had a familiarity with the natural world that attracted attention from observers. Besides the obvious skills necessary to help their parents, children also developed a prescient sense of place, as Ryle Teed recounted:

The Gleason Station was in dense and utterly primitive forest. Allie Murray had a brother, Archie Newcomb, who, with his wife and two kids, lived within a mile of the station. We used to marvel at those kids. I'd say the boy was maybe seven and the girl five. They went anywhere and everywhere in that dense forest without fear, or even attention. They would show up out of the brush around the station from any direction, except by the road, and take off again the same way. When we were on stem analysis, maybe a mile or so away, we would hear their incessant chatter and here they would come to hang around a bit before starting out again.

These perspectives are the views of the men in these relationships. Clearly women had their own perspective, sadly not recorded, and most probably it was far different than that of the men. The kind of conduct at which Teed marveled could be disconcerting to a parent. The freedom that the foresters so clearly enjoyed could be threatening. Despite their closeness, husband and wife could have dramatically divergent points of view.

Personal safety was only the most obvious issue about which their perspectives could differ. Although a forester may have thought that his wife's primary concern while he was away was his safety, she may have been equally concerned with her own—but afraid to tell him for fear of impeding his ability to do his job.

The circumstances of rural life added inherent dangers, which her husband might not recognize, to the position of any woman alone in the woods. The ranger's home or field office was the logical stopping place for anyone who needed directions, wanted to file a claim, might need something, or just wanted to talk. The official position of the forester made his home public property, and as testimony to this, many rangers at small stations used their front rooms as their office. Strangers and others often stopped for meals and overnight shelter, in the same manner as did rangers when they traveled. In an era before widespread or dependable telephones, communications were erratic. This could mean that a ranger's wife might be left alone overnight with a stranger or two in the barn, or in the case of rarer winter visits, in the house. Although this kind of boarding was a common custom at the time, it had the potential to be dangerous as well, a reality surely not lost on women of any time but quite clearly beyond the conception of a number of the men who wrote of their experiences. E. A. Woods of the Lewis & Clark National Forest offered one example of a situation with the potential for a difference in perspective:

Not only the men in the Service underwent adventure and thrilling experiences, but the women also had a share.

One fall I started out on a deer hunt with three other hunters. Night overtook us and so we decided to lay out for the night. The spot selected was a deep canyon, the timber there, an open growth of lodgepole pine forty to fifty feet high. All during the night, regardless of our sheltered spot, the trees swayed violently back and forth. We remarked several times that the wind must be blowing pretty hard out in the foothills.

As we approached the ranger station cabin the next afternoon on our return, we noticed that the place had a strange appearance. (This ranger station was located in the North Fork of Dupuyer Creek. The location of the station was changed some years later.) Sure enough, the wind had been blowing in the foothills. It had been so violent that the rocks and pebbles flying through the air had broken the windows on the west side of the house and had scattered things right and left in its fury—pictures, books, dishes on the table. And it started to move the roof, including the first round of logs.

Fortunately for my wife's safety, two hunters had come by earlier in the evening asking for a night's lodging. They had supper and later went out to sleep in the hay loft. The wind kept blowing harder and harder, and when the top half of the barn door was torn off and the barn began to rock, they decided that they had best seek shelter in the cabin. By the time they had reached the cabin the windows were broken, so they went back and got the door section and somehow managed to find hammer and nails in the shed beside the cabin and nailed the door over one window and an old canvas over the other. Had it not been for their assistance, I fear my wife might have been seriously hurt or perhaps killed.

Woods appreciated the fortuitous presence of the hunters, but in other circumstances, their appearance might have posed a danger to his wife and family. Although an unspoken code of honor seems to have governed relations in rural areas and the women of these places were clearly self-sufficient and capable of defending themselves if necessary, the possibility that a stranger could do harm could never be far from the mind of a woman alone. Yet the men who wrote about their wives did not mention this risk, either from a lack of understanding or perception, an unwillingness to mention delicate or threatening subjects, or simple nostalgia.

The importance of family in the woods meant that familial considerations had an even higher priority than in other circumstances. Albert E. Cole described one such situation:

> The year 1919 was a very hard one for me, as I had to have all my teeth removed the last days of May and was hospitalized for nine days with hemorrhages from my gums. This weakened me very badly, and to top that, when we could get back to the Ranger Station both my wife and I came down with influenza and were very sick. The result was that I did not get back to work until the last part of June.
>
> I rode my saddle horse down to Gregson, a distance of about five miles, to get mail and discovered a fire south of there. I rounded up two men and we worked on the fire all that afternoon and night and got a trench around it. As neither of the men could stay on the fire to watch it and I was completely worn out, I returned to the Ranger Station to rest and to put my wife at ease, as I knew she would be very much worried because I had not returned.

Although in some circumstances this could be considered dereliction of duty, Cole recognized that in the case of a minor fire, his wife's mental well-being was paramount. They had both been sick, and his health remained fragile. When he weighed the damage that the fire could do against his wife's mental anguish and his own possible collapse, he placed the needs of his family first.

By the 1920s, conditions for rangers and their families improved a little. There was a change in the perception of incoming rangers. More and more of them finished their education, got a job with the Forest Service, and married. Their wives were sometimes surprised at what they found, as C. B. Hand of the Nezperce and Coeur d'Alene National Forests remembered:

> In 1921 and '22 I worked for Ranger Vern Collins, Grangeville, Idaho. I was assistant ranger. I owned my horse and I packed and built telephone lines. After three years I took the ranger exams. Supervisor Fallaway was in charge of the district.
>
> On September 22, 1922, I married Miss Mabel Folden of Clearwater, Idaho. We were the first couple to be married in the new Lewis and Clark Hotel, Lewiston.
>
> In October of that year I was assigned to the Graham Creek ranger district. Charles K. McHarg was supervisor. Accordingly we set out for our new home. It was near Carter. It proved a difficult trip for my new bride and myself. We left Coeur d'Alene by boat, crossed over the lake to Harrison. Previously I had left the Forest Service speeder at Enaville, but a couple of other men had broken the lock and taken the little car. We had thirteen miles to go to reach our destination. What could we do? Pearl Bailey came along and took us in his speeder twelve miles to Coal Creek. There we met Oscar Hopkins with his speeder and he took us to our destination.
>
> The house was large but there was no electricity or water in it. I bought myself a horse and one for my wife as she often accompanied me when I rode to the lookouts and camps. At that time we were allowed to keep a cow and chickens. These we bought. We also had a garden for our own use. My crew lived in small cabins and did their own cooking.

Families learned to cope with the realities of life in the Forest Service. Improved roads and automobiles made their lives easier, but much of the burden of forest work continued to fall on the wives, as Bert Cramer of the Flathead National Forest, reported:

> During the school year of 1922 I married Johanna Guettler of Missoula and at the end of the winter quarter of school I accepted

Making a home in a ranger cabin, circa 1920. The automobile attests to the changes in the lives of rangers. (Photo courtesy USDA Forest Service)

a probational appointment as Surveyor Draftsman ($1,220 per annum) with headquarters at Missoula. I was just three months from graduation. I planned on going back to finish within the next year or two but never made it to this day. Just had to keep my nose on the grindstone, it seemed. During the field season of 1922 I helped Harold Townsend, Dick Hilleary and Jack Ray revise and improve the drainage map of the Kootenai. Art Baum was the boss on the Kootenai at that time. Bob Byers, who was the Ranger at Rexford, had his eye on that cute little gal in the Supervisor's Office (Adelaide Erdman) but still didn't convince her that she should change her name to Adelaide Byers until some time later. Spent the winter of 1922–23 in the district engineer's office in Missoula, completing the office end of the Kootenai mapping job. Took the Forest Assistant and Forest Ranger Civil Service examination during the calendar year 1922. Got a grade of 65 in the Forest Assistant exam and 95 in the Forest Ranger examination.

On April 23, 1923, I accepted a $1,220-per-annum probational appointment as Forest Ranger and was assigned to the Wolf Creek District of the Blackfoot Forest with summer headquarters at Fairview Ranger Station, and winter headquarters at Kalispell. I loaded my young wife, Jo, my young son, Albert, and our dog, Dewey, into a second-hand Model T and headed for Fairview Ranger Station, located on Wolf Creek 60 miles by dirt road west of Kalispell. Les Vinal was supervisor and Charles Hash deputy supervisor of the Blackfoot at that time. A two-room log cabin, located on the bank of Wolf Creek, served as living quarters, office, warehouse, etc. This is where my good wife served her apprenticeship as cook, clerk, telephone operator, and fire dispatcher, in which capacity she was privileged to serve, without pay, over the next eight years on four different Ranger Districts. Two more sons, Bob and John, arrived while we were assigned to the Wolf Creek District.

As children grew older, parents sought to stay closer to reasonable-sized communities in an effort to assure that the schooling their children received was both practical and useful. Sometimes this required considerable effort by foresters and their wives, as Albert E. Cole of the Deerlodge National Forest recalled:

In the fall of 1923 I was transferred to the Boulder Ranger District with headquarters in Basin, about 36 miles west of Butte. I arrived in October and was quite disappointed with the Ranger Station dwelling and with the poor school there. My wife refused to live at the Ranger Station, so I rented a house in town. I learned in November that the Deerlodge Ranger District was to be vacated by L. D. Williamson, whom I had worked with in 1906–07, and who was moving to Libby, Montana. A Joe Callahan was to be transferred from the Gallatin Forest to the Deerlodge, but after he had looked things over there he said he would rather have the Boulder District, probably on account of having to pay rent in Deer Lodge. It had been the policy of the Regional Office that only one transfer per year of an individual would be authorized, but Supervisor Taylor received permission to let me go to Deer Lodge, and I have lived here since that time.

I arrived on the Deerlodge District on a cold day on December 10, 1923, and found that Charley Joy was in charge, although he was in the field when I arrived.

We were very glad to come to Deer Lodge as both the elementary and high schools were very fine and the teachers excellent; in fact, this has always been the case. My headquarters was the seat of Powell County, and we were fortunate in renting a fine six-room dwelling which we afterward purchased. There were five old Ranger District headquarters cabins that I used for stopping places.

These communities often became home to foresters and their families. In some cases, foresters found spouses in local communities and came to regard these places as home, as J. A. Fitzwater, who spent seven years in Sandpoint, Idaho, explained:

> I was married one year after going to Sandpoint, and two of my youngsters were born there. Somehow Sandpoint has always been home to me, and the friends and associations I made there have always seemed a little closer to me than any other place I have been stationed.

The developing families in the woods, both of rangers and others, signaled the advent of a new phase of forestry and life. Although the roads and trails were incomplete, the amenities infrequent, the dangers real, and the living conditions often horrendous, the growing network of communications made life on the peripheries less remote. The growing number of wives of foresters both indicated that change and furthered it, linking the men of the Forest Service in new ways to their constituents as well as offering a semiofficial stabilizing force in the far-flung communities of the woods.

At about the same time families started to become common in the woods, the development of a structure within the agency began. The USFS valued its decentralized nature, but such organization impeded the spread of certain kinds of knowledge. The agency needed internal mechanisms that communicated the developments in forestry to its people at the grass roots. To spread organization within the agency was crucial and the most effective way to do so was through the supervisors' meetings. Some of these were very informal. John Preston remembered the introduction of science at one such meeting:

During January 1912, a Supervisor's meeting was held at Missoula which was probably the most important to that section of the Forest Service of any meeting before or since, since the whole fire protective and allotment system was worked over and important policies decided which had a far-reaching effect upon the administration of the National Forests. I shall not dwell upon the more or less prosaic matters of administration, although their effect was greater than was the incident which I am going to tell.

Among other things discussed was the problem of controlling insect infestations in the timber—bugs, mostly *Dendroctinus monticola*. Infestations had appeared in Idaho in the white pine on the Kootenai and in various places in Lodgepole, and considerable sums (that is for that day) had been spent following the technical directions of representatives of the Bureau of Entomology. Local concentrations had been assaulted by cutting and peeling infested trees. There were many other spots of infestation which it seemed impossible to reach. The question was whether or not expenditure of money on these relatively few concentration points could have any lasting effect upon the progress of the infestations. There were laymen's arguments for and against, and highly technical dissertations from the trained entomologists supporting the idea of continuing expenditures. It was late in the day of a strenuous session. Everybody was tired but intensely interested in the decision about to be made. Dorr Skeels, the Supervisor of the Kootenai National Forest, arose and was recognized by the chairman. He said, "Gentlemen, I . . . I . . . I want to as . . . ask you this question: if . . . if a town, a whole town, was in . . . infested by rats, you . . . you wouldn't try to s . . . stop the rats by . . . by pu . . . pu . . . putting a gold plug in one rat hole, would you?" That ended the discussion and relieved the tension; the meeting was adjourned.

Clarence B. Swim of the Kaniksu National Forest recognized similar changes:

The year 1911 saw practically the end of June 11th work that had taken so many thousands of man-hour time of Forest officials, particularly at a time when every effort was needed in reconstruction work, for this truly was the real formative period of the Forest Service.

Out of isolated individual homestead-tract surveys grew the problem of land classification, both intensive and extensive. The first project designated for intensive survey [was] the Priest River project [on the Kaniksu National Forest], where blocks of Forest land contained unoccupied and undeveloped agricultural land intermingled therewith that may at some future time, as well as the present, be considered as chiefly valuable for agriculture. I was assigned to this new job as officer in charge. The Priest River project was located along Priest River 12 or 15 miles below Coolin, Idaho, and contained several townships of level to gently rolling fertile land, although for the most part timbered. Some of these level acres were covered with lodgepole pine, while other tracts were covered with excellent stands of young and thrifty white pine. The soil as to depth, texture, types, etc., was classified by a soil expert from the Bureau of Soils, who was a member of the party and worked in cooperation with the Forest Service. His reports became a part of the official report covering the project.

The following year, 1913, I was again transferred to the District Office at Missoula and placed in charge of land classification, both extensive and intensive, for the entire District. My title was changed to the unofficial title of National Forest examiner. Intensive classification projects were scattered from the Kaniksu to the Custer National Forest. This project classification lasted over a period of several years. Finally the big job of extensive classification was gotten under way. Each Forest made a large bulky report on atlas-sized paper, that is, 18 x 22 inches, covering the entire Forest, and dividing the total land acreage into two general classes— land entirely nonagricultural, and land agricultural or possibly agricultural in character. Such latter tracts were to be covered by intensive survey which would be the conclusive classification. My job was that of organization, coordination and final preparation of reports. This forest classification proved to be a big job, requiring seven years for completion.

As the system of management progressed from paper to on-the-ground reality, the scope and scale of the foresters' responsibilities changed immeasurably. J. A. Fitzwater of the Kaniksu National Forest experienced this transition:

In the fall of 1912 I was offered the position of Supervisor on the Pend Oreille in Idaho. I accepted, and reported to Sandpoint, Idaho, October 12. I was on the Pend Oreille from 1912 to 1919, rather a long assignment for a forest office in one location. This was during the period when extreme pressure was being brought to open up the National Forests for agricultural settlement, and the Pend Oreille was one of the hot beds. In order to prevent wholesale eliminations by ranger districts, suspended listing came into being [the suspension of the decision on a June 11 claim, usually so the agency could clear some of the vast backlog of claims that piled up after the passage of the Forest Homestead Act]. Although this procedure somewhat reduced the pressure and no doubt saved much National Forest land, it also put local forest officers on the spot, for just as soon as a claimant was recognized under suspended listing, he brought all the pressure possible to have the land listed. I recall distinctly two very persistent claimants by the names of McGinnis and Heideman respectively who had adjacent claims on Meadow Creek. These two gentlemen made my official life miserable. I managed to hang on to the land and eventually had the satisfaction of seeing the timber cut with the receipts going into the U.S. Treasury and of then personally classifying the remaining agricultural land. Both of these men had 160 acres suspended listing but the final classification gave them about 40 acres each. It has always been no small measure of satisfaction to me that I sold myself to Mr. Heideman and I believe convinced him that I was entirely sincere and was trying to play the game fairly with him.

We did all of our outdoor work—surveying, mapping, estimating and timber marking—on snowshoes, since we had a good timber sale business and there was opportunity for some real timber management. We also had cattle and enough transient sheep to make things interesting. Slash disposal was a big issue and the principal bone of contention between the Forest Service and timber sale purchasers. It was here on the Pend Oreille that cooperative slash disposal was developed, and until this procedure was inaugurated we experienced but little success in proper slash disposal in the western white pine type. Frankly, I feel I made some contribution to western white pine silviculture.

Other administrative developments and policy changes followed in the 1910s. National forest boundaries continued to include significant amounts of land that had other claimants. One major issue was the clarification of the school sections that belonged to individual counties. Ryle Teed, a veteran of a number of forests, the regional office, and the Washington, D.C., office, commented:

Land Exchange. I am the only veteran of the first big land exchanges, in fact, the only forester who was shifted from region to region on these jobs. The basic idea was to clarify the State's title to school sections unsurveyed at time of withdrawal of the forests, and to consolidate their holdings. Special laws were required and these were on the basis of equal areas and equal values. The pilot exchange was with South Dakota. It was small, around 20,000 acres, I believe, and was cleaned up in 1910. I had nothing to do with this exchange.

In the spring of 1912 I visited the office of the Boise Forest to see whether Supervisor Emil Grandjean could keep me occupied pending appointment. He introduced me to Charles L. (Deaf Charlie) Smith, who had been a trouble-shooting supervisor on a number of Region 4 forests but was now detailed to organize an exchange with the State of Idaho. I was the first man hired for the job, on a 6–months' Timber Estimator appointment, the only one retained after the end of the season, and did not get away from land exchange work until the fall of 1927.

In those early years the lumbermen did not regard our professional attainments very seriously, and so our reconnaissance methods were not used. With the exception of myself all the fieldmen were regular commercial cruisers and compassmen and each used whatever cruising method he preferred. The general difference from our method was that in all cases a two chain strip was tallied and usually the average tree method used [a statistical method of determining the number and variety of species in a tract of forest]. Notes were usually posted at each tally (5 chains) only. All employees were investigated, and approved, by both sides. These conditions, established on the Idaho exchange, or possibly the South Dakota exchange, held also for the Montana, Washington and Oregon exchanges which came along in that order.

One of the candidates on the Idaho job, a charming chap named Ben McConnell, was looked at very much askance by the Forest Service selection board, for reasons of suspected instability of character. However, he was the son of Idaho's first Governor, one of his sisters was married to Ben Bush, the State Forester with whom we were working, and another was married to a young Boise attorney by the name of William E. Borah, even then in his second term in the U.S. Senate. With these factors properly weighed Ben qualified with a high score. In the final analysis it developed that Ben had us all sunk for the superb quality of his reports and maps. They should have been good. He had borrowed the forest's extensive reconnaissance report and worked his reports up from that in the backroom of a saloon at Kooskia, Idaho.

As a generalization: The fieldwork on these early exchanges suffered seriously, so far as any individual tract was concerned, from the lack of time and money available. Practically all the school sections were still unsurveyed, and were sometimes 25 to 50 miles from a survey. Nothing less than an official GLO survey could say where a section might fall. The plan used was to take the projection as shown on forest maps and locate the individual sections from cultural, drainage, or topographic features as shown on the best maps available. A thoroughly unsatisfactory system to all of us, but one presumed to average up over the job as a whole.

The Idaho exchange was pushed through to completion in 1912. Since two Regions (1 and 3) were involved, it was handled directly from Washington for the most part. Associate Forester [Albert] Bertie Potter made it his baby and Charlie Smith, in charge, corresponded directly with Washington. Quincy Craft, Fiscal Agent at Ogden, handled the funds. Both regions naturally took quite an interest in the project, and in the final phases we saw quite a bit of E. A. Sherman, then District Forester of Region 4, Ferdie Silcox, District Forester of Region 1, Ovid Butler, Chief of Silviculture at Ogden, and of both Mr. Graves and Mr. Potter. In fact,

Bertie stayed a week or more and dug right in on compilations and tabulations with the rest of us in preparing the proclamation winding up the job.

By the time the Idaho exchange was out of the way the Montana exchange was authorized. This was handled in the same manner as the Idaho job. Charlie Smith was in charge, but now entirely under the regional forester. Through the accident of being the only other career forester attached to the project, I was after only six months on permanent appointment, in effect, assistant to Smith—a job a deputy supervisor should have had. I did handle a field party both years in Montana, however. In 1913 we cleaned up the state base sections on all forests. I cruised out some tag ends on the Missoula Forest in December in 12 below zero weather. In 1914 I ramrodded a party which cruised out the selection area on the West Fork of the Flathead River in the Flathead Forest. This was fairly remote at that time. To reach it we traveled by Model T stage from Kalispell to Big Fork, some 20 miles. Then 8 miles by lumber wagon to the foot of Swan Lake, 7 miles up the lake by boat, then 20 miles or so by pack train. I went in in April and came out in October. But it wasn't bad. We had mail every week or so. A few sessions like that would do wonders for some of these modern J. F. [Junior Forester, a pejorative applied to foresters just out of college] sissies who cry if they have to stay out over the weekend.

Getting lost in the forest is nothing to look forward to. Lone wolfing as much as I did on boundaries, classification, appraisal work, etc., I was lost a number of times. I was never panicked at all, though, and so always got out with nothing worse than temporary discomfort. Some do not do so well. I remember one fellow in Montana. This was on the West Fork of the Flathead in 1914. The country was then utterly primitive. We were camped at Lion Creek. There were several cruising teams of us. One pair, who represented the State of Montana, were what you might call town woodsmen. I mean they knew their stuff reasonably well and were competent but they were Butte boys and their personal lives centered in Butte. Well, one night they didn't get in, and didn't get in. We finally decided they had got lost but that was nothing to worry about. The weather was fine and they would straggle in the next morning. As it turned out, though, they had separated. The cruiser had found a cabin and holed up for the night. The compassman, who was 6 feet 4 inches, had just torn through the brush harder and faster as night approached—a long process up there against the Canadian line in midsummer. We had 3 or 4 tents in a clearing not 50 feet from the trail.

Also, we had a brisk fire in the open and were gathered around it. It was just beginning to get fairly along toward dark, possibly nine o'clock, when we saw Murph coming up the trail with huge and frantic strides, his eyes as big as saucers. Naturally we said nothing as he approached until it was obvious that he wasn't going to stop at all, but to tear right on, practically through the camp. Then we tried to holler him down, but without any more impression on him than our blazing fire had made. Looked like we would have to shoot him to stop him. Some of the boys ran him down and brought him in. That man was a wreck and he hadn't been lost over five hours.

Despite the changes in practice, some aspects of the life of foresters stayed the same. Personnel were still scarce, and even on small fires, the Forest Service had to rely on help. As David Olson of the Lolo National Forest explained, this could often be far more trouble than it was worth:

> I was called from my lookout duties to fight fire. We had a bad one on Dry Creek that kept us busy for a week. At the close of the fire season, I was sent back to my lookout cabin to meet a bunch of fire fighters coming out of Clearwater. When I arrived at the cabin there was three feet of snow and it was snowing so hard one could see but a short distance. I made gallons of mulligan [stew], soup and coffee. Every half hour I would go outside and fire several shots. About three in the afternoon the fire fighters began to arrive and a sorry looking bunch they were, mostly "boxcar bums," shod in wornout oxfords, clad in thin civilian suits. When they reached the snow they had lost the trail and were scattered all over the mountainside. We hollered and fired more shots to direct them to the cabin. Finally all but one were accounted for. I went out in search and found him lying on the snow. He had reached that point in numbness where he only wanted to be left to sleep.

After much prodding, I got him up and carried him piggyback to the cabin. After the men were fed and partially dried out—and had smoked all my cigarettes—I helped them wrap strips of burlap around their feet and legs. Then evergreen boughs were tied to their feet to serve as snow shoes, and they were sent on their way down the ridge to bare ground and civilization.

Timber sales increased in the period following the 1910 fires as well, requiring more USFS personnel. Many men who worked in the regional timber industry became foresters in an effort to meet the demand. One, C. S. Webb of the St. Joe and Kaniksu National Forests, explained a typical pattern and experience:

> I entered the employ of the Milwaukee Land Company, subsidiary of the Milwaukee Railroad. They operated a large lumber plant at St. Joe, Idaho. Here I first came in contact with Ed Holcomb, then supervisor of the St. Joe, and Deputy Supervisor W. B. Willey. Having learned that the Forest Service was selling large volumes of white pine, as a salvage of the 1910 fires, to all lumber mills on the St. Joe River, I called on Ed Holcomb and was offered a job as a log scaler. Ed said that while I might be a pretty fair scaler, there were some skills practiced by the Forest Service with which I might not be familiar. He assigned me to work with Ed Smith, a veteran scaler.
>
> I went to work with Mr. Smith on June 21, 1913, at Branson's camp on Big Creek. We scaled the logs—two tiers of short logs—after they were loaded on cars. By this time deterioration of sapwood had rendered most of it unmerchantable. The timber over large areas had blown down flat on the ground under pressure of the heavy winds ahead of the 1910 holocaust. The timber therefore was not burned, nor checked to any appreciable extent. Some sapwood had blued but was firm. But, most of the logs were scaled inside the sapwood. Nothing smaller than about 14 inches at the top end was removed. We scaled out many trainloads of short logs which, even under these conditions, averaged 6 logs per thousand feet. It was choice white pine, running a high percent of clear, selects and shop. Stumpage prices—$2 per MBM [1,000 board measure, an older designation of 1,000 board feet].

But, this bonanza was to be short-lived. By the end of 1915, the removal of 1910 burned timber, except for cedar, came to an end. At this time (1913) I was paid $1,020 per annum. I boarded myself. Supervisor Holcomb drew $1,680 and Assistant Supervisor Willey was in the $1,440 bracket. These two boys held college degrees in forestry, but I had to make it the hard way. However, everyone in the organization was kind and would give a fellow worker all the help possible. Associations were congenial, and hopes for the better in material conditions induced us to hang on. The aims and policies of the Service were, even then, on a high moral plane.

The Forest Service in 1913 had one characteristic which it still possesses—it could never get a man placed where it wanted or needed him. And, I think that was good. Fresh challenges developed the fellows, most of whom were natives and, like myself, had no formal forestry education.

One sale, the Dalkena timber sale, was long recognized as the largest in the history of the Inland Northwest, as Henry (Hank) Peterson of the Kaniksu National Forest explained:

The Dalkena Lumber Company—August 20, 1912, Timber Sale: Prior to my retirement I was assigned the job of sorting the very old closed timber sale folders for the purpose of retaining those of historical value and disposing of the others.

Among the hundreds of sale folders reviewed of which many were retained, one sale stands out in my memory which had a note stapled to the folder which read, "The largest sale in the Region." This was the Dalkena Lumber Company 8-20-12 Timber Sale.

The sale agreement was signed May 3, 1913, by E. W. Harris, General Manager for the Dalkena Lumber Co.; witnesses were E. B. Tanner and Meyer H. Wolff. The agreement was approved at Washington, D.C., September 9, 1913, by Henry S. Graves, Forester, and witnessed by R. Y. [Stuart]. James W. Girard's signature appears on many of the cost reports; his title was scaler. I never met Girard but heard of him many times during my early employment. Mallory N. Stickney was the Forest Supervisor during 1912.

Howard R. Flint signed several papers as Forest Supervisor in 1920.

This sale was reappraised periodically and continued until the summer of 1930 when the company sawmill located at Lakena, Washington, burned to the ground and the company ceased operation.

During the spring of 1930, I helped cruise the remainder of the sale which was up for reappraisal. Lester Eddy, Neil Fullerton, and I were in the cruising part.

After our cruise, the sale was re-advertised in January 1931. The total sale volume was 263 million board feet on 18,240 acres. Over half the volume was white pine. There were also 191,000 cedar poles on the sale.

This amounted to about 53,000 modern truck loads. Or, to put it in some perspective, if 20 truck loads went by your house 5 days a week, 52 weeks a year, they would still be hauling from the sale 10 years later. That doesn't count the 191,000 poles either! Thirty poles to the load would be 6300 loads. Add another 10 years of trucks going by.

The Dalkena sale was in the middle of a competitive situation between two lumber companies, as C. S. Webb recounted:

I was instructed to go to Dalkena Lumber Company No. 3 on Cottonwood Creek, as a scaler, for the winter. I walked it via old Camp One, crossing from the East Side road on the Whitetail Butte tote road. When I reached the river the boat was on the opposite side, and I skipped across on the logs then floating in the river.

What impressed me most on this trip was the unbroken stretch of forest which I passed through. From a short distance out of the town of Priest River (the Italian settlement) clear through to my destination on Cottonwood Creek, there was one vast expanse of white pine forest. Now and then the log house and barn of a homesteader would be seen in a small, natural meadow. Around the Whitetail Butte area were a few sections of dense lodgepole type. Otherwise, I passed through a solid uncut stand of old growth white pine type, unmarred by any fires of note. Associated with the predominant pine were large, mature larch and fir trees, occasionally a spruce, and cedar poles in abundance.

It is safe to say that on Priest River there were millions of straight, sound cedar poles 30 to 90 feet in length. Many of the Northwest cedar companies took poles from here. At that time the Forest Service was following the theory that much of this land would, after removal of timber, be listed for homestead entry. This same theory was held for the relatively level area immediately above Swan Lake on the Flathead. As a result, the practice was to cut all timber 12 inches d.b.h. [diameter at breast height] and over, and all cedar poles, and make a broadcast burn of the slash. After burning, when the stony soil was exposed, there was no desire to homestead it. The land that was homesteaded was taken up for the timber values thereon.

Up here on the Kaniksu, logs and poles were skidded up to sleigh roads, and many were decked on the roads from October till the time of heavier snowfall and freezing weather. Sleigh roads were cleared before snowfall, and the little grading necessary was done mostly by hand. When heavy snowfall and cold weather set in, teams and sleighs were employed to keep the snow packed down, thus, smoothing and evening up the road surface. Water tanks on sleighs sprinkled the roads at night, and "rutters" built on sleighs were run in this slush, forming ruts which froze and served as grooves which loaded sleigh runners could follow.

These roads were located on a favorable grade to the river landing. Water grade was most desirable, but if they had to go down a hill from one bench to another there was no hesitancy in doing so. During hauling season the ruts were sanded on the steeper sections to slow up the sleighs and avoid crowding the horse team too hard. Any load that the team and a booster team could start at the woods loading point could be taken into the river landing without trouble. The sleighs running in the ruts were easily steered and there were no adverse grades on these roads.

The logs were sometimes loaded on sleighs with a team in crosshaul, using a decking chain to roll the log up skids, but ordinarily a horse jammer was used. With this device, and using a well-trained team in crosshaul as the motive power, the logs were hoisted rapidly. The crew consisted of a taildown man, two hookers, top loader and the crosshaul teamster. Big loads were hauled, and there was rivalry between camps for the biggest load of the winter.

The Dalkena Company had a hard-bitten old German, a real character, as a foreman at Camp Two. His name was John Speck. Not far away the Humbird Lumber Company, with mills at Sandpoint and Kootenai, had a tough old-time foreman called Moonlight Joe. The moniker was credited to Joe's slave-driving tactics, it having been claimed that he worked his men such long days they often left and returned to camp by moonlight. Great rivalry existed between John Speck and Moonlight Joe O'Meara for the biggest sleighload of the season. Loads of 22 and 23 MBM of short logs were not uncommon, but one time Joe selected logs figured out to best fit a 14-foot bunk, set them aside, and built up a load of 28 MBM, which he landed at the river, beating John's record for this winter of 1914–15.

This type of efficiency and indeed motivation was common among the smaller timber operators of that time but unknown before 1910. Foresters and the domain they supervised had been transformed. In some ways, the fires of 1910 allowed greater access to timber; in others, they compelled better planning and response by the agency. The result was a new vision of regional responsibilities and growing sophistication in management.

Eleven

"Our Modern Truck Drivers Have Missed Quite a Lot"

Building Infrastructure in Region 1

Infrastructure was high on the list of priorities for the Forest Service in the two decades following 1910. The fires of 1910 revealed an important omission in agency practice: Although the Forest Service could claim to manage large areas of timber in the Inland Northwest, its personnel in the field had no quick and sure way to reach much of this land. In most cases, foresters traveled by horse along lines of trapper blazes, a situation that made management haphazard and fire unstoppable. Without an infrastructure and a transportation network, foresters were really visitors on the land for which they were responsible.

In other ways, 1910 was an important year in the Inland Northwest. The establishment of Glacier National Park fulfilled Louis W. Hill's expectations as his Great Northern Railway lobbied for the park and played an enormous role in developing amenities there. A concomitant increase in travel to the new park followed, and some of it began to spill over to adjacent national forest lands. Such travel, growing availability of automobiles, and the increased demands of forest management necessitated the creation of a road-building program within the national forests of the area. The roads that existed were hardly adequate, as John Preston recalled:

> I went up the North Fork of the Flathead River during the winter of 1911. The entrance was through Glacier Park which had only that year been separated from the Blackfeet National Forest. The road ran from Belton on the Great Northern Railroad up past

Lake McDonald over the hills and into the North Fork of the Flathead about halfway up; that is halfway from the Columbia Falls to the Canadian boundary. A farm settlement of pioneers had grown up on the Big Prairie up near the Canadian line. These settlers grew hay and vegetables and ran a little stock and somehow eked out an existence. There were perhaps a dozen or 20 of them. When I went up the road horseback with Ranger [Robert] McCormick the snow was perhaps two feet deep along the road. At one point we encountered a place where the snow was badly disturbed and a log which had evidently been across the road was lying in the timber alongside. The condition of the log and the unusual disturbance of the snow attracted my attention and I asked for an explanation. McCormick told me a story which I have often repeated as an example of lack of cooperation in the back woods. The first settler who came out after a storm for mail and supplies found a tree across the road too large to allow his team and sleigh to pass so he got out, cut the log out of the tree and rolled it to one side, but after he had passed on his return trip with his load of supplies, he rolled the log back across the road. Each succeeding settler who passed this point rolled the log and back again so as to give his neighbors no advantage of his activity. The Ranger had finally rolled the log so far into the woods that it could not be rolled back.

There was timber business on the Blackfeet as the National Forest was supplying logs to a big mill in the Fortine Valley and there was some local grazing but the big job was organizing a fire protective system, building telephone lines and trails. I made one trip with Bob McLaughlin on skis up through the Stillwater burn where we encountered the burning snag which I previously mentioned. That was the first and only extended trip I ever made on skis and we almost didn't come out alive.

Preston's experiences continued to be the norm well into the 1910s, as C. W. Webb explained:

In 1916 there wasn't a road on the St. Joe above St. Joe, Idaho, and the one from that town down to St. Maries was a very rough wagon road. Main transportation was by river to St. Joe and by rail to all points above that town.

This was a situation that had to change. Harley A. Calkins of the Regional Office was instrumental in the process:

Before coming to the Forest Service I had worked at various jobs in many places, from Minnesota to Oklahoma. This included common labor for small firms and individuals, engineering work for five different railroads, and with the Bitterroot Valley Irrigation Company. In all this time I had always been treated fairly and with consideration; however, the moment I joined the Service I sensed a different attitude. The men I came in contact with were more friendly and seemed to take personal interest in me as an individual. That was something new.

I was not educated or trained as a forester; to me this was only a job. For this reason I have felt that my observations might have special significance.

My first full assignment was to run a traverse along the Gravely Range on the Madison forest (now the Beaverhead). This was in June 1914. The job was a transit survey to establish a base line for future range surveys. Stone monuments were established at half-mile intervals. On this work I had two young fellows as assistants and a camp-tender and cook, the latter part of the title being decidedly misrepresentative. I have always suspected that the man who occupied this position had had large experience as a sheep herder and that his culinary ability was limited to sour-dough biscuits and mutton stew.

Our camp supplies and equipment were moved by wagon drawn by a team of horses. No roads were in existence in the area at that time other than rough wagon trails following the line of least resistance.

The survey was completed the last of June and we started moving out to Sheridan [Montana]. On the way out I saw more sheep than I had ever seen before or since at any one time. The bands were just moving in on the range, and in one day it was estimated we could see 40,000 head at one time. The Madison Forest that year had issued permits for 125,000 head of sheep. Mr. Wilson was Supervisor.

Following the completion of this job, I returned to Missoula and was assigned as resident engineer on the Bitterroot–Big Hole road then under construction. I moved to the project on the 5th of July and was there continuously until the 25th of October.

Transportation those days was, of course, much different than now. Very few automobiles were in use. I recall that in going to the project I went by train from Missoula to Darby, and by horse stage from Darby to Sula. From there on it was every man for himself. I eventually landed at the Odell ranch on Camp Creek, which for a short time was my headquarters. There I met for the first time Ranger Than Wilkerson. Than was doing inspection work on the job. At that time the work had been under way for some time and was about fifty percent completed between the county road on Camp Creek and the divide.

This project, extending from the old road on Camp Creek near the Gallogly ranch over the divide and down Trail Creek to the Big Hole River near the historic Big Hole battlefield, was a distance of 25.78 miles.

The next year, signs, painted by Frank Cool, were put up on the road. The wording of two of these I think is worthy of recording here—one, on the sharp curves, "Go Slow and Signal," and the other, on turnouts, "Stop and Look Ahead." As to how well the injunction of these signs has been heeded by travelers, I leave to the imagination of the reader.

A few years later when visiting the job with Than Wilkerson, studying maintenance problems, Than remarked, "We ought to have some kind of an open-top culvert to keep the water from following the wheel tracks." That was revolutionary and was a shock to my sensibilities, but it was several years before the idea came into general use, an opportunity I let pass. They say opportunity is like a bald-headed man with whiskers, you can catch him coming but not going. [Open-top culverts on forest roads still existed in the 1980s.]

For the balance of the season I was on location surveys. The first job was to make a location survey from Prichard, Idaho, upriver to Big Creek. My instructions were to locate so that the line could be used for either a road or a logging railroad. The present road follows substantially the location made at that time. The railroad that came later bridged the river twice to take advantage of flats and avoid sidehill grading. The lumberjack hates a pick and shovel worse than a cowboy hates digging post holes. If he has something to build and can possibly build it of logs he will do so, and in many instances makes the mistake I have seen happen so often in our own work of mistaking cheapness for economy.

The natives had a unique and interesting method of freighting up the river. They would hitch a horse to a flat-bottomed scow loaded with freight and walk it right up the river, then the horse would be brought back on the trail and the boat floated down the river.

The type of survey made was a standard transit location and the crew would consist of six to eight men: an instrument man, rodman, chainman, stake artist and two to four axemen as conditions required.

The methods employed were as follows: I would work ahead with the axeman, establishing and clearing the line and setting the flags for the transit crew to follow. The transit crew followed, staking the line, chaining the distance, etc. After this was done I would divide the crew to run profile levels, cross-sections and topography, take section-line ties, dig test pits, make notes on soil classification, clearing, and cutouts and bridges.

Our next survey was to start at the Fourth of July Canyon schoolhouse at the point where the Rose Lake road turned off and ended at Bennetts Bay, a distance of twenty-two miles.

At this time there was very little travel by automobile, and cross-country travel was limited to an occasional stout-hearted individual in search of a record of some sort. The standards adopted for the location were equal to those in use in Idaho and ahead of anything in use in Montana at the time, yet the road had hardly been built before it was evident that the standard was much too low. No one had any means of estimating the great increase in volume and character of travel that was to come in a few short years.

The matter of finances was another difficult problem. The first section of this road, the Burns Summit section, was constructed by the Forest Service and was financed by the State of Idaho, Forest Service funds, county funds and local subscriptions, and toward the end of the season the job was operating on a shoe string, sort of a "now, if we can scrape up a few dollars we can finish this cut" basis.

The winter following this survey I made the design and estimate, and as I recall the estimate was between $6,000 and $7,000 per mile. This was unheard of; it was heresy or something; who ever heard of spending that much on a road; etc. Booth, Idaho State highway engineer, was in Missoula when I finished the estimate, and, although they [state highway officials] didn't say so, I know darned well they thought (and hoped) I had made a mistake.

In 1916 our first job was a retracement of the Wolf Lodge survey. This was one of the toughest jobs I ever had, due to steep slopes, brush and timber, snow and rain, long hard hikes, and working all the time with grades up to ten and twelve percent. I was soft and about twenty pounds overweight when I went in May 10, and when I came out on July 15 I walked from the camp on Sands Creek over the old Skookum trail (seventeen-percent grade) to the Searchlight mine with a transit on my shoulder without stopping.

The project started on Wolf Lodge Creek at the mouth of Marie Creek and ended at the mouth of Sands Creek on the Little North Fork a short distance above the Honeysuckle Ranger Station. The distance was about 12.5 miles with a total rise over Wolf Lodge Summit of about 2,000 feet.

We camped first at the Pietromuex ranch on Marie Creek, then at the Searchlight mine, and last at Jerry Alcorn's logging camp on Sands Creek.

There were two or three incidents that occurred on the job to break the monotony for the boys. There was the time Jean Ewen rigged up a cigar can with two holes in it for eyes and a candle with an ingenious shutter worked with a pendulum that when swinging would make the eyes blink. When Crell saw this about ten o'clock one night he nearly tore the tent down getting in to get my rifle. He shot at it three times and the third time hit and put the light out. "I got him!" he shouted, and the boys started heaving rocks in the brush to give the impression that it was wounded and headed down the creek. It being dark, he couldn't see what they were doing. They ran Crell nearly a mile down the creek before they gave it up. When they came back Crell began to grow suspicious so he took a lantern and went out in the brush and hunted until he found the can. He brought it in, held it up and said, "Well, anyway, I hit it every time." He was too excited to notice only one hole went clear through the can, but he took it in good spirit and was one of the gang from then on.

Decker Brothers, well-known packers at the time, had a pack base established at the Searchlight mine. They were to pack for the Rose Lake Lumber Company. They moved our camp to the Sands Creek camp and I saw those mules with 200-pound packs climb up over a log obstruction like a bunch of lumberjacks. The packer put his horse up the steep slope around the logs but evidently the mules thought that was too much trouble.

It was during the winter of 1916 that the BPR [Bureau of Public Roads] made arrangements to establish a branch office in Missoula, and it was after much head-scratching and conversation that the four horsemen, Cheatham, Williamson, Gumaer and myself decided to transfer over, which we did effective January 1, 1917. All the time though I felt like a deserter. The BPR was a fine organization with fine men, but something was and still is lacking—that fine idealism of the Forest Service—and so on February 16, 1918, I came back.

Beginning with 1918, the year I transferred back to the Forest Service, I was no longer assigned to seasonal jobs of road surveys but was assigned to minor roads, survey, construction and maintenance. Now, all large jobs, major roads costing over $5,000 per mile, would be handled by the BPR.

In 1918 I spent practically the entire field season on the construction of the Wolf Lodge, completing the project from the end of earlier construction near the Big Spring to the "Little River" at the mouth of Sands Creek.

The work was handled by contract under a cooperative agreement between the Forest Service and the Rose Lake Lumber Company, each providing 50 percent of the cost. The contract was awarded to G. A. Carlson of Spokane on a cost plus 10 percent basis, and the construction was nearly all accomplished through station gangs. These gangs were generally made up of five to seven men. They would contract to build a certain amount of road at so much per station. Out of this they would pay board, rent tools, buy powder, etc. On this project they made from $4.00 to $8.00 per man per day clear of expenses. I have known station gangs to make $24.00 per day, but that was unusual. I have carefully checked them repeatedly and found them averaging 20 cubic yards per day per man for eight hours. At the same time 5 to 7 cubic yards per man was the best that could be obtained by day labor. They would not use a long-handled shovel. They called it the "lazy man's shovel." The entire job was built with pick and shovel.

Calkins's work was even more important than he realized. No single development affected the national forests more than the access that roads created. Without vehicles, and roads upon which to drive them, western transportation proceeded at a nineteenth-century pace. Even reaching nearby locations could be difficult and time consuming, slowing everything from surveys to fire fighting. A lack of vehicles compounded the problem. During the first decade of USFS administration in District 1, no motor vehicles were available to the Forest Service and few roads worthy of the name. This made animal transportation a valued commodity, as Ralph L. Hand explained:

> G. I. Porter tells how he was traded by the Nezperce Forest to the Regional (at that time District) Office for two pack mules. That of course was in the days of statutory salaries and it seems that when G. I. moved from Grangeville to Missoula there was an unexpended balance that had been budgeted for his salary. Instead of an immediate replacement, the Supervisor requested permission to use this surplus to purchase two mules which he said were badly needed at the time. Permission must have been granted— anyhow, the Nezperce got two mules and the District Office got G. I. Porter, but it was some years later that I heard more about it from G. I. himself. At first, he said it seemed just a bit humiliating to have been ignominiously traded off for two mules. They might at least have thought him worth a short string [a short string was 5 mules and a regular string 9 mules, plus the packer and his horse with each string]. But after considering the value of a mule against the salary of a Forest Officer in those days, he felt a lot better. There was no doubt, he said, that from a monetary standpoint the Nezperce got the best of the bargain, but on the other hand he re-

alized that the District Forester must have wanted him quite badly, to have accepted such a deal.

With animals in such great demand, development and protection of the region remained a haphazard process that proceeded unevenly. Gene Grush of the Kootenai National Forest explained:

> I worked on fires for the Forest Service, cleared land, and in August 1916 went to Canada and enlisted in the Army, returning from overseas in the fall of 1919. I made cedar posts that winter and went to work for the Forest Service the next spring maintaining telephone line. While I was away the Forest Service or BPR had built a road from Sylvanite up the Yaak to where the radar station is now—about 18 miles. This was quite an improvement from the old trail I had hiked and snowshoed over a number of times.
>
> John Brobst, L. Dooley, and I moved the telephone line over from the trail to the new road. We used some new wire from half-mile rolls. Jack Baldwin and Johnny would put them on a reel on the back of the wagon and drive up the road stringing the wire out, after which they would hook the end of the wire to the axle and go up the road again, as Jack said, "to take out the slack." I was doing the climbing. One day I had taken the wire across my arms and started up an old burnt fir, a remnant of the 1917 fire. It was on a curve and leaning toward the road. I got up about ten feet and, luckily, wasn't using my belt when they took the slack out. It threw me clear across the road. I was plenty mad and started up the road with blood in my eye. I had gone quite a little way when I realized I still had the climbers on. By that time I had cooled off, had a good laugh and went back to work. Later I was up a tree, had the insulator fastened to my belt, and Jack was under the tree telling me how they used to do it when he worked for the telephone company back in Kansas City. The insulator pulled loose and conked Jack on the head. Jack's hair was rather thin so I imagine it didn't feel so good. I am sure he thought I did it on purpose to get even with him for yanking me out of the tree.
>
> Just before the 4th of July we put a young, newly married couple on Mt. Henry. During the summer a lightning storm came up one night and knocked them out of their tent, or so they said. She

had a rather bad burn and had to eat standing up for awhile. Anyway, they said they'd had enough, and we had to replace them.

Fourth of July night when we got back from the lookout the road crew had completed the right of way to the lower ford and were throwing a party. The settlers were invited, and danced in the old schoolhouse. It was quite a party, lasting most of the night.

From the basin on to Rexford over the Dodge Creek summit the county had built a wagon road, which amounted to only a double trail. Some brave soul, not a native, decided to make the trip through with a car. The boys dragged the car through the river at the lower ford with a team and he took off. Later we heard that after prying out rocks and cutting off stumps in the road, what remained of the car arrived in Rexford behind a team of horses. That was the first car to make a trip up the Yaak and through to Rexford.

Even in the late 1920s, more than a decade later, foresters faced an incomplete set of roads with less than state-of-the-art equipment. W. K. "Bill" Samsel of the Clearwater National Forest described one situation he faced:

[One] morning Ed [MacKay] received word that his F.S. truck, which was in the Missoula Central Purchasing Warehouse, had a two ton load of T.N.T. on it and that the city ordinance did not allow explosives to be stored within the city limits for more than 24 hours. It was therefore a must that it be gotten out that afternoon. Ed said, "How are we going to get that damn truck out of town?" I replied that I could bring it out if I had a way to get into Missoula. "Can you drive that thing [he asked]?" I said, "Sure." However, up to that time I had driven nothing larger than a Buick touring car. Ed's truck was a World War One vintage army type. It had solid rubber tires and would spin out and stall if the road was the least bit slick. My problem of getting to Missoula was solved when a man drove up just then in a Model T Ford. He turned out to be an old army buddy of Ed's who just dropped in to say hello and was going back to Missoula so I rode in with him. Ed had instructed me not to try to get beyond Bob Anderson's Ranch that night, which was about 6 miles up Lolo Creek from the town of Lolo. I made it fine to this point, arriving about sun down. When I called

Ed by phone he seemed happy that I had gotten that far. He instructed me to start on in the morning and he would come down
and meet me. He doubted that I would get much farther as the
road became much worse with mud holes, rickety bridges and
high water. He was sure right, as I had not progressed more than
four miles when the rear wheels of the old truck sunk to the axle
in a bog hole. I started to lighten the load by taking about 20
boxes of powder off the tail end. At this time Ed arrived on the
scene. Looking around he found a dry lodge pole tree the size of a
good sized telephone pole. With his great strength he would get
the end of the pole under the axle of the truck, raise it up while I
blocked under the pole, then pry down and I would block under
the wheel. After a couple of trials and failures Ed said, "All right,
we will raise and block the damn thing above the level of the
ground and see if it will run down hill." We did just that and the
truck came out. We left half the load and came back after it when
the roads dried. Later as we were unloading the powder Ed chuck-
led and said, "That was a rather shaky assignment I gave you. It
was bad enough hauling two tons of T.N.T. on that old wreck of a
truck but, you know, you could have gone through any one of
those old rotten log bridges." Well, I didn't and I am still here. I
feel that our modern day truck drivers, who never wrangled one
of those old pelters, have missed quite a lot.

Building facilities in remote places was a sometimes haphazard
process, as Loyd Rupe of the Nez Perce National Forest recounted:

The building of the Elk Summit cabin was accomplished in a
rather primitive manner. Logs were snaked in by lariat ropes tied
to saddle horns. The timbers were then hewed to shape and lifted
into place. Boards for flooring were whipsawed. To accomplish
this feat, a platform was built several feet off the ground to hold
the log that was to be sawed. The man who handled the top end
of the 8 foot saw had the best of the deal. The tall man on the
ground got full benefit of the sawdust. It filled his eyes, plugged
his ears, plastered his hair, ran down his neck, and filled his boots.
The crew managed to get four or five boards a day. By fall the

cabin was laid up and the cracks were chinked with mud and moss.

These cabins, although remote, were part of a network and often created community not only for foresters but for others in the surrounding area. W. A. Donaldson of the Lewis & Clark National Forest described the process:

On January 1, 1913, due to action by Supervisor Spaulding, I was reinstated to the position of Forest Ranger at $1,200 per annum. I was assigned to string telephone "tree line" up the Fishhook Trail to the lookout at Big Baldy and the packer's headquarters at "49" Meadows, where the horses were kept and from where fire lookout camps were supplied.

We were at the completed end of the line at noon on June 10, 1913, and were eating our lunch when the buzzer on the field set sounded. Ranger Daughs was calling to say he had a telegram for me and that it was very important that I come down to the Ranger Station at once, which I did. The message was from Silcox, and read about as follows: "Report Supervisor Leavitt, Great Falls, at once. Ranger meeting June 13. Permanent. Expenses authorized."

I arrived in Great Falls by train about noon, Sunday, June 12, 1913. The Ranger meeting lasted all the next week. At its conclusion, Supervisor Leavitt instructed me to accompany Ranger Moran to the Belt Creek Ranger Station, thence via Neihart and Kings Hill over the Little Belt Mountains to White Sulphur Springs and the Four Mile Ranger Station ten miles east of White Sulphur Springs. However, due to reports that the Neihart road was washed badly, I took the train to White Sulphur Springs, following a roundabout course.

Supervisor Leavitt had assured me that an allotment would be made after July 1 to complete the house in good shape at the Four Mile Station. My first job was to install the two outside doors and eight windows, after which I hauled out the Government property and records and a good cookstove which the Forest Service had purchased, also a heating stove, stove-pipe, etc. Mrs. Donaldson joined me at the station late in June. She and I fenced forty acres of bottom land that summer, and part of an another forty acres the next spring for extra pasture.

The winter of 1913–14 was really tough, with temperatures from December to March dropping to 50 degrees below zero at times. We had lots of snow and wind, making it difficult to get to White Sulphur Springs with the team and buggy for supplies. My wife bought a small "weaner" pig late in the summer which we butchered just before Thanksgiving for part of our winter's meat. She also bought two dozen hens which we kept in the old log cabin that we heated with an old stove all winter so that the hens would be comfortable and furnish us a few eggs. Our nearest neighbor, about a half a mile from the Ranger Station, loaned us a cow so we had plenty of fresh milk.

There was a fine stand of pole timber about a mile south of the station. Our near neighbor, William Reed, loaned me a bobsled, and I cut and hauled 125 telephone poles 26 feet long, to build a telephone line from the Ranger Station to the Dogie Ranch five miles to the north, where it would connect with another rural line and would give me connections with White Sulphur Springs, John Bonham's Ranger Station at Martinsdale, the Sheep Creek Ranger Station, and Lew Morgan's Ranger Station at Belt Creek. Supervisor Leavitt authorized me to hire a fire guard on June 1, and the guard and I constructed the five miles of telephone line in June, before the fire season started.

Ranger Bonham's district, which adjoined mine on the east, grazed about the same number as my district. Ranger Guy Meyer's district, joining mine on the north and northeast, grazed about the same number as mine, and Lew Morgan's district carried much less livestock due to the fact that there was not as much open grazing land but ran heavier on the timber sale work, as the Neihart mines and several sawmills purchase a considerable amount of timber.

These four Ranger Districts joined corners at Kings Hill, where there was a Forest Service lookout cabin, horse corral and small barn. When we made our monthly grazing inspections, we would meet at the Kings Hill camp with our pack horses and inspect the higher sheep ranges, using Kings Hill camp as Headquarters.

Morgan, Myers and I each had a pair of good Airedale bear dogs, and on our final grazing inspection in September we would take the dogs and make about a three-day bear hunt, which was sometimes very exciting and usually netted us three or four good, fat bears to take home for meat and lard. Sometimes in the spring, before the livestock was taken into the mountains, we would meet at Kings Hill and exterminate several stock-killing bears. The bear very often made it next to impossible to keep cattle on their allotted range since, once they were attacked by bears, they refused to stay in the mountains even for shade, fresh feed, water and salt. A mother bear with two yearlings would sometimes get into a band of sheep on their bedground on a moonlight night and kill as many as 75 to 100 sheep and lambs, "just for the fun of it," it seemed.

Roy Phillips of the Lolo National Forest revealed another dimension in the development of infrastructure in the region:

The year 1914 was a historic year for the Lolo Forest as lookout stations were first established then. The only equipment was a map mounted on what is known as a Koch board, as he [Elers Koch] designed it. Dave Olson, later Chief of Planting in Region 1, was the first lookout man on Illinois Peak. An incident of interest that year was the checking of lookouts by setting test fires. F. A. Silcox and R. Y. Stuart, I believe, set such a fire on Eddy Creek, a distance of over 20 miles from Illinois Peak. When they returned to Missoula they wanted to know if this fire was sighted and if not, why. As I had a horse patrolman in that locality I checked with him at the first opportunity. He informed me that he had ridden up Eddy Creek on the morning the fire was set and saw 2 men engaged in watching the fire but as they had a good trench around it he decided they knew their business and rode on. The fire, he said, was making a lot of smoke but lay close to the ground and did not rise above the tree tops. I reported this fact to the supervisor but heard nothing more about it.

David Olson of the Lolo National Forest told of his experiences on Illinois Peak:

Western Montana had gotten in my blood, so I was back for the summer of 1914, working as guard for Roy Phillips, Ranger of the

Superior District. My wages were $50.00 a month and from this I furnished my own grub. Mainly, I was lookout on Illinois peak that summer but, in addition, I gathered a lot of odd assignments. One morning Phillips said, "Dave, we'll either have to build a new barn or dig out the manure." So I lowered the floor about two feet. I also dug a mile of ditch for the water pipe to the Ranger Station.

The lookout tower on Illinois Peak was a rickety affair with an open platform on top. The map and alidade were covered with a sheet of canvas when not in use. The telephone was at the cabin, half a mile away. Neither tower nor cabin had lightning protection, and the cabin had a corrugated iron roof. Cranking the phone or picking up the receiver to talk to the Ranger during an electrical storm was about as hazardous as reaching for a rattlesnake in a gunny sack. During the early part of the fire season, I made observations from the lookout at regular periods. Between observations I built a mile of trail and a foot bridge, sharpened fire tools and cooked. My cabin was at the main crossing into the St. Joe and Clearwater countries. Packers supplying camps, particularly the large USGS survey camps, used my station as an overnight stop. I was the cook. In those days the only things we got in cans were tomatoes and condensed milk. The rest of the food was dry— dried fruit, powdered eggs, beans, rice, bacon, etc. Since I had to furnish my own grub, the packers repaid me by dropping off a slab of bacon, a sack of flour or some other item of food. I finished the summer with twice as much food as my original purchase. I "sold" this to an acquaintance in Superior, but he never paid me.

Occasionally Phillips would release me on Saturday afternoons to come down to the dance at Superior. I'd hike 26 miles to town, dance all night and hike back to the lookout Sunday morning. Today I wouldn't cross a street for a dance.

Life at fire lookouts remained primitive in character. Ralph Hand recalled the general lack of accoutrements that remained common well into the 1920s:

It was about the Fourth of July when we finally completed our share of the main-line maintenance work and arrived at our summer headquarters—the Pole Mountain Ranger Station. My partner was a Texan named Frank Moore who had worked seasonally on the St. Joe since 1914. With us were two brothers, Slim and Tiger Frantz, who were to occupy the Mallard Lake camp some ten or twelve miles beyond our station.

For the first week or so, we were all busy constructing camp, for, though this was the Ranger Station, there were no buildings except a small, practically windowless log structure supposed to be a tool cache. Frank was a genius when it came to making a comfortable, even luxurious camp, with nothing but a few handtools and what the Lord had provided in the way of native material. We had two tents and a fly, and of course there was no cedar at that 6,500 foot elevation, but we split shakes and puncheon from lodgepole pine with a froe (shake-splitter) that Frank had made out of a broken brush-hook. We walled up the sides of the kitchen fly, made shelves, cupboards and racks for utensils, floored the tents, and even made lockers for our personal gear.

The smaller of the tents was to be the Ranger's office, and though Frank was rather scornful, he spared no effort in making a neat shelf for the manual and files and a stand for the old Oliver typewriter. But he just couldn't help comparing it with the office of one of Brad's [Charles Bradner, the ranger in charge of the Pole Mountain district of the combined St. Joe and Coeur d'Alene National Forests] predecessors. It had consisted of one wooden box to sit on, another to serve as a desk, and two large spikes [nails] driven into a post that formed part of the tent frame. Incoming mail was pegged to spike number one until action had been taken or the Ranger had decided to ignore it. Then it was transferred to spike number two which never became filled because its contents—always dealt from the bottom—was used to kindle the fire each morning.

In contrast, a ranger district office in the 1990s contained as many as ten administrative staff members, all handling paper and none doing field work. No spikes existed in such an office. Computers had replaced them.

We had just about completed our camp when Brad arrived with a wooden mapboard and alidade, an iron telephone that weighed ninety pounds, and a set of lookout instructions that had been prepared in the office at Coeur d'Alene the preceding winter. Brad carried the telephone and alidade in a packsack, while I struggled along with a quarter-mile coil of wire over my shoulder and the mapboard under my arm, up the steep trail to the lookout.

We fastened the phone to a broken-topped snag, made the proper connections, and strung out the wire to establish a ground at a small lake below the lookout. Then we nailed the mapboard to a stump with a twenty-penny spike; Brad handed me the alidade and the instructions, shook hands and was gone. I saw him only once afterward until the Pole Mountain District had been blanketed under a foot of snow in early September.

The instructions which Brad had handed me in a somewhat offhand manner, consisted of two or three mimeographed pages and a couple of blueprints. One was of a standard garbage pit, the other a simple but adequate toilet. Since Frank and I had completed the latter to a considerably higher standard than required, we ignored the directions and eventually the chipmunks chewed up part of the pamphlet. It ended up, finally, alongside an outdated saddle catalogue on the wall of that ornate structure that we had built. Ours had four walls, a roof, a door and a ventilator, while the plan had called for nothing but a shallow trench and two forked stakes, spanned by a stout pole.

Despite such inadequate accommodations and provisions, foresters continued to do the many jobs for which their agency was responsible. Development continued at its characteristic uneven pace, supported by the small USFS regional road-building appropriation, efforts by other agencies such as the Bureau of Public Roads, and needs of timber companies. Additional railroads were built to support timber management throughout the 1910s and 1920s, as H. A. "Hank" Peterson of the Kaniksu National Forest described:

During the fall of 1926 the [Diamond Match] Company started construction of an in-between gauge (between narrow and standard gauge) railroad extending from Kalispell Bay on Priest Lake, up Kalispell Creek to Deer Horn Creek in the extreme upper part of the drainage, a distance of approximately 17 miles. Clarence Griggs was the engineer who located the railroad grades. Griggs later had charge of the construction of the Bonners Ferry municipal power dam on the Moyie River.

The railroad grades were constructed by hand labor on a station to station gypo basis [paid by the cubic yard or per foot, a sort of piecework]. Most of the crews were Swedish and White Russians. As logging was completed in the upper drainage, camps were moved up lower country. Rails and ties were picked up and branch lines extended up Chute, Hungry, Rapids, Virgin, Nuisance, and Bath Creeks.

They had two logging trains consisting of a locomotive and nine log cars each. The locomotives were 20-ton, gasoline powered Plymouth with extra ballast. The engineer shifted gears more or less like a truck. Roger Morris of Sandpoint, retired and a long time employee of Lou's Auto Parts, was one of the locomotive engineers. Logs were dumped into a boomed area of Kalispell Bay.

During the annual spring log drive on Priest River the logs were towed to the outlet of Priest Lake and headed for the Cusick Mill. Humbird Lumber Company owned the Diamond Match Company's Newport mill at that time.

Peterson also experienced some of the first roads that companies built to support their timber activities:

The first logging trucks in the logging industry were equipped with solid rubber tires. It was claimed that those were very destructive to the ordinary dirt roads, i.e., they made deep ruts and chuck holes unless the soil was very rocky. Therefore, much of the hauling was done during the winter after freezeup. Hewed timber roads, commonly called "pole roads," were generally constructed over unstable or wet areas.

The method of construction was to lay two hewed logs approximately 12 inches to 16 inches in diameter side by side with the hewed sides up. The logs were laid on and spiked to cross ties about 8 feet apart. A small pole about 6 to 8 inches in diameter was spiked to the inside of the inner hewed log to serve as a guard rail. It was rather tricky to drive a car or pickup over these pole roads since they were built for trucks with a wide wheel base. One was lucky if he negotiated a long stretch without one front wheel climbing over the guard rail. Meeting a loaded truck was terrifying since backing up around curves was very difficult. They had so-called jay-holes, or passing areas, as often as feasible. The best method was stop and listen at each turnout, proceed, and hope for the best. The first logging roads in Goose Creek, Lamb Creek, and Fedar Creek were of hewed log construction. There were many others too numerous to mention.

Each lumber company usually had at least one hewed log construction crew. Those that I knew were of Swedish extraction. Usually one of the crew was an expert with the broad axe. Hemlock, if available, was used in construction. If the timber was green, the Forest Service scaler had to scale and stamp it and the company was charged for brush disposal. The construction crews gypoed [worked on a piecemeal basis] the work. Prices averaged from 50 cents to $1 per foot. I suspect that sections of these pole roads are still identifiable even though they must be well rotted. How times have changed.

The roads of which Peterson spoke were only the beginning of change in the region. However limited, the infrastructure created corridors of access for foresters. Areas along newly developed roads received inherently better fire protection. They also were logged more comprehensively, for the cost of transporting cut timber was far lower than in isolated areas without access to a river. As a result, a patchwork of usable areas became more pronounced as roads facilitated greater economic use. There were still remote places, but the insularity that characterized them before the construction of roads now had temporal limits. It was clear that as roads were built, most areas that had the potential for profit would be utilized.

Trucks, cars, and roads gave foresters easier, quicker access to their lands, but they offered the same advantages to anyone else. As David S. Olson of the Lolo National Forest recounted, a new breed of individual came to the forests—the tourist:

I got my first car, a used Model T roadster in 1916. The Mullan Trail [later to become Highway 10 and then I-90] was barely passable from Savenac to Missoula. From Savenac west was no-man's land as far as car travel was concerned. To make the 90-mile trip to Missoula I would first spend a day overhauling the car—new clutch bands, brake bands, valve grinding, etc. Loaded with three or four extra casings, an extra spring and commutator, repair kits and every conceivable tool—oh, yes, and carbide for the lamps—I'd start out at daybreak and if lucky, make Missoula by midnight.

The first car purchased by the Forest Service for Region One was a Model T touring car for the Ranger of the Ekalaka division of the Custer. This was about 1917. Shortly thereafter Savenac Nursery purchased a Model T, one-ton truck. This was of the vintage with the solid rubber tires on the rear wheel. It took me two days to drive the new truck from Missoula to Savenac. The most difficult section of the road was a place called Nigger Hills, near Alberton. This stretch was a series of short, steep, roller-coaster-like pitches strewn with boulders and rock outcroppings that defied modern transportation. It must have been here that the 24 boxes of MacIntosh apples in the truck changed from solids to liquid.

About this time the Mullan Trail was opened to Wallace. This was accomplished by some county patch work and, at least in one case, by contributed help of local people. The final stretch blocking through passage to Wallace was made a public event. With picks, shovels and wheelbarrows (and free beer furnished by local saloonkeepers), residents of Saltese and Taft scratched several miles of road across the hillsides to forge the final line for car travel from Missoula to Wallace.

To publicize the opening of the road now designated the Yellowstone Trail, a Missoula man named Beck raced against time from Missoula to Wallace. Preceding the day of this event, notices were sent out the inhabitants along the route to fill chuck holes, remove serious obstructions and keep their livestock off the road. We cheered as Beck went thundering by the nursery in a cloud of dust at 30 miles an hour.

Painted yellow bands on poles and fence posts were the first highway markers for the Yellowstone Trail. They served only to locate the route like tree blazes in the woods. It wasn't long before the first roadside advertisement appeared. This was in the form of a directional sign shaped like a hand with the index finger pointing the way of the route. These signs contained mileage information to the next town and warnings, such as "sharp curve," "railroad crossing" and "steep grade." I recall one of these signs that I liked. It read "Step on the gas for the next half mile." The only hint of advertising on these signs was the name "Dolbys." No one knew who or what "Dolby" was until he reached Spokane. There in the window of a men's clothing store was a large replica of the highway sign with the words, "Safe at Dolbys."

After the opening of the road, autos appeared in ever-increasing numbers. The route went through the nursery so we saw them all. In those days a large percentage of the tourists stopped to look over the nursery. There were, of course, no established campgrounds or motels and many were the requests to permit them to camp within our fenced enclosures. They were scared of wild animals. Many stopped to drink and fill their canteens with the tepid water from the surface sprinkling pipes. They were familiar with tap water but were hesitant to use clear, cool water from the streams along the route.

Ranger Frank Haun bought a new Model T about every two years. It was fascinating to watch him get into his car. Frank was a big man with an unusually large paunch. To get behind the steering wheel, he had to cinch up his belt. That made a deep groove for the rim of the steering wheel to travel in. He took great pride in each new car that he purchased and kept it clean and shiny until fire season. Then it really took a beating; axes, shovels and saws were tossed on the back seat and firefighters crammed the frail running boards. From then on deterioration was rapid. A Model T didn't last long on those roads—at about 4,500 miles they were ready for a trade-in. Tires costing $30.00 apiece (3½ × 30) would last no more than 3,000 miles. We bought four-inch-wide leather bands, studded with steel discs, to slip over the casing as a means of prolonging their life, but the sidewalls continued to blow out. There were no garages or auto mechanics to help in our troubles. The spark coils seemed to give the most trouble. It became pretty exasperating cranking the car when things were not working right. I recall coming home one evening and seeing our local station agent's car stalled in the middle of the road. He was off to one side throwing rocks at it.

A Ford was responsible for a mystery on the St. Joe Forest that puzzled the Forest Service for several years. A messy log deck was developing along the old Emida road and no one seemed to know who was doing the logging. [A log deck was a collection of logs usually used to make it easier for wheeled vehicles to cross soft ground. In this case, a log deck simply accumulated.] When the case was broken, the local Ranger was found to be the culprit. Ranger Bill Dawes, of the Palouse District, was one of the early recipients of an official car. He often traveled the Princeton-to-St. Maries road, where he had to negotiate the steep Emida Hill. The brakes on his Ford would not hold going down this hill, so before making the descent he would stop and fell a tree, cut out a section, and chain it to the rear of his car. Dragging this down the hill relieved his brakes. At the bottom of the hill he unhooked the log and rolled it to one side.

We gave a lot of our time helping the early tourists. It seemed to be expected of us at Savenac since we represented the Government. I usually allowed an extra two hours on my travel schedule going east over Camel's Hump, or west over Ford Hill, to help clear the stalled traffic. These were big hurdles for a Model T. The Fords overheated on the long pulls and unless the gas tank was near full a Ford would stall on steep pitches because the gas feed to the carburetor depended upon gravity flow. When one car stalled it usually held up a line of cars from both directions because there were few turnouts on the mountainous roads in those days. Sometimes those traffic jams were pretty difficult to untangle.

The so-called tourists of this early period were largely local travelers and people on the move to new locations. Many were farmers driven from eastern Montana and North Dakota by the severe 1917 drought. With the improvement of road conditions and the sprouting of gas stations and garages in the small towns along the way, came the sight-seeing tourists. My first realization of this change came one day when I was walking along the road toward the nursery. A large black sedan drew up from behind and stopped. A liveried chauffeur asked if I wanted a ride. I thanked him and said I'd stand on the running board since I had only a short way to go. Looking into the car, I saw two elderly ladies sitting in rocking chairs. They smiled and one of them said they were seeing the wild West for the first time.

The West these travelers saw was already transformed, in no small part by the efforts of the men and women of the United States Forest Service. The saga of the early foresters and the trials and travails they faced were part and parcel of an economic and cultural transformation that applied a set of values, rules, and laws distinctly of the twentieth century to a physical world that—without the technologies, infrastructure, and surplus created by industrialization and concomitant population growth—resisted human intervention.

Few foresters rued the passing of the early days of their agency in the region. Although some nostalgically remembered the freedom old-timers experienced and others mourned the changes in the way the USFS did its business, they knew well the hardships that existed prior to the coming of even spotty infrastructure in Region 1. No one who fought the 1910 fires could romanticize an uncontrolled natural world.

In this, the foresters most clearly showed how different they were from most of the people of the nineteenth century. They did not long for an open pristine world; instead a managed and controlled world was their objective. Initially plucked from the rural world of Montana, Idaho, and eastern Washington, foresters became professionals who respected the places they came from and the people with whom they worked. Always torn between their roots and the profession they chose, these foresters became enforcers of a twentieth-century value system in a world that more resembled preindustrial times. That was their contribution, for better and worse.

Twelve

Epilogue

Social History and Agency Identity

The social history of the United States Forest Service broadens considerably the existing picture of the agency: a monolithic entity with strong leadership issuing directives from the top and compliant—but autonomous—field representatives carrying out policy at the grass roots. Instead, a different kind of picture begins to emerge of foresters who faced issues and situations that their leaders had not anticipated, that required quick decisions often without the opportunity to consult a superior, and that reflected on the individual and the agency. In these circumstances, foresters in the Inland Northwest as well as elsewhere had to fashion a doctrine that both worked and of which their superiors would approve. A middle ground emerges from the reminiscences of these early foresters, a time and series of places in which rigid doctrine fell apart and enterprising and creative grassroots-level staff members fashioned compromises that were essential to successful interaction with the people who used the domain of the Forest Service.

This kind of autonomy differs from the more standard view of the way in which the agency operated. Instead of executing orders, grassroots foresters were compelled to make policy and carry it out; at the same time, they had to maintain the respect of local people. That need for community respect speaks volumes about the limits of federal reach at the turn of the century as well as about the efficacy of the selection process carried out by Elers Koch and others. Federal directives from beyond the locality meant little unless someone on the spot could command respect.

Prowess remained salient, as the agency sought to find people who stood out and who had the wherewithal to accomplish difficult tasks.

With more than one million acres in their charge, early foresters were dependent on the people around them for support and sustenance. In nearly every case in which foresters pursued someone, battled inclement conditions, and traveled, they relied on the resources of local communities. Homesteaders helped in the foresters' work, sheltered foresters overnight, participated in "posses," and of course, fought fire. As a result, foresters had to be aware of local needs; they had to respect custom and practice. Even with the growing power of the "Pine Tree Badge," they had to tread lightly for fear of alienating their most important constituency, the people who lived in the woods.

This made for a truly intermediary status for foresters. Mostly of the places or areas in which they worked, they were nevertheless loyal to an outside force with the power to—if necessary—heavy handedly change local custom and practice. Foresters in the field became mediators in the process of applying newly created standards to oftentimes recalcitrant individuals and communities. They announced and implemented change while simultaneously softening its impact by keeping new policy as much as possible within the bounds of local practice.

Forestry taught an unfamiliar ethic for backwoods people at the turn of the twentieth century. To those on the margins who had never shared much in the miracles of the modern age, the very concept of conservation was foreign. Foresters had to explain the ideas of their new discipline time and time again to local people, the regional press, and anyone else who would listen. At the inception of the agency, young foresters were missionaries, pitching in with locals as they proselytized for their new secular faith.

The foresters rightly saw themselves as part of a vanguard. For $100 per month, they endured such difficult conditions as separation from their families, poor housing, bad transportation systems, unruly individuals, and natural calamities in the same manner as did the people who lived in the woods. In most circumstances they had to supply their own horses as well. Despite the wage, they embraced the dominant ideal in national

consciousness at a time when their neighbors were only marginally aware of its existence. Camaraderie characterized their relations with each other; they were men and women with a mission. Arrogance and a sense of superiority would have been easy
to acquire but seemed largely absent, at least in the accounts of
the foresters who chose to record their experiences.

The tremendous interdependence of foresters and local communities played an important role in maintaining harmonious relations. Foresters simply could not do their job without the cooperation of the local community; conversely, locals needed the
amenities and short-term employment opportunities in trail- and
road-building, timber-cutting, brush-cutting, and fire fighting
that foresters made available. Particularly after the summer of
1910, when the survival of everyone in the region depended on
activities coordinated by the Forest Service, the people of the Inland Northwest—foresters and nonforesters alike—felt they were
in the same situation together.

That summer, with its terrible fires, was also a pivotal moment
for the Forest Service. Not only in Region 1 in the Inland Northwest but throughout the nation, the "Fires of 1910" created a
folklore that supported the existing agency cosmology. The response to those fires shaped Forest Service policy long after it
should have, long after roads, trails, telephones, trained crews,
and fire breaks offered a level of technology and communications that could have allowed for a different response.

In many ways, that reflexive acceptance of folklore and history was a drawback for the Forest Service. As national currents
changed, it continued to embrace the same values. Until 1943, its
leaders were members of the initial generation of the Forest Service, those whom Gifford Pinchot had personally trained and
most of whom had personal experience with the fires of 1910.
When Earle H. Clapp, who appears here as a mentor to a candi-
date for the Forest Service, was replaced by Lyle F. Watts, it was
the first time that someone who did not play an important role in
Region 1 at the founding of the agency held its highest position.
When Ferdinand Silcox took over the agency in 1933, the two
previous chief foresters had simply carried out Pinchot's doctrines of 1910 as if they were carved into stone. Formative experiences and folklore permeated the evolution of the Forest Service,

giving it fidelity to a series of tenets but robbing it of flexibility to respond to a changing cultural climate.

No geographic area had a greater impact on the way the Forest Service operated and defined itself than did Region 1. The Inland Northwest became the crucible for the agency. There in eastern Washington, northern Idaho, and western Montana, its staff, from fire guard to chief forester, learned the realities of their trade. There they fashioned responses to its issues; learned to understand and respect local sentiment; and developed the tools, structures, and modes of operation that would define the agency for generations to follow. In this context, the social history of the time, the nature of day-to-day living and experience, and the lessons learned from it take on vast significance. The reminiscences recorded here reflect the groundwork of the value system of the modern Forest Service, the ideological and mythical roots to which the agency owes fealty. In these stories are sources of the strength of this agency as well as its conflicts.

Index